# The Theatres of Japan

# The
# Theatres
# of Japan

## PETER ARNOTT

Macmillan

LONDON · MELBOURNE · TORONTO

St Martin's Press

NEW YORK

First published 1969 by
MACMILLAN AND CO LTD
Little Essex Street London WC2
and also at Bombay Calcutta and Madras
Macmillan South Africa (Publishers) Pty Ltd Johannesburg
The Macmillan Company of Australia Pty Ltd Melbourne
The Macmillan Company of Canada Ltd Toronto
St Martin's Press Inc New York
Gill and Macmillan Ltd Dublin

Library of Congress catalog card no. 74-81567

Printed in Great Britain by
R. & R. CLARK
Edinburgh

# Contents

# List of Plates

The author and publishers wish to thank Kokusai Bunka Shinkokai for permission to reproduce illustrations 14, 17, 19, 20, 22 and 23. The other photographs were taken by the author.

# List of Figures

# Preface

This book is the product of a long interest in the Japanese theatre, and, more immediately, of an intensive study of the 1966–7 season. I write the word 'intensive' with feeling. Whatever other claims Tokyo may have, it is certainly the busiest theatre centre in the world. Like Bunthorne in his franker moments, I am not pleased with all one sees that's Japanese; like him also, I have tried to renounce the uttering of platitudes in stained-glass attitudes. The Western discovery of the classical Japanese theatre was, by necessity, as late and as sudden as the Japanese discovery of Western industrialism, and has tended to produce the same over-enthusiastic response. Re-reading the earlier critical accounts in English, one wonders that incomprehension could turn so quickly to idolatry, and if, perhaps, the two are not aspects of the same position. It should be possible to respect the serenity of *noh* while admitting its lack of theatrical vitality, and the technical expertise of *kabuki* while deploring its lack of content. The same is true of the Western influence on the Japanese theatre. At its best it has resulted in 'creative translation', an illumination and expansion of foreign material by indigenous techniques. At its worst it has produced limp imitations, parrot-productions by actors incapable of adjusting to the style the text demands, and prohibited from using their own.

This book attempts both to trace the development of the classical forms and to show their influence on modern production. *Noh*, *kabuki* and *bunraku* lend themselves to easy classifications, but the contemporary theatre does not. Its manifestations are so diverse that any grouping would be arbitrary. I have therefore composed Chapter 6 as a series of reviews of individual productions, drawing attention to consistent lines of approach and development where they occur. In dealing with the classical theatre I have inevitably had to cover some already familiar ground. In this respect my debt to earlier authors, particularly Earle Ernst and A. C. Scott, needs no less acknowledgement for being obvious. I have tried, however, to temper this repetition with amplification of fundamental points, which, it seems to me, cannot be made too often or too simply for a culture whose dramatic expression is still primarily naturalistic. I have also used plentiful analogies with Western drama forms, which are helpful as long as their limitations are recognized. The Japanese theatre, though unique, closely resembles that of other cultures at various points in their developments, and the suggested parallels will, I hope, make the classical Japanese forms more meaningful to those who may not be able to see them for themselves.

Not the least barrier to the Western understanding of the Japanese theatre is its formidable and unfamiliar technical vocabulary. The terms cannot be translated, for they rarely have a precise English equivalent. To render *hanamichi* as 'bridge' implies that it is simply a means of getting to one place from another. It is not. To translate *sh'te* and *waki* as 'protagonist' and 'deuteragonist', as is often done, introduces a false frame of reference and suggests a dramatic interaction that does not in fact exist. The only hope, then, is to romanize and annotate. Even this has its problems. *Romaji*, as the Japanese call it, admits several variations. An angry letter to a newspaper recently pointed out that there are three different romanized versions of the same Tokyo place-name, each authorized by a different government department. In the same way Zeami, the great figure of early *noh*, often appears as Seami, his father as Kwanami, Kannami or Kanami, and the play *Yamamba* as *Yama-uba*. In this book I have tried to follow the more familiar forms, though aware of having failed to achieve consistency.

My thanks are due, first, to the Hill Family Foundation, working through the University of Iowa, without whose financial support this book could not have been written. In Japan itself I have been immeasurably assisted by the *Kokusai Bunka Shinkokai* (Society for International Cultural Relations), and in particular by two of its officers: Mr Ichiro Suzuki, equally at home in European and Japanese scholarship, and Miss Yuriko Inoue, who, besides disproving the *canard* that the Japanese have no sense of humour, put me in touch with many things I might otherwise have missed. Some portions of Chapter 6 have already appeared in the journal and bulletin of the K.B.S., in Japanese and in English respectively; I am grateful for permission to reproduce them here. Individual debts are too numerous to be listed, but I must mention particularly Professor Gunji and Professor Toita of Waseda University, gifted scholars and able critics, who gave to me generously of their time; Professor Eleanor King, for information about performances I was unable to attend personally; Mr Dacre Balsdon, for various classical reassurances; Mr Dennis Johnston for illuminating sidelights on Yeats's *noh* adaptations; and Mr Robert Hall for drawing the figures that appear in the text.

Stage directions, unless otherwise specified, are given from the actor's point of view: thus, 'left' = the audience's right. 'Upstage' is furthest away from the audience, 'downstage' closest to it. 'Director' is used throughout in the American sense (= British 'producer'). Modern prices are given in yen; at the 1967 valuation, 360 yen = $1, 1008 yen = £1.

In the body of the text Japanese names are given according to national custom, with the family name first and the personal name second; though it should be noted, in connection with the Bibliography, that many Japanese whose works have appeared in English reverse these positions to conform to Western practice.

P. D. A.

# I

# *Historical Perspective*

The theatre is the microcosm of society, and the history of any drama is bound up with that of the audience for which it was written. This is nowhere more true than in Japan, where social and artistic movements have gone hand in hand, and it is impossible to discuss the one without reference to the other. *Noh* and *kabuki*, the two main forms of the traditional drama, came to be identified with distinct social groups and mirrored their tastes, philosophies and aspirations. The modern theatre was born from the enthusiastic *rapprochement* with the West, and its manifestations have often worn a political label. Those in power, whether Shogun or Emperor, native or conqueror, have viewed this connection with alarm, recognizing its strength and its dangers. Accordingly, the Japanese theatre has been a perpetual ward of court, growing up under the watchful eye of the law and plagued by restrictions – sometimes on political, sometimes on moral grounds, though the appeal to morality has more often than not concealed political manœuvring. Foolish though many of these restrictions now appear, their imposition – whether by the Shogunate in the sixteenth century or the American Army of Occupation in the twentieth – was dictated by the common realization that for the Japanese the theatre has always been more than an entertainment. Such attitudes, of course, are not peculiar to Japan. They have appeared, sporadically, in other times and places – in the Greek theatre of the fifth century B.C., for all its vaunted freedom; in the England of Elizabeth and that of Walpole; in Napoleon's France; and in totalitarian Russia.

But in Japan they have been consistent. *Kabuki*, the popular theatre, with its early reputation for lawlessness, was particularly liable to interference. Segregated by the Shogunate, lectured on its morals in the Meiji Restoration, banned or censored by the American Occupation, it has rarely, until the last few years, been left to ply its trade in peace. And yet it has thrived. There are many who feel that a theatre which flourished amid restrictions will wither and die in freedom. Even *noh* had its troubles from censorship during the Second World War, while the new plays, many of them identified with Leftist movements, served as ideological battlegrounds in which the quality of the production was a minor consideration. All these things spring from the perception of drama's intimate contact with society, and its function as a rallying point. To know the plays, therefore, we must know something of the history. The brief summary which follows is concerned, primarily, with the periods from which the plays took their subject-matter and the social conditions under which they were composed and performed.

Japanese history begins in myth. For a long time there is no distinction between myth and history. The sky is full of deities. Gods beget gods in diverse and fantastic ways: through the nostrils, by parting the fingers, or by the act of undressing. They reach down from heaven, stir up chaos like a pudding, and create the earth. From the water-drops spilling from the divine spear the islands of Japan are formed, and they are populated by the gods' descendants. Anthropologists talk more soberly of a pre-historic race, the Ainu, and of their subjugation by various waves of migrants, mostly by way of the Korean peninsula, but also from the south. The people organized themselves into clans, one of which, centred on Yamato (its exact location is now disputed), emerged as the imperial line. 660 B.C. is the traditional date of the first Yamato Emperor, though most historians would place him several centuries earlier. The Imperial House claimed direct descent from the gods, and its power was transmitted in un-broken succession. Hirohito, the present Emperor, is by Japanese reckoning one hundred and twenty-third in line; he is also the first to have renounced his divinity.

The Yamato dynasty did not command absolute allegiance. Other clans were strong, claimed similar divine descent, and at times paid only formal respect to the Imperial House. This foreshadows the position of the emperors in much of Japan's subsequent history, not least in our own day. Although their titular power was protected by tradition and religious sanctions, the real power was usually in the hands of others. Around the noble families, skilled workers formed their own clans or guilds, though the life of the times was centred around agriculture and warfare. Farmer and soldier were one. The same man served in both capacities, working the fields when possible, taking up arms when necessary. This intimate connection became the basis of the Japanese economy. Later society recognized only two classes, the farmer and the warrior, the latter acting as the former's overlord. The merchant class, when it developed, was regarded as an irregular intrusion into the traditional pattern.

Early religion was animistic. It saw gods and spirits everywhere: in streams and mountains, in animals and trees. It worshipped the forces of nature. These beliefs survived the introduction of later cults, produced a wealth of folklore, and greatly influenced the drama. In *noh* the spirits of the iris and the cherry can take human form and speak, and dead lovers assume the shape of trees. In *kabuki*, men can be metamorphosed into animals, and animals into men. Even material objects were regarded as invested with a divine presence. The imperial sword and mirror possessed their own sanctity, distinct from that of the Emperor who used them. This attitude persists. The treasure-house of the Meiji Shrine, in Tokyo, houses relics which are not 'treasures' at all, in terms of their material value. They are the simple domestic objects used by the Emperor and his Empress during their lifetime – desk, books, mirror, inkstand, *kimono*. The visitor is commanded to venerate their austerity and apply to his life the virtues of dignity, simplicity and devotion which the royal family applied to theirs and strove to inculcate among their people.

This religion, at first anonymous, came to be called Shinto, 'The Way of the Gods'. It owned no sense of sin; the guilt-feelings which pervade Christianity had no place here. It was concerned more with uncleanness in the purely physical sense: with the health of the body and the avoidance of acts which might be considered contagious. Ceremonial ablution was important. Certain acts, notably death and childbirth, were regarded as bringing pollution and had to be followed by purgation. The gods themselves were said to have separate abodes in which they cohabited and gave birth, to avoid contaminating the others. Shinto accordingly became prolific in ritual, and concerned itself largely with etiquette and propriety. It taught reverence for the dead and for the past, and worshipped the Emperor as divine. By its own diffuseness it was tolerant of other religions. When, after some centuries, Buddhism was introduced into Japan, it found little real opposition. On the contrary, the two religions soon merged, for it was perfectly conceivable that one could be a Shintoist and a Buddhist at the same time. Shinto thus forms the substratum of the Japanese religious life. It has never disappeared, and from time to time, encouraged for political or militaristic reasons, has enjoyed high peaks of popularity.

Japanese society in its formative years could hardly avoid influence from its larger and more venerable neighbour, any more than the emergent Greeks could escape contact with Egypt and Asia Minor. By A.D. 200 China had developed her distinctive philosophy, literature and art, her own industry and commerce. The Chinese rulers of the Han dynasty brought their civilization to Korea, and established diplomatic contacts – sometimes testy, usually benign – with Japan. Korea thus became a path of cultural, as it had been of racial, transmission. From the Chinese came writing and the precepts of Confucius. This influence received enormous impetus from the spread of Buddhism, which was to leave an indelible mark on Japanese culture and give its classical forms their philosophy.

The new religion had been founded in northern India in the sixth century B.C. by Goutama Buddha, normally known simply as the Buddha. Born into a noble house, he could look forward to eminence as a temporal leader. All this he renounced. The tradition represents him as looking at the world about him, seeing its poverty, pain and suffering, and giving up earthly ambition for the work of the spirit. After long contemplation he decided that the cause of suffering was earthly passion and desire. Only by eliminating these could the individual liberate his spirit and attain Nirvana, the blessed afterlife. The material world was impermanent, corrupting and delusory. Buddha's disciples deified him, propagated his teachings and amplified them with non-Indian elements, often to the embarrassment of Christianity, which found Buddhist ceremony and doctrine so akin to its own that it was forced, in self-defence, to attack the foreign faith as a diabolical parody. In the latter part of the fourth century A.D. Buddhism had already reached Korea. In 552 Buddhist monks, travelling from China to Japan, advised its adoption. This did not come about immediately. The first conversions were followed by a pestilence, interpreted as a sign of divine anger. When the pestilence continued after the converts had recanted, a new interpretation was offered: this was the wrath of Buddha himself at the half-hearted Japanese. Shrines were erected for the new cult, and leading families took responsibility for maintaining them. Prominent among these were the Sogas (a name famous in Japanese history), who survived the rioting and civil war that followed to control the imperial throne and ensure the success and continuity of Buddhism.

Bound now by a common religion, Japan seized eagerly on Chinese culture and adapted it to her own needs. Buddhist temples proliferated, and large monastic communities, charged with important ceremonies, grew up around them. The priests undertook long journeys as missionaries; the travelling priest who sees visions or hears stories of the holy places is a familiar figure in the *noh* play. Shinto was not abandoned, but lived side by side with Buddhism and learned from it. The traditional respect for the past, already reinforced by Confucianism, was now extended by the Buddhist doctrine of reincarnation, by which a soul may undergo a series of mortal existences before attaining Nirvana. Learning followed religion. Chinese writing brought a new vocabulary, and access to Chinese history, poetry, philosophy and science. This period saw the beginnings of Japanese literature, leaning heavily on Chinese precedent.

Prince Regent Shotoku, a strong supporter of Buddhism, introduced various civil reforms to reorganize the government,
strengthen the power of the Imperial House and apply Buddhist
principles to official life. Set out in a 'constitution' promulgated
in 604, they gave new importance to the monarch, whose position had by this time become ambiguous. Identified with the
deity, he was safe from overthrow, for rebellion was tantamount
to sacrilege, but exercised little control over the actions of his
supporters. Now a new civil administration was erected around
him, which took the law out of the hands of the old ministers
and created a new governing class. Its members were chosen
partly by birth, but principally, as in the Chinese system, according to ability. Codes of law were formulated and military
conscription made universal. The land was declared state property, though every man and woman was entitled to a share. Redistribution every six years prevented individual aggrandisement.
(In a country as small as Japan, with an ever-increasing population, land-ownership has been a continuing problem: the redistribution system has been periodically revived, with the last
taking place a quarter of a century ago.) Japan began to mould
Chinese traditions to her own ways, instead of swallowing them
whole. A native syllabary (each character standing for a syllable)
supplemented the Chinese characters, which each represented a
whole word. This combination has continued in use to the
present day. The syllabary is known as *kana* ('substitute letters')
and is itself complex; coupled with the Chinese characters, it
presents a written language of formidable difficulty, mastery of
which, as in so many things in Japan, becomes a mark of breeding and education. Using *kana* alone, though not impossible,
brands the writer as inferior. One other important event of this
period was the relocation of the Imperial Household. In 794 it
was moved from Nara to nearby Kyoto, where it remained until
the nineteenth century.

The real seat of power, however, usually lay elsewhere, for the
governmental reforms backfired. Far from increasing the power
of the throne, they surrounded it with an inner circle of power-
hungry nobles who juggled for prestige and influence. The

Fujiwara family, the second most illustrious in Japan and boasting of its own divine descent, controlled the emperors through a series of regencies. Controlled, but did not remove them: the throne was still sacrosanct. They gradually acquired most of the important offices, and made them hereditary. Their women were chosen as the emperors' wives, and royal heirs from the sons of Fujiwara mothers. An Emperor who became too independent was forced to retire, and replaced by a younger, more tractable figurehead. Often there were several retired emperors alive at the same time; the conflict between allegiance to them and to the present incumbent, or the royal house and the *de facto* ruler, is the background to many plays.

The governmental class thus became self-centred and evolved its own luxurious life around the court, losing contact with the provinces. *Genji Monogatari* (*Tales of the Genji*), written by the Lady Murasaki in the eleventh century, and one of the most famous works of Japanese literature, describes this aristocratic life though the adventures of its hero, the Don Juan-like Prince Genji, whose amours figure prominently in later plays. Local lords took advantage of the preoccupation of the court to increase their holdings. The six-year redistribution plan fell into abeyance, and a handful of powerful figures secured new and ever larger estates. Often these lords were exempt from taxation. Small-holders, seeking the same relief, surrendered their lands to the aristocracy and received them back as fiefs. By such means the country in time came to be made up of huge fiefs owing allegiance to a local landlord and outside direct governmental control. The landowners themselves, though bound by formal allegiance to the Emperor, were largely independent. Japanese society had assumed a pattern very like the feudal structure of the European Middle Ages, and, by the end of the eleventh century, the central government was on the point of collapse. The lords were free to fight for power among themselves.

Each had a private army, professional soldiers who had come to think of themselves as a separate military caste. Some of these *samurai* had been recruited from the police, others from the lord's dependants; some came from the younger nobility, others

were *ronin*, unemployed men; but they were united by their
source of income and way of life, and evolved their own code,
structure and hierarchy. It was with such armies that the lord
struggled for power. Their aim was not the deposition of the
Imperial Family, but the right to dominate the country in the
royal name. The history of these feudal wars is long and extremely complex; there is no need here, fortunately, to consider
it in detail. Military families assumed control in turn. Particular
rivalry existed between the Minamoto and Taira houses. The
former was almost completely suppressed, but a few escaped,
led a successful countermovement and eventually triumphed.
Prominent among them were Yoshitsune and Yoritomo and the
former's retainer, the warrior-priest Benkei. Their names live in
Japanese history and drama. *Heike Monogatari* (*Tales of the Heike*),
written in 1233, told the story of the rise and fall of the Taira clan
in fact and legend, and served as a source-book for several *noh*
plays and a great deal of *kabuki*. The work is still popular, and has
recently appeared in a modern version by Yoshikawa Eiji.

Yoritomo did not use his victory to interfere with the Emperor,
or even to unseat his administrators. While preserving the form of
the Fujiwara government, he established a separate military administration, loyal only to himself and the real centre of power.
His name for this was *bakufu*, literally 'tent-office'. In 1192
Yoritomo was named Shogun. This was not a new title – it meant
'general' and had been frequently held – but it now assumed a
new significance, that of generalissimo, or military dictator.
(The word 'dictator', with its shift of meaning from early Roman
times to the present day, is, in fact, roughly analogous.) The
centre of the *bakufu* was removed to Kamakura, near Edo (modern
Tokyo), which became a separate capital.

Yoritomo was supplanted by the Hojo family, who presided
over a period of civil strife and important cultural advances. Zen,
one of the many sects of Buddhism, flourished at this time. More
will be said about this in its proper place. For the moment, it
need only be noted that Zen found particular favour with the
warrior classes who were now in power, because of its simplicity
and insistence on self-reliance, and had a major influence on *noh*,

the form of drama that they espoused. In this period, *noh* began
to shake off its rustic antecedents and emerge as a distinct, and
highly sophisticated, dramatic form: taken up by the *samurai*,
and protected by them as the Imperial Household preserved the
old court dances, it was to flourish in comparative seclusion and
to face its first real threat only with the Shogunate's demise. It
was in this period, too, that Japan faced its one major threat of
foreign invasion. The Mongols, sweeping over Asia, attacked and
were repulsed. The Japanese won through shrewd generalship
and luck. They were aided by a storm which scattered the enemy
fleet, and which they gratefully called *kamikaze* – 'the divine
wind' – a name later to be given to the suicide pilots of the Second
World War, and, by analogy, to Tokyo taxidrivers.

There were further upheavals. The Emperor tried to regain
control, in vain, and a reconciliation was eventually worked out
with the Ashikaga family in power. They ruled from 1392–1603,
and established their Shogunate in Kyoto. Though weak rulers,
they were great patrons of the arts; under their influence *noh* was
brought to its perfected form. Rival lords, however, were almost
as strong, and further interference came from monastic communities whose religious interests were, to say the least, per-
functory. Armed monks operated as private armies, and were as
great a menace as the *samurai*. Although Japan has never produced
a dominant priestly caste, the religious organizations were important both in politics and in cultural transmission. They fought,
but they preserved; in the anarchy of civil war the monks, like
their less aggressive counterparts in Europe, treasured precious
manuscripts and passed them on. The ordinary people paid for
the wars, as ordinary people have always done, and protested un-
availingly against the increasing oppression. More money was
needed to support the government, and the burden fell upon an
increasingly narrow segment of the populace. The riots which
ensued did not make the task of the authorities any easier. One
desperate Ashikaga Shogun even accepted Chinese suzerainty in
return for trading rights.

Out of this anarchy came three remarkable leaders, Nobunaga,
Hideyoshi and Ieasu, who brought peace by a series of military

and political *coups*. Hideyoshi is frequently called the Japanese Napoleon, the unique example of a commoner rising to supreme power. Ieasu re-established a central government and, in 1603, founded the Tokugawa Shogunate, with its capital at Edo. This marked the beginning of more than two centuries of peace for Japan – but peace at a considerable price.

At Edo Ieasu had a firm base, surrounded by fiefs under the control of *daimyo* (lords) from his own family, and secure against surprise attack. But this was not enough. He saw that, to retain power, he must eliminate the factionalism that had so often brought down the central government. One source of danger was the Imperial House. Although the emperors were personally powerless, others might use their name. It had happened before. He therefore decreased the royal family's influence, paradoxically, by increasing their importance; he debarred them from participation in practical politics by emphasizing their sanctity. The Emperor, being divine, must not be soiled by mundane affairs. Cut off from profanation by the common people – and therefore deprived of any effective contact with them – he was to content himself with his proper business, the distribution of honours and the ordering of religious ceremonial. Access to him was rigidly controlled, and the Emperor became virtually a prisoner in his own palace. Seeing only a few high officials, he was carefully segregated from the larger world. Thus the Imperial Family developed an increasingly rarefied life, pursuing its own amusements (notably music and the dance), and speaking its own language; a pampered symbol, a prestigious anomaly.

The Emperor was not the only one to be so treated. The Tokugawas' political philosophy was 'divide and rule'. Since combination spelled danger, all channels must be closed. Since alliances brought revolution, they must be prevented. Ieasu strove to divide the country into the largest possible number of self-contained units and to restrict all communication between one and another.

His task was made easier by the deep-rooted clan instinct of the Japanese people. Once again he turned a potential danger into an advantage. Family loyalties had brought about the feudal wars; the idea of the closely knit, self-sufficient group could now be used to stifle rebellion at its source. In the new order, the interests of the individual were confined within a narrow and strictly regulated sphere. He was given no opportunity to look wider, or to acquire allegiances other than to his immediate superior. This held good for all ranks of society, which led in an intricate chain of command to the virtually inaccessible position of the Shogun. Provincial lords (*daimyo*) were carefully watched and kept within their own domains. Conspiracy was impossible. They could not travel unobserved, for barriers and check-points brought any movement to the attention of the police. Thus the towns were largely segregated from each other and developed artificially what classical Greece developed naturally – distinct local styles, traditions and attitudes.

Since Edo has now come into the picture, and is, with Kyoto and Osaka, one of the cities principally concerned in the emergence of the Japanese theatre, it may be appropriate to say something about the characters of these places. Each was different; and the difference is easily apparent, even today, beneath the superficial similarities of modernization. Kyoto had the oldest traditions. Refined by association with the Imperial Household, which resided there for centuries, it claimed a polish and courtliness which its rivals lacked. These qualities are still there. They are not obvious on the grand boulevards, choked with cars and clattering trams, but one need only turn off into a side street to find a pool of quietness that has known no disturbance for hundreds of years. Kyoto is a city dedicated to worship and contemplation. It is said that one could stay three years and visit a different shrine or garden every day. Some of them have fallen into disuse now, and others have passed from private into public hands. The Abbot of Ryoanji, site of the most famous garden of them all, is currently waging war against the hordes of school-children brought on educational trips and who, he says, disrupt the serenity of the place and make contemplation impossible. But, in spite of the tourist traffic, Kyoto on the whole maintains its calm and sophistication. Sheltered by the mountains which surround it on three sides, it remains proud and exclusive. In the centre of the city stands the Old Imperial Palace, where the emperors still come to be crowned and visitors must still be vetted by the Imperial Household before they gain admittance. Kyoto, as we shall see, was instrumental in preserving the courtly arts. Behind the toy walls of the palace, dances and ceremonies were treasured and kept free from profanation by the outside world.

Osaka, by contrast, is a merchant's town. It profited from its position. On one side was Kyoto and the luxury of court; on the other the port of Kobe, one of the principal centres of foreign trade. Osakans were brisker and noisier than their Kyoto counterparts. It is a depressing city now, full of factories and overhung with smog, but its pulse is still lively. The traditional Osaka greeting is 'Are you making money?' and the traditional lying answer, 'Not at all.' Osaka jokes are the Aberdeen jokes of Japan. It is no accident that the favourite form of entertainment, and one which, supposedly, was born there, is *manzai*, quick-fire repartee between two stand-up comedians. Osaka is now the city where most things in Japan are made. One of the things it helped to make was a traditional form of theatre.

Edo was a brash newcomer. Though it has changed its name and was legitimized when the Imperial Household left Kyoto and settled in Chiyoda Castle, the former stronghold of the Shogunate, in the nineteenth century, it still has this reputation. It first became important when the Shogunate seized power, and its population rose sharply. Ieasu had some eighty thousand retainers, not all of whom could be accommodated in the city as it then stood. They were joined by the families and retainers of more than three hundred *daimyo*, and thousands of priests flocking to the new shrines and temples. Traders and artisans followed, and by 1731 the citizen population had already passed the half-million mark; by 1787 it had risen to 1,367,000, larger than the London of that time, and nearly twice as large as Paris. It is now a staggering eleven million. Edo was a city that had to be constantly on the defensive, alert to any rumour of trouble. This was also the one city in Japan where a man might rise through his own merits. Its illegitimacy and its arrogance fostered what came to be known as the typical Edo spirit – flamboyant, where Kyoto was suave; full of braggadocio, where Osaka came straight to the point. These qualities became important in the development of *kabuki*, and produced a distinctive Edo style.

Within the cities the formation of the merchants into guilds (*za*) was encouraged, and areas were set apart for each trade. Something of this still survives – for example, in the bookshops of the Kanda district in Tokyo or in Osaka, where whole streets are devoted to the sale of electrical goods; it survives, too, in the modern equivalents of the 'gay quarters', of which more will be said later. The life of the average citizen was so hedged about by minute rules and regulations that he had no opportunity to protest, and no initiative. Bureaucracy in its worst form was the major instrument of government policy.

One small example may stand here for the whole. One of the most impressive buildings in Kyoto is Nijo Castle, built by the Shogun in 1603 for use as a residence during his conferences with the Emperor. The building exemplifies the conditions under which he lived and ruled. Visitors were conducted through a series of rooms, each with its own precise function, and linked by a 'nightingale floor', so constructed as to squeak musically at the slightest footfall. A familiar ornament of Japanese domestic architecture, it had an ulterior motive at Nijo, to betray any unauthorized approach. It is a small but significant example of how often, in this age, art served politics. In the first room, visitors were searched by the Shogun's inspectors. Next they were ushered into a waiting-room, the golden walls of which were appropriately decorated with crouching tigers, beasts known to the Japanese from Korea. Finally they reached the reception chamber where the Shogun's ministers interviewed them. This was the closest most of them could come to the Shogun himself. More important visitors, the hereditary lords, passed into another anteroom and, at last, into the presence chamber. Even here they were forbidden to look upon the Shogun, or to address him directly. The ruler sat in solitary state on a dais at the far end of the room, surrounded by secret doors from which guards could rush out at the first sign of an attempted assassination. At the other end knelt the lords, eyes fixed on the floor; between them and the Shogun sat the intermediaries, his ministers, through whom all questions were put and answered. This inaccessibility of the Shogun's person and the harsh punishment reserved for those who ignored it provide the background for one famous protest play, *Sakura Gimin Den*, which will be discussed at greater length in Chapter 4. It deals with a courageous farmer who, ignored by his immediate superiors, commits a massive breach of protocol by presenting his petition directly to the Shogun. For this crime he and his family are crucified.

On the far side of the suite was still another chamber, reserved for meetings with the imperial messenger; and in the heart of the castle were the Shogun's private rooms. Here he was attended by the ladies of the court; no other man was permitted access. The layout of the castle epitomizes the history of the country as a whole for over three hundred years. In the centre the Shogun, secure behind barriers of protocol and etiquette, no less strong for being intangible. Around him, in an immutable hierarchy, the officials, from the highest to the lowest, each with his carefully defined authority and responsibilities. On the fringes the people, divided and subdivided so that any popular impulse would be dissipated before it could gain momentum. The atmosphere of the police state is often felt in the plays. Works of actual protest are rare: to question the authorities was to invite immediate retribution. *Sakura Gimin Den* could be written only in the nineteenth century, when the Shogunate was already tottering. But the mechanics of state supervision are often present – the police patrols, the guards at the bridge, the popular hero who escapes arrest by disguise. There is often a sinister undercurrent to *kabuki* stories which now appear merely picturesque, like the grim realities of the Terror romanticized in the exploits of the Scarlet Pimpernel.

At the same time Japan was firmly cut off from the outside world, and entered the long period of seclusion which was not to end until the late nineteenth century. Only an island could have initiated such a policy, and only a police state could have enforced it. To us this segregation seems arbitrary and disastrously shortsighted. For the Shogunate it was essential if the internal equilibrium was to be preserved. People would accept the new order if they had no basis for comparison. Foreign influences, however benign, could only confuse and distract, and might set up new bonds of sympathy running counter to the approved associations. In the Shogun's defence it must be said that a closed-door policy was the only hope of healing the country after its bout of civil war. The rulers knew their subjects and the essential contradiction inherent in the Japanese character: on the one hand reverence for the past, on the other susceptibility to whims, fads and crazes. The Japanese are somewhat akin to the Welsh in temperament, capable of enormous bursts of enthusiasm followed by equally sudden disillusionment. This tendency is strongly marked in the history of the theatre, particularly in the evolution of *bunraku*. But such fanatical enthusiasm could be dangerous when applied to political ideas. Novelty must be prohibited.

In its foreign contacts the Shogunate had some grounds for apprehension. The events of the preceding century had been disturbing. In 1542 Japan had been accidentally discovered by three Portuguese traders, shipwrecked on a neighbouring islet. This led to organized trading visits and, in 1549, to the arrival of Francis Xavier and two other Jesuit missionaries, who landed at Kagoshima and began to preach Christianity. At first the authorities were sympathetic. They saw the commercial advantages of religious contacts and hoped particularly for a source of Western firearms. There was no hostility to the new religion as such. The nebulous concepts of Shinto could embrace virtually any belief, and Buddhism, in many of its observances, was sufficiently similar to Christianity to offer a common meeting-ground. Some Japanese were, in fact, ordered to turn Christian, just as their ancestors had been ordered to become Buddhists. Nobunaga continued well disposed, but his successor, Hideyoshi, saw in Roman Catholicism a new loyalty that might diminish his own authority. In 1587 he declared all missionaries *personae non gratae*, though traders were still admitted. The missionaries clearly paid no attention, and the following years saw increasing animosity to-

wards them, fostered by Hideyoshi's suspicions that they were
working as political agents. Nine were executed. From 1612
Ieasu pursued a consistent anti-missionary policy, which came to
include traders as well. Finally Iemitsu (1603–51) closed Japan
to the rest of the world and the rest of the world to Japan.
Nationals were forbidden to leave the country. This prohibition
has substantially continued in force until the present day.
Though the regulations were eased with the coming of Meiji,
strict exchange-control has kept the majority of Japanese at home,
and it is only in recent years that travel agencies have been able
to woo them with the delights of Honolulu and Las Vegas.

The remaining Christians were massacred in 1638, the victims
of a political ideal. The Shogunate distrusted Christianity for the
same reason that the Romans had done. While prepared to tolerate the new god, they could not countenance a group that cut
across existing class loyalties and claimed a higher allegiance.
After 1641 Japan was almost completely isolated. Chinese merchants were allowed to trade at Nagasaki, and the Dutch remained on a small island in the harbour, but could not penetrate
inland. The limited circulation of Dutch books was Japan's only
surviving contact with Europe.

The new order, rooted in ancient prejudice and formulated by
law, shaped the arts of Japan and the habits of its people. An
almost pathological resistance to change sanctified the old and
inhibited experiment. In the Imperial Palace ancient dances
continued to be performed in their original form. *Noh* drama,
the increasingly esoteric nature of which had already removed it
from the larger public, was soon to be restricted by edict to the
*samurai* class. The development of *noh* stops, to all intents and
purposes, at the beginning of the sixteenth century; from this
point it was simply a question of imposing a rigid form on old
material and codifying what had previously been left to the
artist's inspiration. History records that commoners erected an
illicit *noh* stage and hid it with the same care that bootleggers
devoted to their stills. Any sort of popular theatre was suspect.
The playhouse and the *geisha* house were danger-spots where
social barriers might be broken and the orders mingle and con-

spire. They were therefore forbidden to the *samurai*, who had to taste these furtive pleasures in danger and disguise. But the Shogunate found, like every other government, that the theatre can never be completely suppressed. The lower orders evolved their own entertainment, *kabuki*, and countered the exclusiveness of *noh* with a snobbery of their own. This was their theatre, their self-expression. But even *kabuki* recognized its boundaries, developing and guarding traditions at least as complex as those of *noh*. Subjected to continual harassment, building restrictions and sumptuary laws, it adopted a defensive posture, created its own hierarchy and became as closely identified with one class as *noh* was with the other.

The stratified society, with its intricate subdivisions, created a taste and need for classification. Identified with a recognized group, the individual was safe, and the appropriate social distinctions were embodied in language, dress and deportment. Spoken and written Japanese evolved distinct levels of formality: nothing so simple as the French *tu-vous* or German *du-Sie*, but drawing on different vocabularies and honorific affixes. One modern play, *Gozonji Isshin Tasuke* (*The Famous Isshin Tasuke*), turns these distinctions into comedy. It is a story of the third Tokugawa Shogun, the young Iemitsu, who escapes his assassins by changing places with his double, an Edo fishmonger. The humour arises from their differences: ruler and merchant in those days were worlds apart in speech and behaviour. Not the least difficulty of *noh* is its preservation of a highly formal language completely divorced from ordinary usage. These speech distinctions endure in today's society, though the modern tendency is to simplify. The most famous example is Emperor Hirohito's radio speech announcing Japan's capitulation at the end of the Second World War. Everyone listened, and no one understood, for the Emperor was speaking in High Court Japanese.

The habits inculcated by the Shogunate have left other enduring marks on the national character. Official business is still transacted through a labyrinthine bureaucracy. In spite of the enthusiasm for Western ways, official suspicion of the foreigner remains. Japanese visa regulations are set up on a complicated *quid pro quo* basis. Resident aliens in the United States may report changes of address by mail to a central bureau; in Japan they must report to the local ward office in person. Social behaviour is still governed by the need to identify with the group. In Japanese practice the family name is given first and then the personal name: you first establish the group to which you belong and then which particular member of it you are. In business it is the same: the Japanese must ascertain his milieu to know which rules apply. All Japanese of professional standing – and many with no professional standing at all – present their cards at first acquaintance and expect a card in return.

This explains the apparent inconsistencies of Japanese etiquette and the boorishness of people in the mass. Five minutes in a Tokyo rush-hour induce an agonizing reappraisal of Japanese courtesy. But the private formality and the public rudeness are part of the same pattern. Etiquette involves introduction and identification. By these standards the casual passerby does not exist, and it is every man for himself. It follows logically that the Japanese are the world's most dangerous drivers.

It often seems impossible to trace an address in Japan. Towns are divided into wards, wards into districts, districts into blocks; within each block houses are numbered haphazardly, in order of erection. The resident is familiar with the arcana of his own district, but outside may easily be lost. Taxidrivers need detailed local maps, or have to stop several times for directions. Journeys to any but the most familiar landmarks assume the hazards of a trek across the uncharted Kalahari. When the destination is, after several errors, located, the driver is modestly triumphant. He never expected it to happen.

In restaurants the same is true. Most Japanese eating-places specialize in a single dish. For *tempura* you go to one place, for *sukiyaki* to another. Even in those which operate on the Western pattern, individuality is frowned on. Order the set lunch without one item and you cause consternation. Out-of-towners keep their group identity even when eating; there are restaurants which cater to local preferences and allow the commuter to keep the habits with which he was brought up. Everywhere one sees the love of clinging to a pattern, even though the pattern may be outmoded.

This fondness for classification has complicated theatre scholarship. Plays are divided into types, and though the divisions may be arbitrary and inaccurate it is thought good that they should exist. The traditional grouping of *noh* plays into five categories, for example, is often misleading. This is particularly true of the Fourth Group, usually labelled 'madman' or 'obsession' plays. They might more properly be called 'miscellaneous', for any play which does not obviously fit the other categories is included here. Similarly *kabuki* is conventionally divided into historical and domestic plays, with a subdivision for works dealing with low life. This ignores the fact that many plays involving historical characters deal solely with domestic intrigue. The categories are, in fact, often interchangeable. Another venerable *kabuki* classification is based on merit: the so-called 'eighteen best plays', an honour roll of the finest productions. The classification of masks is often complicated to the point of absurdity. There are in fact only a few basic types, but scholars have elaborated the list to over a hundred. Scholars and critics themselves specialize to a degree unknown in the West. There are *noh* specialists, *kabuki* specialists, *bunraku* specialists; they confine their critiques to their adopted field, and are wary of committing themselves, even on the most elementary points, on matters which lie outside their narrow province.

Japan's isolation lasted over two hundred years, and was finally broken down by increasing pressure from the West. As long as access was difficult, the country could remain aloof. Now, with improved communication, the probing became more urgent and ultimately irresistible. In the first half of the nineteenth century other countries had multiplied their requests for trade relations. Russia was close at hand and vaguely threatening, while the acquisition of California by the United States removed another barrier. In 1853 Commodore Perry made his famous visit to Japan, returning the following year to support his requests with armament. Japan took its first tentative steps towards reunion with the world. Trade agreements were signed in 1854 and 1859, an American consulate was established in 1857, and Townsend Harris, consul-general, continued by finesse what Perry had begun by threat of force. It was at this point that the Imperial House came into its own.

The Shogunate, as we have seen, had removed the throne from the political arena by emphasizing its sanctity. To this end, Shinto, which worshipped the Emperor as divine, was revived and encouraged. It proved to be a two-edged weapon. The respectful attention directed towards the Imperial House and the study of its history showed up the Shoguns for the usurpers that they were. In the turmoil of the 1860s, with Japan under increasing external pressure, many turned for support to the Emperor, the man they now regarded as their legitimate ruler. There were three principal factions. One accepted the superiority of Western, as their remote ancestors had of Chinese, culture, and argued that Japan must inevitably bow before it. A second hoped for some sort of compromise, in which Japan could accept what was best from outside and blend it with her own traditional ways. A third, the diehards, urged the maintenance of the *status quo*, and tried to keep the door as tightly shut as it had been before. Each faction sought support from the personal dignity of the Emperor, and it was the reactionaries – unhappily for them, as things turned out – who were most vociferous, seeing in the antiquity of monarchical rule a safeguard against the Westernizing tendency of the Shogunate.

They received indirect support from the British, who, in their own demand for treaty rights, insisted on negotiating directly with the Emperor and not with the Shogun. Yielding to popular sentiment, the Shogun resigned in 1867, and in the following year the Emperor Mitsuhito was restored to full power. The Imperial Household was moved to Edo, which under its new name of Tokyo ('Eastern Capital') continued to be the centre of government.

Mitsuhito promptly disappointed his supporters by initiating sweeping governmental reforms. Feudalism was abolished, and local administration reverted to him. Most of the lords surrendered their fiefs voluntarily: there was some armed resistance but it was soon put down, and in 1876 those *samurai* who had not already laid down their swords were compelled to do so by law. The breaking up of the Shogunate, and the wanderings of the new *ronin*, the unemployed *samurai*, have provided the modern Japanese film with many of its plots. Numbers of them were, however, retained in the new elaborate bureaucracy. It was inevitable that they should be; they were the only class that had been trained to rule. In this way the military caste continued to dominate the Japanese government and was responsible for much of its later policy. Political parties came into existence, and the Constitution was proclaimed in 1889.

The reign of Mitsuhito, later given the name of Meiji ('Enlightened Government'), saw the sudden and often painful transformation of Japan from a feudal state to a modern industrial power. For all the vast amount that has been written about the era, the most impressive testimony is pictorial. It may be found in the Meiji Memorial Picture Gallery. Enshrined after his death, the Emperor continues to be worshipped in one of the most beautiful gardens in Japan. Somewhat apart in a park of its own, the Picture Gallery records the principal events of his life. Eighty large canvases show the Emperor's career from birth to the grave. They begin by recording ceremonial events in the flat, formal style of traditional Japanese painting. We see his birth, his growth, his investiture as Crown Prince, and his accession to the throne. In the last the Emperor sits in state on a dais, clad in full and formal robes, with the court prostrated on the steps below. In 1868 we see him giving audience to foreign diplomats: the Emperor is still in formal Japanese attire, the ambassadors in frock coats. In 1871 Prince Iwakura sails on his mission to Europe and America. Japanese and foreigners crowd the shores and some of the frock coats are now worn by Japanese. In 1872, for the formal opening of the Tokyo–Yokohama railway, the Emperor has abandoned the palanquin which carried him in earlier pictures for a horse-drawn carriage. The first conference of prefectural governors, in 1875, shows the rapidity of the revolution. All are wearing Western dress. The officials are no longer prostrated,

B

but standing respectfully, and the Emperor presides from a small table. The elaborate court ceremonial is succumbing to Western procedure. In 1877 the Empress visits the Tokyo Charity Hospital; by this time she too has forsaken the *kimono* for Western dress. So we move through the realistic scenes of the Russo-Japanese War, to the final picture which obliterates change; the palanquin bearing the Emperor's body, surrounded by weeping, parasol-carrying mourners.

The subject-matter of these paintings is fascinating enough. Modern industrialism suddenly intrudes. We see the Emperor at the railway and in a coal mine, and his Empress visiting a silk mill. These modern scenes are continually juxtaposed with others rooted in Japanese tradition. Among the conferences and the flaming battleships we find 'the Empress, sending a poetic epistle to the Emperor, who was travelling in the North-Eastern provinces. The poem is on the flight of Autumn geese.' But hardly less fascinating is the way the style of the paintings changes. We move from the flat decorated panel to the heavy textures of Victorian realism. Looking at the earlier pictures, we could only be in Japan; with the later we could as easily be at Balmoral. And in this shift of attitude we see the transformation of a country.

The artistic upheaval caused by the Meiji Era will be traced at length in the chapters which follow. The change of rule was the first serious blow to the traditional dramatic forms, and one which they survived only after considerable heartsearching. In comparison, the restrictions and censorship imposed by the American Occupation were no more than a trivial annoyance and produced few lasting consequences. In some ways, indeed, the Americans helped: their enthusiasm restored the flagging popularity of the *kabuki* and created a wider audience for the traditional art. The effects of the Meiji reforms have been more durable. Divorced from the social background which assured their prestige, the traditional dramatic forms have been forced to justify their existence on purely artistic grounds. It is to their honour that they have, so far, continued to do so, though not without considerable sacrifice. How long they will continue to survive is another question. There are many who argue that *noh* is already moribund and predict the imminent demise of *kabuki*. The introduction of the Western theatre created a new and for- midable rival. This sometimes merged with the old, to produce the bastard forms known as new, or mixed, *kabuki* and *shimpa*, modern treatments of traditional themes. More often it has sup- planted it; on rare and valuable occasions, as in some of the pro- ductions described at the end of this book, new inspiration has fertilized old forms to create a theatre which is at the same time distinctively modern and characteristically Japanese.

The state of the theatre is the state of the country; as usual, one mirrors the other. Japan now lives in its own past and in another's present. To call it a land of contrasts is to use the weariest of travel-book clichés; but when the cliché is so patently founded on the facts, and the facts so constantly obtrude on the attention, due respect and acknowledgement must be paid. The segregated state leapt with a bound into the nineteenth century and since then has made up in industry what it lost in time, with results that are everywhere apparent. Modernity, sometimes beautiful, often strident, jostles, overlays or mingles with tradi- tions hallowed by the centuries. On every side there is testimony to the two contradictory strains in the Japanese character: the abiding reverence for the past and the wild enthusiasm for the new. Japan is a museum of living history, though largely stocked with replicas. Shrines, temples and pavilions still stand where they have stood for centuries, but only rarely are they the ori- ginal structures. Buildings destroyed by war, fire or natural disaster have been rebuilt, again and again, exactly as they were. The impressive feudal pile of Osaka Castle has been reconstructed in concrete. Most of Nara has been rebuilt, plank by plank, stone by stone, as it originally was. Tokyo, delighting in its antiquity, has almost twenty times transplanted or rebuilt the shrine of its seventeenth century Shogun, Ieasu; at the same time, defiant in its modernity, it has torn down the Imperial Hotel designed by Frank Lloyd Wright, one of the few buildings to withstand the earthquake of 1923.

Often, modern practices cloak old assumptions. In the north- west corner of the city stands Tokyo's newest hotel, glittering,

Westernized, efficient. It would be equally at home in Los Angeles. It is called the Otani unofficially and the New Otani officially, since the latter combination of letters is numerologically more propitious. In its shadow stands the Kyo Ine, a traditional Japanese inn. To enter it is to cast off a hundred years. The walls are paper, the floor is covered with *tatami* mats, there are no chairs, the table stands a foot off the floor. In one corner, in the alcove reserved for the traditional scroll and the guest of honour, stands a tiny transistor television. In a curious way it harmonizes. An overhead expressway is being built, cutting through the heart of the city. Shrouded in bamboo scaffolding, its towers of structural steel contrive, somehow, to resemble a giant's calligraphy.

Other things do not harmonize so well. A technology which has imitated, borrowed from and often surpassed its Western rivals is still bound to a written language which is a preposterous amalgamation of Chinese and indigenous script, and where the average typewriter has 2300 characters with more in reserve. In a country which has traditionally paid grave respect to age and learning, a nucleus of fifty dissidents, as I write, has closed a university for months and driven professors from the campus with stones and broken bottles. It is not enough to sigh nostalgically for the past, to blame the urban ugliness on New York or the student riots on Berkeley. These things are inherent in the Japanese character. From the beginning the Japanese have been both imitative and seclusive, keen to adopt the latest fad and jealous in guarding the old ways, obedient to order without question and prone to violence without warning. The ugliness, the grotesquerie, the love of the freakish, abnormal and bizarre, is often present in the plays beneath the surface tranquillity. Whatever we may think, as historians or sociologists, about the three centuries of restrictive rule imposed by the Shoguns, in which every activity was policed, every journey controlled and every gathering suspected, no-one has ever suggested that the Shoguns were fools. They knew the national temperament and sought to restrict any loyalty other than to themselves by forestalling combination and breaking down the social structure into the maximum number of component parts. The Japanese insistence on protocol, obedience and discipline is somewhat akin to the ancient Greek reverence for moderation: both strove to encourage by artifice virtues to which they were not prone by instinct.

It is against this background that the contemporary Japanese theatre operates, and it is in the theatre, perhaps, that the contrasts are most clearly revealed. It is an amalgam of the most ancient and the most modern, reproducing its own past and simultaneously copying the West. As *Hello, Dolly* opens in Osaka, a *noh* theatre in Kyoto performs a play that has been in the repertory for six hundred years, and whose present form would be almost immediately comprehensible to the original audience. In the Asakusa district of Tokyo a chorus line kicks its legs a garter's throw from shrines preserving dramatic rites of immemorial antiquity. The Bayreuth Opera brings Wieland Wagner's production of *Tristan und Isolde* to Japan as a Japanese company takes *noh* to Norway. It is hard to say which audience is the more puzzled, though both are polite. 'We do not need to go anywhere else,' a proud Tokyoite said to me, 'because, in the end, everything comes here.'

Japan, obviously, is a theatre historian's delight. It has preserved its rites and performances as assiduously as its shrines and palaces. One may see, in living performance, the whole gamut of the country's theatrical history, from the *kagura* dances which began it all to the present day: on one stage *Okina* and on another *MacBird*. The sense of felicity is tempered with the sad knowledge that it cannot last. There is a growing fear that the oldest shrines will soon decay from lack of interest and support. Already, dances that were once performed by adults are now being performed – and not so well – by children; women may be seen as *noh* musicians, because there are not enough men to go round. Japan is full of societies for the preservation of *noh*, *kagura* and *bunraku*. Experience unfortunately teaches that the formation of such societies is the last kick of the dying art. It is all the more necessary to record and compare, and to suggest the analogies and the differences, between the traditional Japanese concept of theatre and our own.

# A NOTE ON CHRONOLOGY

The history of Japan, particularly during the feudal wars, is already complicated enough without the complications that have been added by historians. A notable source of confusion is in the various ways of naming reigns and eras. Some writers distinguish periods by reference to the presiding family (e.g. the Ashikaga Shogunate, the Tokugawa Shogunate). Others use the conventional chronology in which eras are named after the seat of the *de facto* government (not necessarily the residence of the Imperial Family, which was most of the time in Kyoto). A simplified scheme follows:

| ERA | | DATE |
|---|---|---|
| Legendary | A.D. | –604 |
| Yamato | | 604–710 |
| Nara | | 710–794 |
| Heian | | 794–1185 |
| (from Heian-kyo, the old name of Kyoto, remembered in the Heian Shrine. Kyoto simply means 'Capital') | | |
| Kamakura | | 1185–1333 |
| Muromachi | | |
| (a quarter of Kyoto, seat of the Ashikaga Shogunate) | | 1333–1568 |
| Momoyama | | |
| (on the outskirts of Kyoto, site of the Fushimi Palace) | | 1568–1600 |
| Edo | | 1600–1867 |

As Tokyo (Edo) continued to be the centre of government after the Imperial Restoration, succeeding eras, beginning with Meiji, are distinguished by 'auspicious names'.

# 2

## *In the Beginning was the Dance*

Of all my memories of the performing arts in Japan, one of the most vivid concerns something that was slight, accidental and not connected with the professional theatre at all: a visit on 5 May to a Tokyo kindergarten. This is Boys' Day in Japan, the fifth day of the fifth month. Every family with a male child hangs out paper carp, the symbol of courage and manliness. Miniature suits of *samurai* armour are on display in schools and houses, with all the accoutrements of the warrior – his sword, spear, drum and fan. The kindergarten had arranged a dance programme for us, and I went, like most of my fellow-guests, in a mood of amused condescension. It turned out to be enthralling. There was none of the oafish romping that passes for children's dancing in the West. These Japanese tots were perfectly disciplined and amazingly precise. There were more than sixty five- or six-year-olds involved, the boys in blue shorts, the girls in *kimono* or white frocks. They gave several dances. The first was an ensemble performance, in which two ranks passed, repassed and intertwined with bells and tambourines. Then came a masked mime, a story of an old man and a flock of sparrows; dances by girls with fans; and a short ballet set in a restaurant, where couples chatted and four balletic cooks made omelettes. Japanese children are set to dance as Western children are set to read and write. From the earliest possible age they learn to move to music, and after centuries of tradition the rhythmic sense has become instinctive. You may see it in a gang of workmen erecting a telephone pole;

in a students' protest march; in the flourishes of a waiter in a restaurant. In a country which is, in any case, so small and crowded that all motion must be ordered and contained, the most casual gesture may reveal an innate musical sensibility and a love of harmony and balance.

Dance is central to the dramatic concept, and, in Japanese tradition, takes its origin from the gods. The story has some resemblance to the Greek myth of Demeter and Persephone: in both a vital force withholds herself from the world and has to be tempted back by her peers. The Japanese story tells how the sun-goddess, the prime figure in early mythology, was angered by the foolish misbehaviour of her brother, withdrew her radiance from the world and sulked in a cave. Here is the sequel as recounted by Zeami, the illustrious father-figure of *noh*.

> At the moment when the Great-Goddess-who-illumines-the-sky shut herself in her Heavenly-Home-in-the-Rock, the World-beneath-the-sky was plunged into darkness. Then the eight hundred myriad deities assembled on Heavenly Mount Kagu, and, to captivate the divine heart of the Great Divinity, offered her a *kagura* [i.e. a sacred dance]. Ama-no-uzume-no-miko stepped forward from their midst, holding a branch from the sacred tree, tied with votive streamers. She raised her voice, and beat her feet in a tattoo upon the ground, raising a roll of thunder. In a frenzy of divine possession she sang and danced. The Great Divinity was unable to hear her voice clearly, and opened the door of the rock. Earth was radiant again, and the light glowed on the divine countenances of the gods. The entertainment that the gods devised at this time was, as they say, the first *sarugaku* [i.e. popular dance]. You will find the details in the stories men have told of it from ages past.

In other versions the goddess is lassooed by her peers as soon as she shows her face outside; or the door is closed behind her and made *tabu* with a sacred rope; or the gods hold up a mirror and show the goddess her own reflection, telling her they have found another source of light, so that she is piqued into coming outside to confront her rival. But Zeami was a good theatre man,

and knew when to stop; he also knew the power of his art. Ama-
no-uzume-no-miko has been happily called 'the proto-*geisha*'.
Zeami acknowledges another story, which again derives the
sacred dance from divine inspiration: in this case, from India,
and the direct intervention of the Buddha. As he tells it, the
dedication of a new Buddhist monastery was being interrupted
by heterodox worshippers who conducted a noisy rival ceremony in the courtyard. The loyal priests, acting on divine ad-
monition, set up drums and gongs in the back room, and performed sixty-six mimes. These attracted the attention of the dissidents, and eventually calmed them. Whatever the true origins
may have been, the Japanese mind saw the dance, and dance-
drama, as a fundamental and inseparable part of worship.

*Kagura* was officially adopted as the sacred dance. It may still
be regularly seen, and exists in various forms: some authorities
distinguish as many as thirty or forty variations. It may be danced
by men or women; by one performer or by several; in masks or
without; with properties – specifically, fans, swords and bells –
or with none. Danced with swords, some of its figures have a
strange resemblance to the traditional English morris dance. The
pieces are usually quite short, and may be accompanied by various
instruments – flute, drum or *koto* (the zither, or horizontal harp)
– or by the unaided human voice, chanting a prayer. In its simpler
forms *kagura* is given as an act of thanks and propitiation. Some
shrines hold performances on a regular basis, in gratitude for some
offering or donation.

The festivals held at major and minor shrines at significant times
of the year embody ceremonies which often go back to remote
antiquity. These are usually symbolic acts which have been translated into dance or drama form. The most venerable, as might be
expected, are those connected with the fertility of the soil. In
one, designed to bring divine favour on the planting of the fields,
a man puts on an ox mask and draws a plough, charging at the
bystanders and scattering them. Some of the most impressive
ceremonies occur in the rainy season, mid-June, when the rice
seedlings are transplanted to the paddy-fields. The oldest of these
*otaue*, and certainly the most famous, is held at Sumiyoshi Grand

Shrine in Osaka. According to tradition, it began some 1750 years ago when the Empress Jingo ordered her aides to hold a rice-planting ceremony at the shrine's sacred paddy to commemorate her victorious return from her Korean conquests, and also to pray for a rich harvest. It begins shortly after noon, with a procession of priests, *geisha*, and parishioners in ancient *samurai* costume. The girls receive sacred branches, which they carry to the paddy-field on the outskirts of the shrine. In the centre of the paddy a stage has been built, connected by a bridge to dry land. Stands are erected on the bank for the priests and distinguished visitors, and people come in thousands to watch. An ox splashes through the shallow water with a plough, while lines of girls stand ankle deep to transplant the seedlings. As they work, a continuous performance occupies the stage. *Geisha* and *miko* (shrine maidens) offer ancient rice transplanting dances, in which the gestures of the labourers below are transformed into balletic action. The *geisha* here are performing their ancient and honourable function (though the name *geisha* itself seems not to appear before the eighteenth century), which must not be confused with the shows beloved of modern tourists: the *geisha* party, in its present form, is the silliest entertainment ever devised by the mind of man, and the so-called 'pillow-*geisha*', who are prostitutes with ideas above their station, have degraded the art still further. Then the boys take over. Dressed as *samurai*, they hold a mimic battle on the stage and round the perimeter of the field, with demonstrations of stick-fighting and other martial arts. At the end of three hours the whole field is planted. In October a similar festival is held to celebrate the harvest. Another famous *otaue* takes place at Fushimi Inari Grand Shrine in Kyoto. Here four *miko* dance in costumes of the Heian period, while parishioners, Shinto priests and other shrine girls work in the sacred field, dressed in the clothes worn by farmers centuries ago. These festivals are typical of those performed all over the country at about this time.

Other forms of dance came from abroad. One of the earlier importations was *gigaku* (literally, 'skill-music'), said to have been brought from Korea in 612. It included compositions for

flute, drums and cymbals, and dances and farcical interludes performed by masked players. When the Great Buddha was dedicated at Nara in 752 – the largest bronze Buddha in the world,
over fifty-three feet high and weighing nearly five hundred tons –
*gigaku* formed part of the ceremony. We have few facts about
*gigaku* now; most of the information has been lost. There is one
interesting survival, however, in the *shishimai* or so-called 'Lion
Dance', which remained persistently popular and reappears in
various forms in the traditional theatre. The *shishi*, properly *kara
shishi*, 'Chinese lion', is a fabulous animal with little resemblance
to the king of beasts. It may be seen together with the *koma inu*,
'Korean Dog', carved in stone to guard the temples and other
holy places. The Japanese were fascinated by lions, having none,
and the Chinese themselves knew the animal only from Korea.
The *shishi* reflects this wonderment in his distinctly unleonine
appearance. At the risk of anticipating, it may be worth while to
follow his spoor across the centuries, for it is an excellent example of how the Japanese performing arts, even in comparatively modern times, continued to embody dances from remote
antiquity.

The *shishimai* exists in various forms, more or less complicated.
In one, still performed by the itinerant Yamabushi priests of
north-eastern Japan, the *shishi* is played by a male dancer in a
savage mask, and offered a dipper of water. This is explained as a
ceremony to propitiate the fire-god, and keep the ever-present
danger from the farms and villages. There are sometimes two
*shishi*, with one climbing on the other's shoulders and performing juggling tricks. In another version two young men dance with
mitts, or glove puppets, on their right hands, representing the
head of the fabulous beast. A long red scarf attached to each
glove winds up the dancer's arm round his neck; its undulations
represent the lion's tossing mane. The dance was also adapted for
*noh* play. It appears in *Shakkyo* (*The Stone Bridge*), by Motomasa,
who died in 1432. The play is of a form familiar in *noh*. A priest
is on a journey to China, to visit important Buddhist sites. In the
course of his travels he comes across a ravine spanned by the
stone bridge of the title. As he is about to cross, a mystic child

appears and informs him that the other side is the paradise of the god Monju Bosatsu, and may not be entered without long and arduous spiritual discipline. By way of compensation the priest is told that if he waits by the bridge he will see a marvellous sight. After an interlude in the form of a recitation by a hermit, stage assistants bring in a large property bank, a box covered with green cloth. This is one of the rare occasions when *noh* indulges in scenic display; the box is planted with two enormous sprays of peonies, one red, the other white. The principal actor reappears in the form of a *shishi* dancing among the flowers. He wears a rich brocade costume of blue, white and gold; on his face is a golden mask with grinning teeth, and an enormous mane of white hair trails down his back to sweep the floor. He tosses it from side to side, and stamps fiercely. In a variant version there are two *shishi*, one with a red mane, one with a white, to match the flowers; another variation has four. As so often in *noh* the 'story' is the merest pretext for introducing the dance, and in performance the second part is often given alone as a 'half-*noh*'.

Kabuki, the popular theatre, made its own version in *Kagami Jishi (Mirror-Shishi)*. Though not written until 1893, it still goes back to ancient sources, and is partly patterned after the *noh* play. Once again the text is minimal, and serves only to give a dramatic setting to the dance. After a brief conversational prologue between court lords and ladies on the forestage, the inner curtain rises to show a full orchestra in position: *samisen*, flutes, and three kinds of drum. Yayoi, a young girl of the court, is persuaded to perform an offertory dance as part of the court celebration of the New Year. After an initial show of reluctance, she makes an obeisance to the audience and agrees. She performs a series of dances with increasingly ornate properties – first, empty-handed, manipulating the sleeves of her brilliant robe; then with the *fukusa*, a strip of red silk: with one fan, gold and silver, and with two fans, red and gold, tossing, spinning them and balancing them on her fingers with agreeable dexterity. Finally she crosses to the altar where the sacred brown *shishi* head is displayed among the sacred rice cakes. Putting it on one hand, she moves into the *shishi* dance. Butterflies, manipulated on long poles by the property men, flutter around her. The *shishi* head has an articulated mouth; it comes to life and snaps at them. At first the dancer is unaware of this. When she notices, she tries to stop it, but the head is now so lively that it dominates the dancer, dragging her after it as it chases the butterflies. She falls to the ground, but the head will not be denied, and drags her at a run off the stage.

The *kabuki* version imitates *noh*'s two-part structure. In the second half, both butterflies and *shishi* are metamorphosed into human shape. The butterflies turn into little girls, who rise into view on an elevator through the stage floor, and perform a short dance of their own, each carrying a small shrine drum. Property men bring in huge sprays of red and white peonies, and the principal dancer returns completely transformed into the *shishi*. The costume is that of *noh* except that dead-white make-up replaces the golden mask. The white mane reaches to the ground, trailing behind the dancer for a full two feet. At this point, too, the drumbeats and rhythmic howls from the orchestra are deliberately reminiscent of the *noh* performances. The *shishi* falls asleep among the peonies, and the children, dressed in butterfly costume, flutter round and wake him up. There follows an elaborate *pas de trois* in which he stalks them and they tantalize him by leaping over his swishing mane. As the dance reaches its climax, the *shishi* tosses his mane wildly back and forth and from side to side, and the curtain closes.

The dances which were later to be canonized as classical were almost entirely of foreign origin. *Gigaku*, which became a regular part of Buddhist ritual, was in time superseded in popularity by other forms, which rapidly gained prestige in both sacred and secular uses, and have become associated particularly with the Imperial Court. The general name for the courtly arts of music and dance is *gagaku*, literally, 'elegant and authorized music'. It is a type of entertainment which, very early in its career, received the stamp of official approval, and for this reason has been handed down through the centuries virtually unchanged.

This phenomenon occurs frequently enough in Japanese cultural history to deserve some comment here. Several of the traditional arts have been preserved largely for social reasons, because they function as a badge of class. When any art becomes, like *gagaku*, closely identified with a particular, and unrepresentative, segment of society, its natural process of development tends to be arrested. It is cut off from the mainstream of life, and so, from lack of common handling, loses contact with the variety of experience that would act upon and modify it. In addition its aesthetic qualities tend to be subordinated to its value as a symbol of social status, so that any change becomes doubly suspect. All court arts have, in the end, been sterile. The longevity of the classical tradition in Japan, as opposed to the short life of, say, the masque in Western society, or the essentially aristocratic art of the neo-classical English drama, is due mainly to the artificial restraints that the country imposed upon itself. The long period of isolation preserved the narrowly stratified society, which in turn protected its traditions long after their natural life-span. How artificial this preservation was can easily be seen if we study the turbulence among artists after the Meiji Restoration. The wind of change crumbled the old values like mummified bodies discovered in the Etruscan tombs, which fell to dust at the first breath of air. It was largely owing to the intervention of scholars that the pieces were put together again and the old arts permitted to continue. Another factor which helped to preserve old forms for so long unchanged was the reverence for the past, always a part of Japanese tradition and given additional emphasis by Confucianism. It was felt that once an artistic concept had been refined and stated in definitive form, to change could only be to worsen. The old ways were always the best. While artists, who believe in the vitality of change, and sociologists, who accept its inevitability, must deplore such an attitude, historians can only applaud it, for it permits the preservation of works from the remote past in a way which happens only in the rarest of instances in the Western world. What happened to *gagaku* in its identification with the Imperial Court was also to happen, on a larger scale, with *noh* in its identification with the *samurai*.

*Gagaku* embraces dancing, singing and instrumental music. Music performed without dance is known as *kangen* ('wood and string') from the types of instrument which, with percussion, make up the classical Japanese orchestra. Dance accompanied by music is known specifically as *bugaku*. For the dances the strings are normally silent. Like so many of the Japanese traditional arts, *gagaku* has been preserved by hereditary transmission. It saw its greatest development in the Heian era, after which it was largely 'frozen': *gagaku* as performed today represents the musical values of a by-gone epoch, re-created by musicians who are mostly direct descendants of the original performers and whose families can be traced back some fifteen hundred years. The transmission of arts through real or adopted families – clans or guilds – is part of the Japanese system from the earliest period. The Nakatomi and Imiba families traced their descent from the gods who had respectively recited a liturgy and made offerings before the cave of the sun-goddess and claimed the custody of these rituals; they were the hereditary 'medicine men'. The court performers reflect the same tradition.

*Gagaku* owed its prestige, its form and its security to the favour of the court, and it is primarily as a court entertainment that it has survived. In a more democratic and less leisured age opportunities for seeing and hearing it are rare. Although it is still performed at some shrines and temples, the principal custodians of *gagaku* are now the musicians of the Imperial Household. They number about twenty-five, and normally enter the Music Department at twelve or thirteen, undergoing years of rigorous training before they are thought worthy of carrying on the line. In the past this training was confined solely to the *gagaku* repertoire, containing ancient Japanese pieces, medieval importations from Hindu, Chinese and Korean sources and later Japanese imitations. It was not until the Meiji Restoration that Japan first took serious cognizance of Western music. The court musicians, of their own accord, asked to be trained in these arts as well as their own, and the present generation, at least in theory, is equally proficient in both fields.

Even the court performances are now rigidly restricted. The musicians appear occasionally at the National Theatre, at receptions for foreign dignitaries, and, twice a year, in a small hall in the Palace precincts for a specially invited audience representing

the various cultural societies and the general public. They thus
preserve the isolationist spirit characteristic of old Japan. Because of their guardianship, the music of the past has been artificially segregated from any influence that might modify and in
time subvert it.

The present Imperial Palace stands in the heart of Tokyo, a
living and lonely relic of the exclusiveness that once characterized
the ruling classes. Before the court moved from Kyoto it was the
residence of the Tokugawa Shogunate. Freeways now thunder to
the west and south; to the east lie banks, offices and some of the
smarter hotels. But behind its high stone walls the Palace keeps
its dignity and silence. The general public is admitted on one day
each year – 29 April, the Emperor's birthday, when crowds go
to pay their respects. At other times, admission is limited to
those on official business, determined sightseers who have obtained prior permission, or, as in the case of these performances,
those who carry hard-won invitations. There are, however, signs
that this exclusiveness is being infringed upon. The Palace Hotel
rears up just outside the walls and overlooks them. Within the
precincts a large area is being converted into a public park.

Arriving for the *gagaku* we enter not through the great ceremonial gate with its famous double bridge, but through a smaller
portal in a secluded corner of the walls. It is as if we must be reminded from the beginning that the visit is a rare privilege, and
that we must be carefully segregated from the main body of the
Palace. Inside, the grounds are curiously disappointing. Several
buildings were destroyed or badly damaged by wartime bombing
and have never been restored. Bulldozers are levelling the soil,
and cranes tower above the surrounding trees. But we have little
time for inspection. Policemen check our credentials and marshall
us along a winding path to the north-east corner of the grounds.
Here stands a small theatre, its tower encrusted with mosaics,
erected in honour of the Empress. It is, frankly, hideous. Next
to it is the hall used for *gagaku* performances, where we are
bound.

*Gagaku* was traditionally given in the open air, but this is to be
an indoor performance. The hall contains a permanent stage,

used by the musicians for their rehearsals and rare public appearances. There is a surrounding gallery, which gives the best view. At ground-level the seats surround the stage on three sides. The

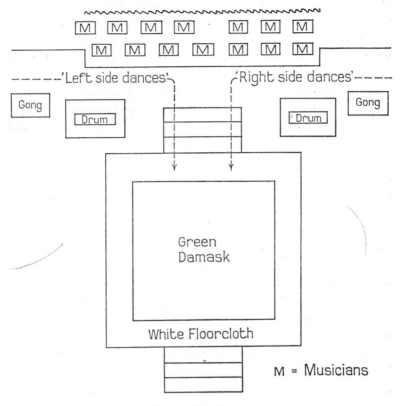

Fig. 1 *Gagaku* stage

floor is covered with fine gravel. Even when making concessions to climate and changing custom the Japanese usually contrive to bring some of the outdoors in with them. What we see is an openair stage transplanted virtually unchanged into a modern concert hall.

The stage itself is square and stands some three feet above the ground. It is draped with black silk and its surface covered with a white floorcloth, on top of which is laid in turn a green damask carpet, covering most of the area and providing the actual dancing surface. Red railings knobbed with gold fence off the stage, and three black-lacquered steps give access to the ground at front and rear. This is the usual but not invariable form. Details have changed over the centuries. A print from the Nara Era, preserved in the Waseda University Theatre Museum, shows four flights of steps, and two booths or pulpits between the stage and the royal audience, from which priests read the *sutras* while dancing was in progress. But in its basic structure the stage remains unaltered. To the rear are two smaller platforms, also with steps and railings. Each holds a huge drum mounted in a flame-like surround and topped by a gold or silver sphere. These drums testify to *bugaku*'s relationship to religious worship. The mountings are of Indian origin, and represent the sacred flames encompassing the Hindu deity Siva, a halo of fire which may be regularly seen on Buddhist statuary. One tradition of *gagaku* traces it back to the drum rhythm with which Siva created the world. The drums themselves are painted with interlocking S shapes, the Chinese symbols of the duality of *yin* and *yang*. Drums of this type may be seen in the inner sanctums of the shrines.

The drum-platform on the spectator's left is draped in orange, that on the right in green. These colours are related to the costumes of the dancers, and thus to the origins of the dances themselves, as will appear. Beside each drum stands a still smaller platform holding a gong. Behind the drums, in an alcove of the far wall, is a long, low platform used by the musicians when the stage is occupied by dancers. It is backed by a curtain striped in orange and black, with a pattern of white medallions. The atmosphere is formal and sedate, disturbed only by a megaphone which, protruding through the curtains, implores us not to smoke.

Most of the audience have been in their places for an hour, and the performance begins on the dot. This sort of punctuality (at least on the part of the performers) is almost invariable in Japan; Western theatres would do well to copy. The concert is in two parts, instrumental music followed by a set of three dances. In procession the musicians advance onto the large stage. Their instruments are the *sho*, a small, mouth-operated organ with seventeen bamboo pipes; several kinds of flute; the *koto*, horizontal harp or zither, with thirteen strings; the *biwa*, the Japanese four-stringed lute; bass and kettledrums, and small gongs. One of the pieces is known as *The Prince of Lan-Ling*, representing the Prince Chang Kuang, a famous Chinese warrior of the sixth century, and composed in his honour after he had particularly distinguished himself in battle. The purely musical part of the concert is short – possibly in deference to the many Western visitors who find it difficult, if not impossible, to grasp the principles of Japanese music,with its six scales and unfamiliar tonality. For most of us the chief interest is in watching the musicians and their strange instruments. They sit cross-legged in solemn dignity, dressed in black mitres and orange robes, not so much giving a performance as engaging in a rite.

After an interval the musicians return, this time to the platform at the rear. They have changed into rich robes of red, white and gold brocade; the plain black mitres are replaced by stiff, pointed hats, almost like helmets. The stage is left clear for the dancers. Interest in the audience rises, for even the non-specialist can find much to admire in the Japanese dance. The costumes are sumptuous and the movements, even if showing little variation to the untrained eye, flowing and graceful. It is now that the giant drums come into use – the left or the right, depending on what sort of dance it is. *Bugaku* remembers its origins in its staging. The dances are divided into two schools or traditions, depending on their provenance. Those introduced from China, India and Indo-China, and their Japanese imitations, are known as *samai*, 'Left Dances', those from Korea as *umai*, 'Right Dances'. The performers indicate this by the side from which they enter, and by their costumes. Left Dances are dressed in shades of red, orange and reddish brown; Right Dances in green. The colour of the costumes thus relates to the drapery of the drum-stands, and the right or left drum is used as appropriate.

Today's programme includes two *samai* and one *umai*. First come four men in brownish robes patterned with lions, trains which sweep the ground, and full white trousers. They advance

onto the stage in slow procession and form a square. *Samai*
dances are usually elegant and stately. The four men turn in and
out; they extend their arms in unison, in full, flowing gestures.
Only rarely do they move from the spot. The footwork is confined to turns and an occasional vigorous stamp. They exeunt still
dancing, each waiting until the man ahead has reached the top
of the steps before moving from his place. Next comes a solo by
a dancer representing the same Prince of Lan-Ling whom we heard
commemorated musically in the first half of the programme. His
robe is orange, with a brocade surcoat trimmed in red and white.
On his face is a grimacing golden mask such as the Prince is said
to have worn in battle to terrify his enemies. The last dance
(*umai*) is given by four men dressed as women, in gree nkimonos
and white masks, and elaborate headdresses in the shape of birds.
*umai* dances are traditionally vigorous and fast-moving, though
this is by comparison only: the tempo, by Western standards, is
still slow.

   It may be appropriate here to notice some general characteristics of these court dances, for they reappear in *noh*, and many of
the ritual appurtenances of that form derive directly from the
dance tradition. We may see, first, the methodical observance of
traditional rules and customs, not only in the dance itself but in
what precedes and follows it. The movements of the dancers as
they approach and retire are as carefully schooled as the posturing
on the stage. In an art as old as this, where every detail has been
meticulously studied and hallowed by time, protocol is rigorous.
Second, although the meaning may be apparent only to initiates,
the dances are customarily based on some concrete character,
historical event or 'message'. A pattern which seems abstract is
in fact conveying a story. For example, the first *samai* dance
described above uses the five notes of *kangen* to represent the five
cardinal virtues, humanity, justice, politeness, wisdom and
fidelity. For those who have eyes to see, dance becomes an
allegorical presentation. Although the movements are usually
stylized to a point where their original meaning is no longer immediately discernible, they are firmly founded on mimetic gestures, and the observation of actual people engaged in real acti-

vities. The classical Japanese dance refines everyday behaviour into rhythmic patterns of movement, just as a painter may translate material objects into studies of spatial and dynamic relationships. This is true of music as well as of dance. It usually has a story. One of the most famous *koto* pieces is a study of the various moods of water. The Greeks would have been sympathetic to such ideas, though our own musical appreciation is founded on rather different premises. Third, we must notice – and we can hardly avoid it – the sumptuousness of the costumes as contrasted with the stark simplicity of the stage. In Western ballet the idea of scenic splendour was originally inseparable from the conception of the dance. It is only comparatively recently that choreographers have sought to remove the dancer from his pictorial surroundings and work in terms of pure movement. In the dance-dramas of Japan the reverse has been true. Simplicity of staging comes first. It is only later, in the elaborate transformation scenes beloved of *kabuki*, that scenery begins to grow up behind the performers, to compete with them, and sometimes to overwhelm them.

Authorities claim that the court dances have become effete through inbreeding, and that their original vigour may now be seen only in the country and at the shrines. Certainly the shrine performances, where they may still be found, return the dances to a more appropriate historical context. They are seen there not as isolated performances, but as part of a rich and varied ceremony which draws on various sources. The shrine festivals offer pageantry as well as dance. They are gala performances, sometimes lasting for several days, in which large sections of the community take an active part. Some are historical pageants. At the Toshogu Shrine in Nikko there are annual processions in which devotees follow the portable shrines dressed in the costume of three centuries ago. Over a thousand participants representing warriors, priests, flag-bearers, page-boys and attendants parade in honour of the Shogun Ieasu. Dances are dedicated on the temple steps, some by the Buddhist priests themselves. The Asakusa Kannon shrine in Tokyo has rites which are far older. Every May, parishioners carry their own portable shrines through

the maze of surrounding streets. There may be as many as a
hundred of them, massive and weighty, jingling with bells and
encrusted with golden ornaments. Each is carried on a palanquin
by thirty or more young men, who gyrate with their burden
through the crowd and stop at fixed points to elevate their load
head-high: all this to the continuous rhythmic chant of 'Hei-a!
hei-a!' Children carry miniature shrines and do their best to
imitate the adults. In a smaller building near by, a sacred dance is
dedicated to Kannon, and other dances are given by amateurs on
the *kagura* stage. Some of these are designated by the government
as 'intangible cultural properties', and preserved as jealously as
treasures in a museum. All this goes on against a constant background of colour, pageantry, movement and noise. Carts full of
drummers jolt through the crowd. Flutes wail in the background.
The temple gong beats ceaselessly. Smoke of incense rises, and
fireworks brighten the evening sky. Out of this turbulence, part
sacred, part secular, the classical theatre of Japan was born.

All parts of Japan maintained such ceremonies. They were
connected with the seasons of the year, with local folklore, or
with specific activities, and contained, as well as the higher forms
of dance, entertainments of more popular origin. The adoption of
*bugaku* by the aristocratic and priestly classes removed it from
popular favour, and other forms replaced it. The names are, as
usual, significant. *Dengaku*, 'field' or 'rustic music', was aimed at
the general public, who had no time or desire to cultivate refinement, and was simpler to appreciate and more acrobatic in
style. We hear also of *sangaku*, 'scattered' or 'irregular music' –
irregular, in contrast to the precise organization of *bugaku* – and
of another type, *sarugaku*. This similarity of names has puzzled
philologists. Some argue that the latter is a phonetic corruption
of the former. Others see it as a deliberate and derogatory
coinage to describe the content of the performances: the name
means 'monkey music'. There is also some confusion of usage.
At some times the words appear to have distinct meanings, at
others to be used interchangeably. Folk arts do not lend themselves to easy definition.

These popular forms, however, had several things in common.

They appear to have had an early connection with *kagura*, and to have been performed as a deliberate contrast to the solemnity of the religious dance, a Japanese equivalent of the Christian 'Feast of Fools'. Looser in structure, they permitted the interpolation of elements which did not properly belong to dance, and which contained the seeds of the later drama. It is impossible to say how much was native and how much foreign. *Dengaku* may have been imported from elsewhere in Asia. A Chinese origin has been suggested for *sangaku* and *sarugaku*. But wherever these dances came from, they were swiftly absorbed into the folk-culture, and came to include indigenous dances as well as turns and performances of various kinds. The earliest comprehensive description of *sarugaku* that we have is *Shin Sarugaku Ki* (*New Notes on Sarugaku*) attributed to Fujiwara Akihira (989–1066), scholar and courtier. He lists such items as a midget dance, 'imprecators', juggling with balls, mimicry of priests and women, a praying-mantis dance and a 'boneless man' – presumably a contortionist. He gives the titles of several sketches: 'Priest Fukko begs for robes'; 'The Nun Myotake asks for swaddling clothes' (she has, presumably, been naughty); 'A country gentleman goes to the capital for the first time'. The author mentions four or five actors in the capital who specialize in these farcical roles, and in the twelfth century we hear of dancers impersonating demons, dragons, gods and goddesses.

The type of entertainment indicated here is familiar in other cultures during the formative stages of their drama. 'Imprecators' suggests an analogy with the licensed abuse of early Greek festivals, which left its mark on Aristophanic comedy. There is an obvious similarity, also, with the early performances of Republican Rome. In that city, as in Japan, there seem to have been two distinct streams of influence. On the one hand were the dances imported from the Etruscans, used first for religious purposes and then taken up by amateur performers from the aristocracy. On the other was the Mediterranean mime, a medley of song, dance, acrobatics and impersonations, which combined with rustic verse-forms to produce a local popular comedy. Or we may compare the mimes, reciters and *jongleurs* of the Middle Ages in

Europe, whose activities infiltrated the sacred chant to contribute
an important element to the later religious drama.

Both *dengaku* and *sarugaku* soon came to include some rudimentary dramatic element. By the beginning of the Muromachi
Period we hear of frequent performances called *noh* – dramatic
interludes in, or variations on, the popular dance forms. *Noh*
means 'ability' or 'accomplishment'; in modern Japanese, more
concretely, 'brain'. We have an account of an open-air performance of *dengaku-noh* in 1349, in the dry bed of a river – a
favourite place in both China and Japan for theatrical performances, just as the Greeks used the level ground at the foot of a
hill. Two teams seem to have performed in competition. The
stage was spread with green and crimson cloth (the colours of the
*bugaku* performances) and decorated with tiger and panther skins.
They gave, among other things, what was quite literally a 'monkey
dance', by boys dressed in monkey-skins. In 1374 the Shogun
himself attended a performance of *sarugaku-noh,* thus greatly
raising its prestige.

If we can see a perfect re-creation of the traditional court
dances at the Imperial Palace, we can gain at least an approximate
idea of their popular counterparts at the modern shrine festivals.
At the Yasukuni Shrine in Tokyo there is held every April a
festival in honour of the war-dead. For several days the shrine
precincts are turned into a fairground. The long avenue leading
to the main gate is lined with booths and tents. There are tea-
stalls, al fresco restaurants, and hucksters selling toys, balloons
and flags. Plastic figures of Batman hang side by side with prayer
streamers, amulets beside goldfish to be dipped for and taken
home. Many bring offerings of food and *sake* to the shrine, to be
displayed and tagged with the names of the donors. The forecourt is the place of entertainment; despite its purpose, this is
no solemn festival. The displays of rocks, flowers and miniature
gardens are sedate enough, but there is also a stage, constantly in
use and the main centre of attraction. It is easy for the casual
visitor to forget the religious associations: what he sees is a
combination of garden fête and circus. Spectators sit on benches
round a temporary stage, put together from slotted poles. Its

plank floor springs under the dancers' leaping, and the straw mats which cover it are damped down between each sequence. It is roofed with branches, and hung with flags and prayer-streamers. A long plank makes a ramp up to the stage; a flautist and drummer stand behind. This simple structure is worth noting. It shows what the *noh* stage must have been in its simpler and more rustic days.

Four men perform a sword dance. Their weapons are real and viciously sharp, slicing the paper banners as they catch them overhead. They interlace in complicated patterns: the dancers duck and weave through and under them, to the pounding of the drum. They are followed by two others, who dance an episode from *samurai* history. One carries a longbow. The other, holding arrows, leaps back and forth through the bow stretched open by his partner. They grapple for the bow and mime a struggle, while the drumbeat rises to a crescendo. One of them collapses from exhaustion. Or is it all part of the dance? Certainly his eyes are closed, and the sweat is real enough. Four stagehands appear opportunely. They hold him upright, mop his brow, set a sword in his hand and go through the final motions for him, manipulating him like a bedraggled puppet. He is carried off amid loud applause.

One programme of dances is now over, and workmen dismantle the stage. Shinning up the high poles, they tear down flags and lashings: in twenty minutes the stage has been reduced to a heap of lumber and carted away. The day's programme continues, on a more solid structure, the permanent *noh* stage in one corner of the shrine. There are *noh* dances, a comic interlude and a complete *noh* play. It is fascinating to see the classical drama restored to the setting of its birth; it is an entirely different performance in the open air. The *noh* is followed in speedy succession by other acts — *koto* and *biwa* recitals, monologues, and a conjurer (in white tie and tails) who performs the venerable but always impressive trick of turning a pigeon into a silk scarf in mid-flight. There are also folk-dances and *kagura* performed by various local groups. Three girls dance with fans, gold on one side, silver on the other; the colour sequence changes constantly as their bearers flip them with careless expertise. There is a *pas seul* with tambourine. Other offerings reveal, much more clearly than the ceremonial posturings of court, the intimate connection of Japanese dance with the workaday rituals of common life. The dancers mime the gestures of farming and fishing; their clothes are work-clothes, worn for ease of movement, not for display. The show continues until late in the evening, and there will be more tomorrow.

Though the trappings of the festival are modern, its core is ancient. It makes little difference that the dancers perform to recorded music, that the monologuist uses a microphone, or that the conjurer is accompanied by a Dixieland version of 'The Old Folks at Home'. In its essentials this sort of festival has remained unchanged for centuries, not because it has been artificially preserved, but because its elements are eternally popular. It caters to the universal need for song, dance, spectacle and wonder; and from these elements, paradoxically enough, the chaste form that we now call *noh* was born.

At festivals like this we may recapture something of the atmosphere of *sarugaku-noh*. In the country districts there are still performances which retain the content of the early drama. The Yamabushi priests include in their repertoire, as well as the *shishimai*, several dance stories which later became familiar in more elaborate *noh* and *kabuki* versions. *Dojo-ji* is one of the more famous. The background is as follows: A girl was told by her father as a cruel joke that a travelling priest who was staying at their house wanted to marry her. Discovering the deception, she pursued the priest to the Dojo-ji temple and found him hiding beneath a huge bell. Changing herself into a serpent, she twined herself round it and reduced it to a lump of molten metal. In the immediate action the girl returns to the temple when a new bell is being dedicated and gains admission by pretending to be a shrine dancer. Once inside, she pulls the bell on top of her. The priests, realizing who the woman must be, use incantations to cast her out. Lifting the bell, they find her in her serpent guise and drive her away with spells. In the *noh* and *kabuki* versions there is a real bell and an impressive transformation. The *yamabushi* have no bell, and the girl changes her costume behind a *kimono* held as a screen; but to all intents and purposes the story is the same.

A form of *sarugaku-noh* is still practised in the village of Neo, in Gifu Prefecture. Some performances are given in farmhouses, others on an improvised stage which is hardly more elaborate than the temporary dance platform described earlier. The acting area is small; performers dress behind a curtain at the rear and make their entrances through this directly onto the stage. There is no sign of the *hashigakari*, or long walkway, that is the characteristic feature of the more elaborate theatres. The plays use the regular *noh* orchestra – two drums and a flute – though music is subordinate to speech. In the more refined performances the musicians are dominant and set the atmosphere of the play; here the words always come first, and the music is introduced only later. A minimal chorus sits at the back of the stage instead of at the side, the more familiar position. The actors are amateurs and perform with a heartiness in comparison with which the professionals seem somewhat over-refined. In *noh*, as in *bugaku*, living for centuries in a protected environment has brought about loss of vitality. The tempo, also, is noticeably faster. Several scholars feel strongly that *noh* was intended to be played at this speed, and that the gradual *rallentando* of the professional performances is a distortion of the art. Whether or not we accept this, the Neo plays give us a glimpse of what *noh* must have been like in the period between its separation from the dance proper and its polishing by master hands; the time when performers were still making do with rudimentary materials, and the various elements of the drama – orchestra, actors and chorus – had not been welded into a unified whole.

Finally there are interesting performances still given annually at Kyoto: mimed farces, in the precincts of the Mibu Shrine, which claim a history of seven hundred years. This would take them back before Kwanami and Zeami, the founders of *noh* proper. Though some of the plays are obviously derived from, or even parodies of, full-length *noh* drama, others must be far earlier, and show the burlesque material out of which *noh* developed.

Once again, there is a tiny stage, with a pit beside it into which people and objects may be thrown. Acrobatics are much in evidence, and one play even includes a slack-rope dance. The targets are the familiar ones. A priest, illicitly married, does his best to conceal his wife from a visiting dignitary. Two shopkeepers compete for the privilege of setting up a tax-free business and overturn each other's goods. The actors make up in enthusiasm what they lack in professional skill. In one play, a version of the *noh Funa Benkei* (*Benkei in the Boat*), the actor playing Benkei had never done the part before, and had to be continually, noisily and angrily directed by a senior. Once again there is a parallel with Roman drama. The early Italian burlesques – the Atellan farces – were, by all accounts, much like this, both creating their own slapstick plots and parodying those of their more serious rivals. The Japanese found such things to their taste. *Sarugaku-noh* and *dengaku-noh* companies competed for the public attention. Their popularity was such that they won the ear of the Shogun and found their way into the shrines.

# 3

# The Theatre Protected

In the battle for audiences it seemed at first that *dengaku* would win; it became a popular fad, one of the earliest of many in the history of the Japanese theatre. The moralists, however, frowned on it. *Sarugaku-noh* achieved a more respectable footing by its association with the temples. Buddhist priests saw in it a potentially valuable medium for propagating the faith and sponsored performances in the temple precincts, often taking part themselves. Temple *sarugaku* acquired a new sobriety, and a new purpose: to expound the principles of Buddhist worship in dance. Its performers assumed a higher professional status, forming guilds (*za*) to strengthen their connection with specific shrines and to foster and protect their art. In this they followed the customary pattern of professional life. Admission to the guilds was restricted, a certain period of training insisted upon, and the size of the group kept within manageable limits. As the popularity of *sarugaku-noh* increased, the guilds multiplied and subdivided. Actors frequently left the *za* in which they had been trained to head a new group of their own.

From the medley of dance and drama came the drama proper. The dancers acquired stories they could act and a Chorus to support them. The evolution is implied in the name: the plays are called *noh* pure and simple. In some cases the change is almost imperceptible. Some pieces classified as *noh* and contained in the official repertoire are almost wholly dance, with dramatic interest so slight as to be negligible. The most famous example is *Okina*,

generally recognized as a survival of a far earlier tradition. It
consists mainly of a group of dances said to have been in existence
in the tenth century and has a place of honour in the *noh* repertoire. Modern performances are comparatively rare, and restricted to times of special celebration or commemoration, but in the
daylong *noh* cycles of earlier periods *Okina* headed every programme as a propitiatory rite. When given now, it still comes
first, and is preceded by private ceremonies in the dressing-room.
*Okina* has a clear religious function. It invokes the help and support of the gods, calls down prosperity on the land and prays for
long life for the people. There are three characters. Okina, the
principal role, who is both god and patriarch, is played by the
head of the *noh* school. He enters barefaced, with his mask in a
box (a significant difference from customary practice), and puts
it on in full view of the audience. The mask, which has previously
been offered on the dressing-room altar, represents jovial old age,
with a smiling mouth, laughing eyes and wrinkled cheeks. Okina
then engages in an antiphonal dialogue with the Chorus. The
sense of the words is now lost; derived from remote sources,
possibly Sanskrit, they had already, by the Middle Ages, hardened
into a meaningless formula – *tu tu tarari tararira*. Actor and
Chorus exchange wishes for eternal life : 'I pray that our lord may
live for ever without end, in high prosperity.' This is followed by
several dances, first by the second character, Senzai (1000 Years),
then by Okina himself, revealing his divine nature, and finally by
Sambaso (Third Old Man), who is something of a comic relief to
the others. His dances, first unmasked and then with mask and
bells, represent sheer animal exuberance, the blind faith in
existence. This sequence is said to be a symbolic representation
of the cycles of earthly existence according to Buddhist philosophy, but its interpretation must remain obscure : the ancient
text, handed down by rote, is now largely meaningless, even to
the performers. *Okina* also exists in several *kabuki* forms, where
the role of Sambaso has been enlarged to the detriment of the
others. In his later manifestations he appears virtually as a clown,
with white face, eyes rimmed with red and cheeks lined with
green. On his head is a tall cap striped in black and gold, and in

his hand the inevitable bells. His mouth is painted in a fixed smile, and his protruding tongue shows his exhaustion from the dance. His dances are often performed, alone and out of context, by both men and women. There is even a puppet Sambaso, whose solo regularly introduces the *bunraku* performances and appears in folk-forms also. This is probably the closest the Japanese puppet-drama has come to providing a popular folk-figure on the lines of Guignol, Kasperl or Mr Punch.

*Okina* stands in a class by itself, but there are several later plays which show early dance forms in a dramatic setting. One obvious example is *Shakkyo* (*The Stone Bridge*), discussed in the previous chapter. This is no more than a dramatic framework for the *shishimai*, and the dance is usually performed alone, without the play. In *Ema*, a slight dramatic incident serves as a pretext for the dance which is the body of the piece, and which itself recalls ancient origins. A messenger from the Emperor is on his way to the Great Shrine of Ise. (The use of a messenger or pilgrim to introduce a play is a favourite *noh* device, as will be seen.) He spends the night at the near-by village of Saiko to observe a traditional custom. On the last night of winter, votive tablets are hung out to foretell the fortunes of the coming year. The messenger meets an old couple who put out such tablets, and they reveal to him that they are really gods in disguise. In the second, and principal, part of the play the sun-goddess appears in her own shape. She and other gods dance for the messenger, re-enacting the old legend of the withdrawal of the goddess into her cave, and the trick played by her fellows to entice her out. What we have here is, in effect, a refinement of the original *kagura* dance with a dramatic setting and a prologue. *Miwa*, too, em-bodies a *kagura* dance. A priest lends a cloak to an old woman, and afterwards learns that it has been found hanging in the branches of a tree. When he goes to see, the god Miwa no Myojin appears to him in the woman's shape, tells a story con-nected with the site, and gives the familiar account of the entice-ment of the sun-goddess, accompanied by *kagura*. These examples are particularly interesting in the light of the tradition deriving the *noh* from the *kagura* stage and the latter from the upturned tub on which Ama-no-uzume-no-miko danced; the characteristic stamping of the *noh* dance is said to originate from the pounding of the feet that lured the goddess out. In other plays, of course, the dramatic interest is far higher, and may sometimes (as in *Shunkan*, discussed at length in Appendix I) almost eliminate the dance. Normally, however, and whatever the story, the dance remains central. In modern performances the *noh* dances (*shimai*) are frequently taken out of context and given as separate pieces. It is in them that the interest chiefly lies and the skill of the performer most reveals itself.

The classical civilizations of the West regarded certain individuals as having taken the vital step of giving plot and form to disorganized and semi-dramatic elements. Greece so recognized Thespis, the Romans Livius Andronicus. The Japanese attribute the same honour to a minor Buddhist priest, Kwanami, on more solid grounds. Thespis is a shadow on the fringe of Greek history, and Livius at least as much fiction as fact, but with the creation of *noh* we are talking of the fourteenth century A.D., well into the era of accurate records. The facts are well attested. Kwanami lived from 1333 to 1384, and at the performance of *sarugaku-noh* attended by the Shogun in 1374 danced the role of an old man. By Western standards – even when we remember the origins of our own religious drama – this may seem a surprising activity for a priest. By Oriental standards it was normal. Dance had always been an integral part of worship, and the Buddhist priests of Japan never formed a separate, aloof caste. On the contrary, they have always been prominent in the arts. One of Japan's leading modern sculptors, Nishikido Sinkan, is a Buddhist priest: Eda Kazuo, an *avant-garde* director in Tokyo, is also a Zen priest. An authority on Zen studies and the history of *noh*, he has incorporated some of Zen philosophies into his basic theatrical theories and successfully integrated jazz with the stylizations of the classical theatre. The priesthood and the fine arts continue to combine.

Kwanami was born at an opportune time for artistic experiment. At various periods in its history Japan has been highly susceptible to, and has indeed invited, influence from China. It was in such an age that Kwanami lived. His country was enjoying a cultural renaissance which owed much to the glories of its larger neighbour in the two hundred years preceding. In the middle of the twelfth century the Chinese capital had moved to Hangchow, the 'Chinese Venice', which became the centre of a civilization as culturally powerful as it was politically weak. The reign of the fourth Hangchow Emperor, Ning Tsung, marked its summit. This was the age of the glorification of nature in painting, and of the propagation of Zen Buddhism to inspire and inform the arts. Japan observed and emulated this cultural leap forward. The Ashikaga Shogunate produced men who, like the Hangchow emperors, were indifferent rulers, but discerning patrons. The Shogun Yoshimitsu abdicated in 1395 and devoted the remaining thirteen years of his life to aesthetics. Yoshinori, his son and successor, was assassinated in 1441. Yoshimasa, who came to power two years later, was immensely concerned with beautifying his domain and increasing its cultural prestige. Scholars have compared him to his Italian contemporary Lorenzo di Medici. These reigns saw the evolution of three things which in their separate but related ways are held to typify the classical spirit of Japan: the *noh* play, the Zen landscape garden, and the tea ceremony.

*Noh* drama, like Greek tragedy, takes its vitality from the tension between sacred and secular. The creation of *noh* proper begins with the separation of the plays from the religious festivals and their re-establishment in a secular context. Nevertheless they never entirely lose their Buddhist associations. The priest is a familiar figure in them, and the *sutras* are frequently read; the deities appear, and the action assumes a Buddhist philosophy, insisting on the transience of the material world and the struggles which the individual must undergo to attain Nirvana. Sometimes the didacticism is embodied in a powerful harangue: *Eguchi*, by Kwanami's son Zeami, embodies a sermon, delivered by the ghost of a former courtesan, on the blessings to be found in the power of Buddhist law. Buddhist aesthetics, particularly, as developed in Zen, had a major influence on the stage form as well as on the content of the plays. Kwanami's contribution was to illuminate Buddhist doctrine with dramatic material drawn from secular sources. Coming from a family which had wide connec-

C

tions with the performing arts, he functioned more as a selector
and adaptor than as an original composer, providing the dances
with stories and librettos and seeking appropriate material in
popular sources.

The tales and legends already current in medieval Japan provided a limitless source of supply. Many were well known in
literary form, through such works as the *Heike Monogatari*. This
source alone provides forty-one of the plays in the current repertory. *Taiheiki* and *Gempei Seisui Ki* each furnish seventeen, and
the *Genji Monogatari* and *Kokinshu* eleven each. Others were
popular as ballads. They had already proved their dramatic adapta-
bility, and some had been embodied in the older *sarugaku* performances. One such form was *kusemai*. The name had various
meanings and could be used of both song and dance, but in the
fourteenth and early fifteenth centuries had come to refer chiefly
to a type of popular ballad in which dancers performed to the
melodic recitation of historical tales, on the whole far longer
than those of *noh*. *Kusemai* had its own schools of players, none of
which survived for very long; Kwanami gave it a new importance
by studying it and appropriating it for *noh*. The ballad line, with
its strong musical beat, is generally used to narrate the main
story of a *noh* play, and is almost always found at the main point
of the development section.

*Sarugaku* also included a choral form, *kowaka*, which attracted
performing schools if its own. *Kowaka*, like *noh*, is credited with
an individual founder, one Momoi Naoaki, but his date and
genealogy are obscure, and he is a far more nebulous figure than
Kwanami. *Kowaka* is epic on the verge of becoming drama, choral
recitation with a minimal amount of dance. Flourishing in
Kyoto, it was transplanted in the late sixteenth century to the
village of Oe on the island of Kyushu. There it has enjoyed a
freak survival as a local and hereditary art; the texts have recently
been collected and published, and some of them translated. In
*kowaka* the text takes precedence. Dance, in the present performances, has atrophied to a stamping walk by one of the reciters
in the closing stages of the piece, but the text has still stopped
short of turning into drama. In *noh*, although the dance pre-

dominated over the text, a happier *rapprochement* was effected.

This type of development again suggests an analogy with the supposed beginnings of Greek drama. Many scholars now believe that Greek tragedy evolved from the fusion of two distinct elements, the non-dramatic Chorus (if anything Greek could ever be non-dramatic) and the public recitations of the Homeric poems and similar works, easily adaptable into dramatic form. From the combination of these two – perhaps by a man called Thespis, perhaps by the tyrant Peisistratus – came the Chorus and the actors of the drama proper. Japanese history reveals the same process, of which *noh* and *kowaka* are different manifestations. In *kowaka* the reciters do all. In *noh* there are actors, who may speak for themselves – Kwanami is credited with introducing *monomane*, impersonation – but the reciting tradition is still strong, far stronger, in fact, than in the Greek. In Greek tragedy the actors speak their own lines and the Chorus sings about them, embroidering on what we have just heard from their lips. In *noh* the Chorus may speak for the actor, in his person, as well as about him. Sometimes even the flute may speak for the actor, and words are replaced by music. In the popular forms, *bunraku* and *kabuki*, the reciter has an even larger part to play.

Some ninety plays have been attributed to Kwanami, but his fame has been far overshadowed by that of Zeami, his son (1363–1444). Both left an indelible impression on the theatre they helped to create, but the son's contribution was the larger. Kwanami and Zeami were not the first writers of *noh*, any more than Homer was the creator of the first Greek epic, but their work overwhelmed that of their predecessors. Of the two hundred and fifty-six plays in the current repertory, Kwanami has contributed ten, and Zeami possibly one hundred and twenty-six; there is some doubt about the authorship of twelve of them. Zeami's life was not entirely a happy one. At first enjoying the patronage of the Shogunate, he later lost his position to more successful rivals and towards the end of his life went into exile. Nevertheless his influence was enormous, and his personality continues to excite interest. A play by Yamazaki Masahazu based on his life was written as recently as 1963, won honours in its own country and was the first full-length Japanese play to be presented in English in New York. Its theme was the identity of the performing artist.

Zeami took up his father's work and built upon it. The extent of his debt is obvious from his own writings. Both father and son wrote treatises on their art, of which Zeami's alone have survived. They were intended as 'secret books', and so preserved for many years. We must interpret 'secret' perhaps in the sense of the 'mysteries' of the medieval guilds – that is, a body of professional lore fully appreciable only by those already initiated in the art, and with little meaning for outsiders. When we read them now, much of their advice seems either obvious or hopelessly obscure. Zeami's works were jealously guarded and distributed through several branches of the family, for *noh*, like other arts, became a hereditary affair. His own son, Motoyoshi, withdrew from the profession in 1430 to become a priest. It is possible that Zeami did not transmit the works to his successor, Onami; this would account for their long disappearance. At any rate some were preserved, others scattered and lost. A few were published in 1665, but in altered form. It was not until 1909 that they became fully available. As part of the scholarly interest that came to *noh*'s support when governmental protection had declined, sixteen manuscripts were edited and published. Translations followed – notably an English version by Arthur Waley – and the texts are now easily available in several languages and have been widely commented upon.

In a series of long articles Zeami deals with the principal elements of *noh* writing and production and the training of the actor. Formulating the ideas inherited from his father and illuminated from his own practical experience, he divides the play into its component parts and suggests the ideals to which it should aspire. The result is not abstract dramatic criticism – though Zeami is vitally concerned with the aesthetic basis of his art – but a practical handbook, written by an actor who knew his trade. It is our primary source for the history of *noh* in its formative period, and fundamental to any subsequent criticism.

In discussing the form of *noh* it is important to establish from the beginning what *noh* is not. Kwanami gave the dances a greater dramatic interest, but this statement needs considerable quali- fication. The spectator who comes to *noh* expecting a plot in the Western manner will be sorely disappointed. A number of the plays, it is true, contain a recognizable conflict or a quest ending in solution. Some involve death in battle or by assassination, although in production these actions are so stylized that they may not be immediately recognizable. A recurring theme, no doubt given greater interest by years of war, is the reunion of a divided family. A parent identifies a long-lost child or a husband finds a wife who has lost her wits and sees her restored to sanity. In other plays there may be a conflict which is primarily spiritual rather than physical. *Aoi no Ue (The Lady Aoi)* is a good example of this, dealing with the familiar theme of unrequited love. Usually the thwarted woman in such plays dies and returns as a ghost to persecute her rival. *Aoi no Ue* is unusual in that one woman is persecuted by the spirit of another who is still living.

Princess Rokujo, the former mistress of Prince Genji, has been supplanted by Aoi in his affections. Aoi's servants gave her additional offence when their coaches jostled for position at the Kamo Festival. (A panel painting by Kano Sanraku (1559–1635), now in the Japanese National Museum, delightfully illustrates this sort of incident. The court ladies wait in haughty indignation in their closed carriages, while their servants fight with um- brellas for the best places.) Rokujo tries to control her jealousy, but it manifests itself in spite of her, appearing in physical form and afflicting Aoi with a strange illness. Here the animistic basis of Japanese religion may be clearly seen : jealousy assumes material shape. The spirit first appears in sympathetic guise as a lovelorn woman. When a priest is summoned to exorcise her she assumes her true shape and reveals herself as a demon. A vigorous combat ensues over Aoi's prostrate body. The priest rolls his beads and chants incantations; they dance back and forth across the stage. Depending on which school is presenting the play, this duel of minds may have considerable physical excitement. The demon resists, then succumbs, and is almost driven from the stage. At the last moment she recovers her strength and attacks again. It is a long conflict. At one point the priest is on one side of a pillar and the demon on the other, reaching for each other across the railings of the stage. Finally, as she sits poised over her rival's body, the priest wins over her heart to love and forgiveness. 'Hearing the voice of the incantation,' chants the Chorus, 'the demon's heart softens.' Rokujo has transcended the frailty of human emotion and attained Nirvana.

Plays of this type, however, which present a story in terms of direct action, are outnumbered by those in which the action is merely reported or seen indirectly through a vision or a dream, and where the stage action, such as it is, is confined to the entrances and exits of the principal characters and the obligatory dance. A familiar pattern, accounting for about one-third of the repertory, is the following. A wanderer – usually a priest on pilgrimage, sometimes a warrior, sometimes an ordinary traveller – stops at some spot for the night. He is greeted by a local inhabitant, who tells him a story connected with history of the place or its religious associations. Often the informant turns out to be a god or spirit who has assumed human form, and who appears in his own shape to dance the conclusion. *Ema*, described earlier in this chapter, is one play of this type. In another, *Kakitsubata* (*The Irises*), the action is even slighter. This play is based on a story of the poet Ariwara no Narihira, who stopped at Yatsuhashi on his journey to the east, and was so impressed by the beauty of the irises blooming there that he commemorated them in a poem. This story is told in the play in the form of a reminiscence. The action of the play begins with the arrival in Yatsuhashi of a wandering priest who lodges in the house of a local woman. He is surprised when she appears before him in a magnificent robe and asks who she is. She tells him that she is the spirit of the irises and repeats the story of the poem. Narihira, she says, was a Buddhist god of music and dance who had taken mortal form. According to Buddhist dogma even the irises have spirits; they too may attain Nirvana. The play closes with her dance. Or, to take another example, *Yamamba* (*The Old Woman of the Hills* or *The Mountain Hag*) opens with the arrival of a woman dancer and her attendants in a remote country district. The woman has won fame for her performance of the Yamamba dance, the story of a spirit who inhabits the mountain-tops in the shape of an old woman. Night falls suddenly, and the travellers look for shelter. An old woman appears and offers hospitality; she reveals that she is the real Mountain Hag, and in the second half of the play comes back as a demon and dances.

Many plays hold a promise of exciting action which is never fulfilled; the playwright, in the end, is content with reporting it. In *Morihisa* a captured general is being taken to the Shogun at Kamakura. He seeks consolation in religion and occupies his journey by reading the *sutras*. Falling asleep, he sees a wonderful vision, the content of which is narrated by the Chorus. When he arrives at Kamakura (the journey is represented by a walk round the stage), he is sentenced to execution, but the headsman is dazzled by the light shining from the *sutra* in Morihisa's hand and drops the sword. In the second Act Morihisa appears before the Shogun Yoritomo (not represented on the stage) and relates his dream. Yoritomo, who has had a similar vision himself, is so impressed that he orders his release. Wine is poured, and Morihisa celebrates with a dance. What seems from the description to be a visually exciting moment – the frustrated execution – is, in performance, reduced to practically nothing. There is no attempt to create suspense or build to a climax. The executioner simply raises his sword and, almost in the same gesture, throws it away. The whole emphasis of the play is on the long narrative speeches and the choral recitation.

Such plays, in which the direct action is minimal and the characters' movements serve only to introduce a story and a dance, form the greater part of the *noh* repertoire. To make a crude division, about a hundred plays show the crucial action directly, and over a hundred and thirty prefer report or reminiscence. Even in the former category many plays are borderline cases, in which the characters spend most of the time discussing their past history and relating it to the immediate action. Authors, of course, varied in their approaches. Zeami preferred the contemplative plays, and some of his successors the more violent kind. But for the most part we are presented with a sort of trun-

cated Greek tragedy, containing a prologue, a messenger scene
and little else. This preference is in part a natural consequence of
*noh*'s self-imposed limitations on the number of its actors. It also
rests, however, on a more profound philosophical basis, which
will be discussed at greater length later in this chapter.

In his writings Zeami devotes considerable space to a structural
analysis of *noh*. Some of his conclusion are, necessarily, tentative.
It is clear that, when he wrote, certain elements had not yet
fallen completely into place, and that he was formulating some
things for the first time. He frequently cites the oral traditions
of his art, for which he has great respect. The drama that Zeami
knew was, apparently, not so refined as it has since become.
Acting could still be acrobatic – reflecting its *sarugaku* origins –
and left more liberty to the individual performer. In particular,
Zeami's works make it clear that, in the first half of the fifteenth
century, the Chorus was still a novelty which had not yet been
completely assimilated.

Zeami recognized a threefold division of the plays. In its
simplest form, this is as follows:

1. INTRODUCTION: *Entrance of the waki, or subordinate actor.*

The *waki*'s task is to set the scene, relate any necessary background information, and, in general, prepare for the entrance
of the *sh'te*, or principal actor. He thus functions as a sort of
prologue, though in fact a great deal is left to the audience's
understanding. The *noh* author can assume (like Sophocles,
when he wrote *Oedipus the King*) that the story is well known
beforehand and spare himself the labour of setting out the background in full. He may, however, make numerous passing
allusions to this background in the body of the play, safe in the
knowledge that an initiated audience will appreciate them.
Thus in *Aoi no Ue* the story of the unfortunate encounter between Princess Rokujo and Aoi at the festival is nowhere set
out at length, but Rokujo's language, using imagery drawn
from wheels and carriages, constantly alludes to it. Henry
W. Wells, in his analysis of the 'lyric capsule' of *noh*, points
out that the opening lines of the play are often a cryptic sum-

mary of the play's message. Here we may, perhaps, see a further instance of the influence of Zen, which contributed so much to the plays. Zen teachers traditionally taught in riddles: 'What is Zen? Zen. What is Zen? Not Zen'; and it is with a 'riddle' of this sort that the play often opens. Greek tragedy uses something of the same technique, but less cryptically: its prologues often serve not merely as introduction to the play, but as summaries of the theme.

2. DEVELOPMENT

(a) Entry of the *sh'te* or principal actor.
(b) Interchange between *sh'te* and *waki*.
(c) Account of the main story.

The Chorus, it will be noticed, does not intrude upon the action at regular and predictable intervals, as it does in Greek tragedy. Its importance varies widely from play to play. It may speak impersonally, narrating those parts of the story which are not shown; it may repeat and emphasize the lines of the *sh'te* and *waki*; or it may speak in their persons, reciting passages which are assumed to be spoken by them.

3. CLIMAX (usually in the form of dance).

In practice these three sections are rarely distinct, but merge imperceptibly into one another. In the longer plays, where the *sh'te* has to change roles or costumes, an Act break is introduced between 2 and 3. The musicians put up their drums and turn aside, and a minor actor fills the interval with a monologue – often a summary of the play in simpler language for the benefit of a less erudite audience. Such passages were originally improvised and unscripted. Later they assumed a fixed and traditional form, but there has been some disagreement as to whether they should be considered part of the text of the play proper. The earlier translations of *noh* therefore often omit them, while later versions take them into account.

It is essential at this point to say something about the production of *noh*, as in these plays, more than in any other, presentation is inseparable from content. *Noh* is today usually seen on an indoor stage, apparently simple, but in reality highly sophisticated,

C 2

the conventions of which must be understood if the play is to be meaningful. It reached this form only after centuries of development. In the history of any drama the plays come first and the theatre buildings later. Performers begin by using whatever comes to hand. They work in whatever space is most convenient, using buildings designed for other purposes and influenced by local custom and topography. It is only comparatively late in the development of the art that buildings are erected specifically for the performance of plays, and these normally inherit many of the features of their temporary predecessors. Thus the earliest Greek actors performed against the wall of a temple, or built a temporary stage on the rim of a threshing floor, which made a good level place for dancing. The Elizabethans played in inn-yards, the French companies in indoor tennis-courts; and when they felt secure enough to build permanent premises of their own, they embodied in them the features to which they were accustomed. In the same way *noh*, which evolves from dance, inherits several of the physical features of the dance performance. In particular the orchestra continues to be assigned a prominent place on the stage, and the *sh'te*, who dances, remains the centre of attention; the whole performance is arranged to bring him into prominence and leave the other elements comparatively obscure.

*Noh* in Zeami's time was still a popular art form. It had not yet become the exclusive property of the upper classes. Zeami makes a point of this in his writings, and stresses the importance of adhering to local customs and traditions:

> Our art depends on the favour of the masses. With their blessing, we may establish our schools in the happy confidence that they will have a long life. Consequently, if our performances become too remote, the applause of the great public will be lacking. That is why, without ever forgetting *noh*'s beginnings, we must adapt to the times, conform to the place, and, in short, interpret *noh* in such a way that the most obtuse spectator will say to himself 'Yes, that's how it really is.' That is the key to a long and prosperous career.

The plays themselves contain frequent allusions to local rites and customs, in much the same way that Euripides, himself a great popularizer, ties his mythic stories to some tradition or festival familiar to the audience in their everyday lives. The esoteric quality which is now generally associated with *noh* came much later, when the patronage of the *samurai* severed its popular associations, choked its development and preserved outmoded forms which, left to themselves, would undoubtedly have

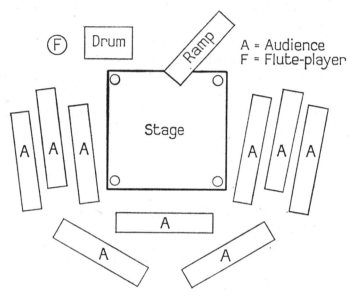

Fig. 2  Temporary dance stage, Yasukuni Shrine

changed. Performances were given in a wide variety of places. In the temples the actors found *kagura* stages already built and adaptable for their use. Elsewhere they had to start from scratch. We hear of performances given in the country districts and of open-air cycles given, in the summers of 1413 and 1464, in the dry river-beds. There were also private performances at the palace or in noblemen's houses, which imposed still different conditions. By supplementing historical records with observations of existing open-air performances, we can reconstruct with some probability the evolution of the *noh* stage from its crude beginnings into its perfected form.

Figures 2–9 suggest the main points of this development. The earliest dancing places must have been quite simple: probably no more than special areas of the shrine precincts marked off with bamboo poles, straw ropes and paper streamers. This is still common Shinto practice; compare Plate 12, where the same device is used to mark off a temporary outdoor *noh* stage. Dances could, of course, be given on the temple steps or in the shrine and it was more desirable to bring them outside where the crowd would see them.

Figure 2 is a plan of the temporary wooden dance-stage at the Yasukuni Shrine, described in its festival context in Chapter 2. The earliest *noh* stages would have been no more complicated than this: a trestle platform, a pole at each corner, and a crude roof of branches hung with flags and streamers. In the *kagura* stages, which are still a regular feature of Shinto shrines, we see this crude structure translated into permanent architectural

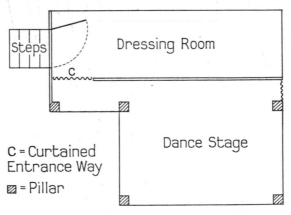

Fig. 3   Covered *kagura* stage, Asakusa Shrine

form, with a dressing-room added and a curtained entrance-way connecting the two. Figure 3 shows the *kagura* stage at the Asakusa Shrine in Tokyo. The more important shrines have several stages of different sizes, the larger being used for more complex *kagura* and for *bugaku*. These are of the type already illustrated in Fig. 1 (p. 49), set up in the shrine courtyard and protected by a canopy roof. Early *noh* performers could have accommodated themselves here; the *sarugaku-noh* stage still used in the village of Neo (see p. 59) is basically a *kagura* stage adapted for dramatic performance.

Early *noh* was therefore performed in the round, or at least with the audience on three sides. Away from the shrines the

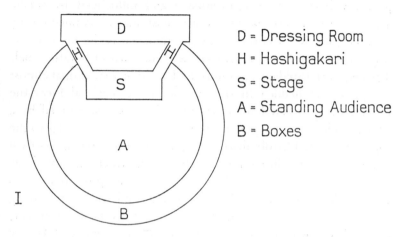

D = Dressing Room

H = Hashigakari

S = Stage

A = Standing Audience

B = Boxes

Fig. 4. 1 *Dengaku-noh* performance, 1349

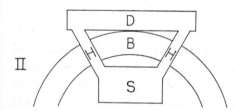

Fig. 4. 11 Suggested alternative arrangement of *hashigakari*, dressing-room and audience

players had more space, and could build to their own requirements. The first stages designed exclusively for *noh* seem to have been those used for *kanjin*, subscription performances to raise money for religious causes and public works. Figures 4.1 and 4.11 show the stage built for a *dengaku-noh* performance in 1349 to finance the construction of a bridge at Kyoto. Its main features are clear, though opinion differs over details; it has strong

affinities with the stage still used for mime-farces at the Mibu
Shrine (see p. 59). Here the audience almost completely surrounds the action, and we see for the first time a characteristic
feature of the classic *noh* stage, the *hashigakari*, bridge or walkway, connecting the stage with the dressing-room. This was
probably born out of convenience and influenced by shrine
architecture, where buildings are customarily connected by
covered galleries. Another possible influence is the *sumo* wrestling stage. *Sumo* is an ancient art with its own elaborate ritual.
The ring is elevated on a mound and defined by a straw mat almost
completely embedded in the ground. In its original form the
mound was protected by a canopy, which was supported by a
post at each corner; in other words a structure very similar to the
*kagura* stage and hardly distinct in purpose, for *sumo* has its own
Shinto affiliations. In modern tournaments, which cater to huge
audiences, the canopy has been modified. The posts have been
removed to improve the lines of vision, and the roof is slung
from the ceiling of the stadium. Traces of the posts, however,
may still be seen in the practice-rings of the *sumo* schools (see
Plate 11). What happened to *sumo* also happened to the later *noh*
stage: a building designed for outdoor uses was moved indoors
and modified to suit its new environment. More important, the
*sumo* ring has its own 'bridge', a narrow path used for ceremonial
occasions and for fans to present tributes to their favourites, and
this has been suggested both as the antecedent of the *noh hashigakari* and the similar structure used by *kabuki*. Whatever its
origins, the *hashigakari* came to acquire an important artistic
function. In perfected *noh* it is much more than a means of getting
from one place to another. The arrangements for 1349 show two
*hashigakari*, which is unusual. It has been suggested that there
were two troupes engaged in the performance, with separate
entrances. One accident marred this entertainment: the grand-
stands for the audience collapsed.

Figure 5 is the plan of a stage in the dry river-bed at Kyoto, for
a performance attended by the Shogun in 1464. There is now only
one *hashigakari*, running straight back from the stage. The audience occupies the banks, and the Shogun has the place of honour.

Musicians sat at stage left, and the Chorus possibly at stage right. Figure 6 shows approximately the same arrangement as it may still be seen at Sumiyoshi Shrine in Osaka. The dance stage is built in the sacred paddy-field, a bridge connects it to the bank, and the audience sits around the edges to watch.

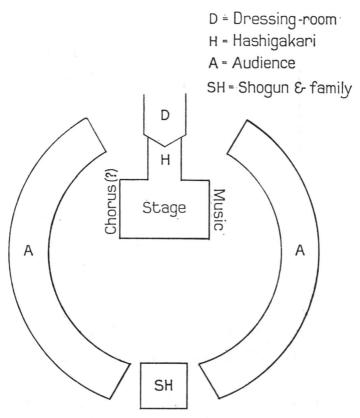

D = Dressing-room
H = Hashigakari
A = Audience
SH = Shogun & family

Fig. 5 *Noh* stage at the river-bed at Kyoto, 1464

The three principal elements of the classic stage-platform, dressing-room and *hashigakari* have now appeared. In the years that followed, their relative positions were changed and the whole complex was given a different orientation. As the performances grew more complicated and the Chorus became a permanent feature, staging in the round was no longer practical.

The musicians were moved to the back of the stage and the Chorus to its present position at stage left; the *hashigakari* was relocated at the side of the stage, so that the actors could utilize its length to advantage in their movements. Figure 7 shows an outdoor *noh* stage as presently in use at the Heian Shrine, Kyoto;

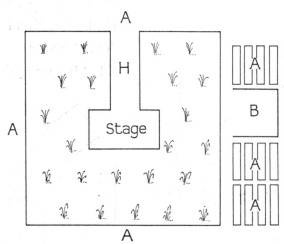

H = Hashigakari

B = Boxes for priests and other distinguished guests

A = Seated or standing audience

Fig. 6  Dance stage in sacred paddy-field, Sumiyoshi Shrine

we know that by at least 1599 the stage must have evolved to approximately this point. Here the mass of the audience is concentrated round two sides of the stage and along the *hashigakari*. Few seats remain at stage left, where vision is blocked by the Chorus. The stage itself is on trestles and one can see the point of Zeami's admonitions to his actors to check the platform carefully beforehand for rough spots and projections. No such care is needed on the indoor stages, the platforms of which are immaculately preserved and polished with the natural oil of the wood.

Temporary outdoor stages, however, have one considerable advantage; they resound like thunder to the stamping of the dance. Indoors, even with the acoustical aid of hollow vessels set below the floor, the noise is not nearly so impressive.

This arrangement became standard and was imitated in the

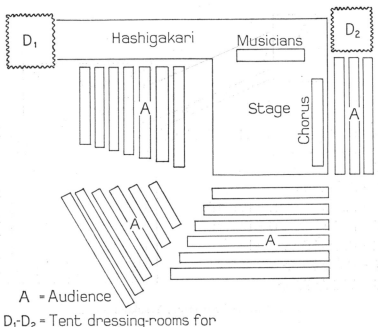

A = Audience

D₁-D₂ = Tent dressing-rooms for actors and chorus

Fig. 7   Open-air *noh* stage, Heian Shrine

permanent buildings that followed. The temporary structures became fixtures. Stage and *hashigakari* acquired a roof supported on pillars which defined the limits of the acting area proper. Solid timber and elaborate carving replaced straw rope and bamboo. The Chorus area and *hashigakari* were railed off, a gravel path (nowadays often cement) surrounded the stage, and the play withdrew perceptibly from its audience. It customarily happens that when a folk-art turns professional and divorces itself from its popular origins, it begins to shrink from physical contact with its

public. The stage withdraws and the audience is kept at a respectful distance. We see this, for example, in the Greek theatre of
the late fifth century B.C., when the growing professionalism of
the drama is accompanied, in the theatre buildings, by a shift of
the centre of interest. The emphasis in early plays had been on the
Chorus, which performed in the midst of the audience; in the

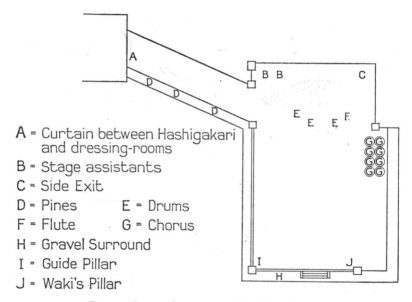

A = Curtain between Hashigakari
    and dressing-rooms
B = Stage assistants
C = Side Exit
D = Pines        E = Drums
F = Flute       G = Chorus
H = Gravel Surround
I = Guide Pillar
J = Waki's Pillar

Fig. 8  Covered *noh* stage, Yasukuni Shrine

later it was on the actors, who performed on the rim of the
*orchestra* (dancing-floor) and away from the audience; the *orchestra*
gradually fell into disuse and provided a 'mystic gulf' between the
public and the players. We see the same phenomenon in the transition between the Elizabethan public stage and the Restoration
playhouses. The open platform which carried the actor into the
heart of his audience was truncated, as the drama grew more
aristocratic and more refined, to a deep apron stage; this in turn
withdrew more and more inside the proscenium, until the
'fourth wall' became a rigid convention, dividing the playhouse
into two, with the actors on one side and the audience on the
other. In the same manner the surroundings of *noh* grew more

artificial as the plays grew more remote. The open stage acquired a rear wall, which acted as a sounding-board for the performers' voices. On it was painted a gnarled pine-tree, in token of the natural vistas that audiences had once been able to see.

Many shrines now have their own *noh* stages, though few are in regular use. They often do double duty, being used also for *kagura* dances: the wheel has come full circle. Figure 8 shows the stage at Yasukuni Shrine, which may be taken as typical, and re-presents the perfected *noh* form. The shape of a theatre often indicates the way in which the various elements of the performance developed and their relative importance. This holds good for *noh*; the dance is central and the Chorus (representing the literary element) relegated to the outskirts. Greek tragedy and *noh* both developed out of dance, but in the former the dancers became the Chorus and actors were a later addition. In *noh* the dancers became actors and the Chorus appeared later. Thus in both theatres the nuclear importance of the dance is signified by its central location, but where in Greece the Chorus is the focal point with the actors, at least originally, on the fringe, the reverse is true in *noh*. The *noh* Chorus usually numbers eight (though some performances make do with less; trained personnel are hard to find) and sits on stage left, in a shallow annexe beyond the pillars supporting the canopy; that is, outside the acting area proper. The musicians, usually three in number, sit upstage. One plays a flute, another a small drum (*kotsuzumi*) held on the left shoulder and struck with the hand, and the third a large drum (*otsuzumi*) held by the left side and also struck with the hand to give a sharp wooden tone. The drummers also punctuate the music with rhythmic howls which help to dictate the tempo of the performance. Their music normally begins and ends the play; to applaud an actor's exit before the music has finished is as great a social *gaffe* as applauding between the movements of a symphony. It is clear from the way in which they enter that the musicians are distinct from the Chorus and constitute a superior social group; their association with *noh* is more ancient and more prestigious. They enter formally, like actors, up the *hashigakari*, in the same grave processional motion as the *gagaku* musicians at the Imperial

Court. Their formal exit, after the actors, marks the close of the play. The Chorus enters, almost furtively by contrast, through a sliding panel, the 'hurry-door', at upstage left, which is too small for dignity. This door is also used to bring on properties, and occasionally for the exit of an insignificant character.

There is no scenery of any kind. The decoration is limited to the pine-tree painted on the rear wall, a formalized bamboo pattern round the Chorus door and three miniature pine-trees planted at fixed intervals along the front of the *hashigakari*. Even these have no scenic function; they allude to no precise time or place, but serve merely as a reminder of the drama's outdoor origins. As in the Greek drama or in Shakespeare's plays poetry replaces scenic artifice. The actors or the Chorus give the necessary indications of the setting.

Thus the *noh* stage is, potentially, as flexible as its classical counterparts in the West. Unhampered by realistic settings and the time needed for changing them, the action can move from one location to another with no perceptible break. The stage is conveniently neutral. Successively redefined by the actors' words, it can represent different places as the play proceeds; it is no place and therefore any place. A long journey, for instance, is indicated by a walk round the stage, or, more simply still, by a single step forward. The actors end where they began, but the journey is assumed to have been accomplished: the only scene-change takes place in the mind's eye. Some plays, like *Shunkan* (see Appendix 1) call for a 'simultaneous setting', in which the *hashigakari* and stage represent two different locations. In practice, however, the stage is rarely called upon to exercise this flexibility to the full. The action of *noh* is so restricted – and in many plays, as we have seen, virtually non-existent – that a simple indication of place at the beginning of each play suffices. In matters of time, however, *noh* is infinitely flexible. The action is not governed by clock or calendar. Dramatic value is the sole criterion, and the duration of an action is controlled by its importance. A journey or a battle may be compressed into seconds, but a single reaction indefinitely prolonged if the meaning warrants it. The *noh* stage is a void beyond the laws of space and time in which past may merge with present, dead history turn into a living reality, visions become actual, and actuality turn to dreams.

When the place must be more precisely defined, properties are introduced as needed. They may be quite large, like the swordsmith's forge in *Kokaji*, the wicket gate in *Hajitomi*, or the boat in *Funa Benkei*, but like the setting they are not intended to be realistic or to do more than hint at the object required. Normally, the outline is suggested by a light bamboo frame. This simplicity is dictated, at least in part, by stage necessity; on an open stage more solid objects would obstruct the spectators' view of the play. But there are more important considerations. The properties subscribe, like every other aspect of the performance, to the overriding aesthetic principle of *noh*: that the function of drama is not the representation of the actual, but the revelation of the metaphysical; that the material world is deceptive and ephemeral, so that to reproduce it on the stage would only perpetuate a delusion; and that the play works more effectively by suggestion, allowing us to transcend the evidence of our senses and reach for the greater truths beyond. Smaller properties are consequently often left to the imagination or suggested by the actor's play with his fan. An evocative gesture indicates a sword-thrust (deriving to some extent from the warrior's use of the iron-ribbed fan as a defensive weapon, as well as a battle-signal) or the pouring of wine; to show the actual objects would be distracting and redundant.

The properties are handled by stage assistants, in full view of the audience but conventionally invisible. These men are more than stagehands; their responsibilities are enormous. As well as handling the major properties, they place stools for the actors as required – always of the same pattern, black lacquered drums – and remove any discarded objects, to leave the floor uncluttered for dancing. The properties are governed by the same law that governs stage time: an object is retained only as long as it is dramatically useful, and is removed once it has served its purpose. Stage assistants must be expert dressers. They help with on-stage costume changes, some of them extremely complex, and step forward from time to time at a point of rest, to adjust an actor's *coiffure* or the folds of his robe in mid-performance. When not in action they take their places behind the musicians and so are conventionally 'off-stage'. Their silent presence is unquestioningly accepted by the audience; they are as much part of the stage machinery as the lights and curtain of our own theatre. They move with such graceful unobtrusiveness that their work looks easy. It is nothing of the kind. The leading assistant is often a trained actor himself, ready to substitute for the *sh'te* in an emergency. Even the handling of the properties requires much skill and rehearsal, and an acute sense of timing. At one performance I saw a small child work as stage assistant. He was the youngest member of an old *noh* family, making his first appearance on the stage. His only task was to walk across and retrieve a discarded fan, but the tense concentration of every muscle in his body and the care with which he picked his steps suddenly made clear the skill and discipline which underlay the apparently effortless ease of his elders. Every movement in *noh*, even those which are seemingly the most trivial, requires and receives the same devoted attention.

We have dealt with the periphery of the stage: now to its centre and the actor. Four families, or schools, assumed early eminence in the performance of *noh*: Kanze, Kongo, Komparu and Hosho. All four are still in existence, together with a fifth, Kita, which was founded in the early seventeenth century, and the Umewaka school, of less importance, which dates only from the Meiji Era. The Kanze school was Kwanami's own; it operates the Kanze Kaikan, still one of the most active Tokyo houses, and another theatre in Kyoto. There are, of course, no actresses. Women had no more place on the *noh* stage than before the Buddhist altar and are still barred even from back-stage during important pre-performance ceremonies.

The principal actor, almost invariably masked, is the *sh'te*. In a sense he is the only actor. *Sh'te* is related to the verb *suru*, 'to do', and the *sh'te* is the actor in the literal sense of the word, the doer, the agent. He holds the key role, and it is by his performance that the play stands or falls: it is he who performs the crucial dance, and the others are there merely to provide a

dramatic context and throw his performance into relief. Those
who assist him in the main role are known as *sh'te-tsure* and wear
masks only when impersonating female characters. These actors,
together with the Chorus and stage assistants, belong to the same
school. The actor who plays the secondary part comes from a
different school and is known as the *waki*; his assistants are *waki-
tsure* and are never masked. His name, meaning 'bystander',
precisely expresses his function. The relative functions of *waki* and
*sh'te* may be seen most easily in the 'reminiscence' plays described
earlier in this chapter. It is normally the *waki* who appears first,
as priest, traveller or inquirer, and the *sh'te* who appears sub-
sequently as his interlocutor. Once the *waki* has introduced
himself and asked the questions which prompt the *sh'te's* story,
his job is over. The stage is then left to the *sh'te's* recitation and
dance, and it is by this that the performance is judged. The
*waki's* only remaining function is to make himself as unobtrusive
as possible. In action and language the *waki* role is strictly subordinate to that of the principal, and this is emphasized in the conventional positioning of the characters. Even when the *waki* has a
large part, he is still no more than 'feed' to the *sh'te*, and his performance must never distract from that of his principal. For this
reason the common translation of *sh'te* and *waki* as 'protagonist'
and 'deuteragonist' respectively is misleading; it implies a
dramatic interaction between them that does not exist.

Child actors (*ko-kata*) appear in some plays, either in children's
roles (though those may sometimes, as in *Kokaji*, be played by
grown men) or in adult roles of a special nature. Strict conventions govern the portrayal of the Shogun or the Imperial Family
on stage. The actor must be wary of *lèse-majesté*. In *Morihisa* the
captured general, after his miraculous escape from execution,
relates his vision to the Shogun Yoritomo, whose presence is
assumed but not shown. Instead, the actor comes downstage
centre and addresses his narrative to that part of the theatre
where, in the early performances, the real Shogun would have sat.
The same reasoning explains the playing of the Emperor, in
Kwanami's *Soshi-arai Komachi*, and of Prince Yoshitsune, in *Funa
Benkei*, by children: the convention removes the possibility of

offence. Arthur Waley has pointed out that, in addition, such characters raise a delicate question of dramatic protocol. If represented on the stage by full-grown actors they might carry the aura of the originals with them and inhibit or overshadow the *sh'te*'s performance. As long as they are played by children, the *sh'te* is still dominant by virtue of his size. Some minor parts – soldiers, messengers, servants, boatmen, attendants – may be played by *kyogen* actors, who belong to yet another group and whose principal function is to present comic interludes between the *noh* plays. They are easily distinguished on the stage by their yellow *tabi* (socks); the regular *noh* actors wear white. Although some plays have large casts, involving a number of *kyogen* actors and *tsure*, they do little more than dress the stage. The core of the performance is the *sh'te*'s recitation and dance; all else is peripheral.

The *noh* actor has always accepted rigorous discipline and a long and arduous training as a condition of his art. He is probably the most disciplined actor in the world. The *sh'te*'s role makes exacting physical and mental demands. Zeami cautions the actor to avoid debauchery, frivolous amusements and over-indulgence in alcohol; to 'practice hard, avoid pretentiousness, and be wary of vanity'. He lays down a detailed scheme for the actor's training, which, critics have pointed out, parallels the main divisions of the modern school and university education. From the age of seven to twelve or thirteen the fledgeling actor should be allowed to develop spontaneously, without undue guidance or restriction. The real training begins with the next stage, which lasts for five years. This, says Zeami, is the appropriate time for the boy to learn the repertoire, to which he can bring a youthful grace in interpretation and a good voice. Such youthful actors may even seem to possess the 'flower' (*hana*), the supreme quality of their art, but this, if it occurs, is only an accident of nature and will pass. The true 'flower' is not granted to all, and comes only when the technique has been completely assimilated. At seventeen or eighteen the actor enters the third stage, a period of crucial importance. The temporary 'flower' of youth disappears: the natural grace of body and voice are gone, and must

be replaced by art. Many abandon the profession at this point.
When the actor reaches twenty-four or twenty-five, the artistic
faculties of his career begin to be determined. The voice is established, and the potentially great actor manifests his promise. But
there must be no relaxation of training: exercises should be
multiplied to keep pace with the growing development. Still
greater severity is needed when the actor has reached his thirties.
At forty-four or forty-five comes the dangerous age, when the
faculties begin to weaken. Actors must select impersonation
suitable for their years, though the truly great among them will
now be at their peak: 'If an actor in his fifties still possesses the
"flower", he will certainly have won universal fame in the years
preceding.' But fifty, for most, marks the end of the career; at
this point, the actor should stop. There are many *noh* actors who
have conspicuously failed to take Zeami's advice. Umewaka
Rokuro, now over sixty, still acts and dances as robustly as a man
of twenty. Nomura Manzo, a *kyogen* player born in 1898, is still
active, and in 1967 was designated by the government as an
'important intangible cultural property'.

Kwanami is said to have introduced the art of *monomane*, or
imitation; Zeami amplifies his father's work with detailed instructions on what the actor is to imitate, and how, which give
the key to the acting style of *noh* as well as to its social pretensions.
It is important to find worthy objects to copy. The noblest examples – the Emperor and his court – are inaccessible, but the
actor must find out as much about them as he can, and study their
speech and etiquette. Zeami cautions him to concentrate on
people of quality, and not to take his models from the lower
orders or the working classes. Though these too have their part
in plays, their characteristics should not be reproduced too
exactly. Women are suitable objects for imitation by young men,
but very difficult. Here it is vital to get the externals right. The
actor must study how a woman wears her robe and carries her
fan, and imitate the movements of her neck and body. For
women's parts the exterior is all-important. Old men, however,
are another matter. Exact imitation of the bent and palsied
stances of senility are aesthetically unpleasing. Imitation must be

tempered by art. The same is true of mad roles. There are many types of frenzy, and the actor should learn to distinguish between them; nor should he allow his violence to become excessive, and consequently ugly. Once again, the actor must be discreet in selecting the right degree of imitation. When playing a person possessed by a demon, he should try to show two things at once and distinguish between the character of the possessor and that of the possessed.

Coming from Zeami to an actual performance, one is conscious, at first, of an apparent discrepancy between the theory and the practice, between what one has read and what one hears and sees. Zeami insists throughout that *monomane* is fundamental: 'First of all, be a perfect image of the person you are imitating, and then you will be like him in action.' But the *noh* actors are clearly not 'imitating' in the common sense of the word. They do not speak, but chant, and their language, partly prose and partly verse, is an artificial survival, preserved in isolation on the stage, of the elaborate honorific cadences of fourteenth-century Court Japanese. Known as *sorobun*, from its habit of adding the honorific *soro* to each main verb, it reads, in literal translation, like something from *Les Précieuses Ridicules*: the simplest phrases are endlessly complicated. Even in Zeami's time the language that the audience heard from the stage differed markedly from that of their everyday life. Nor are the actors' movements and gestures in any sense naturalistic. They may be derived from the gestures of real life, but, like the dance-postures of *bugaku*, are refined until only a vestigial resemblance remains. In many cases the meaning is still clear enough, without a key. When the ghost of the bandit Kumasaka, in the play of that name, dances the story of his last battle for the familiar inquiring priest, his performance needs no interpreter. He relates how, with his band, he broke into the house where the young Ushiwaka was staying, and after a fierce duel was killed by him. The duel is then portrayed as a solo dance. The *sh'te* circles the stage, whirling and leaping, stabbing and lunging with his halberd; he plays both victor and vanquished, and at the close is brought to his knees. But other gestures may not be immediately decipherable. One step signifies a journey.

A single gesture with the fan indicates a death blow. This allusive, almost cryptic, quality of the *noh* gesture has no real equivalent in the West. Ballet has produced its own choreographic short-hand (hand on heart means 'I love you'), but this is crude by the standards of *noh*. How may such artifice be reconciled with 'imitation'?

The answer, of course, lies in Zeami's own words, once one has acquired the eyes to see. Imitation is the foundation of the art, but not its sum. 'First of all, be a perfect image of the person you are imitating . . .' The key words are 'First of all'. *Monomane* is the actor's starting-point, but Zeami makes it clear that imitation must be selective, not indiscriminate, and informed by art. The actor must select from the gestures he observes only what is meaningful, relevant and aesthetically pleasing; the rest may be discarded. Even ghosts and demons must be things of beauty. For this reason the studied deportment of the upper classes is an apter model than the less inhibited gestures of the lower. One must see Zeami against the background of his times. To an audience already largely petrified with etiquette (increasingly so, as the plays came to cater to a less representative selection of the populace) the formality of the stage must have seemed only a slightly heightened version of the formality of everyday life. But any discussion of this subject must proceed with caution, and two provisos must be borne in mind. First, there are indications that the acting of Zeami's time was less inhibited than what we now see, and that the artist still had considerable liberty for improvisation. Donald Keene has recently advanced the theory that it was not until the Tokugawa Shogunate that the movements, gestures and music were completely codified. Second, such words as 'realism' and 'imitation' have a shifting currency in dramatic criticism. Their meaning varies according to the preconceptions of the audience and the existing conventions of the stage. Burbage was counted as a naturalistic actor in his time: so was Betterton; so was Garrick. Queen Victoria found Irving horrifyingly realistic, though we would call him stilted. What was imitative by Zeami's standards may need considerable qualification by ours. But, when all is said and done, it seems clear that, even at the beginning, the gestures of *noh* were no more intended to reproduce the details of ordinary behaviour than the *noh* boat was intended to sail upon a lake. The same principle applies to both: having found the source, to select from it what is meaningful and appropriate; to reduce this to an aesthetically pleasing pattern; and to integrate it harmoniously into the composition of the whole. *Noh* takes life and reduces it to ritual; the gestures, by hinting at real actions, not representing them, allow the mind to penetrate their temporal significance and perceive a higher reality.

The actor, in other words, transcends the surface representation to find the essence, and prefers the spirit of the gesture to its substance. His movements, like his speech, evolve into a private language, meaningful only in its theatrical context and making increasingly heavy demands on the spectators' understanding. *Noh* assumes, as a condition of its existence, a knowledgeable audience. Far from imitating the outside world, it creates a world of its own, responsive to its own laws and logic, to which only the initiated may gain access. It works within its own frame of reference. Even the simplest gestures and the most basic movements are subordinated to a rhythmic pattern which divorces them from crass associations, gives them symbolic value and sets them firmly in their own rarefied world. The characteristic *noh* walk is the product of choreography, not of nature. It involves a curious gliding step with the head erect and looking firmly to the front; the knees are slightly bent, and the foot never completely leaves the floor. (When it does so, as in the stamping of the dance, it is always highly significant.) A character disembarking from a boat has a set method of progression: one foot out, pause; turn, pause; walk off. This is not the art which must conceal art. In *noh* the art is always apparent.

Technical virtuosity and physical discipline, however, are not ends in themselves. The actor aspires to a higher quality, to which Zeami gives the name *yugen*. It is an untranslatable word; the more pretentious renderings ('transcendental phantasm', 'beauty of reverberation or suggestiveness') only confuse the issue; *yugen* implies something dark or obscure, a beauty that lies beneath the surface. Zeami uses it for the artistic quality that

infuses an actor's performance when he has so completely
assimilated his techniques that they become an unconscious part
of himself; the inner beauty that transcends the visual grace of
motion and deportment. The techniques, once mastered, make
a springboard by which the actor may attain the heights. He
works from an intuition which is the product of his technical
expertise. Zeami lays down strict rules for the interplay of voice
and gesture, but admits that, at the last, the actor perceives the
correct balance and the precise moment by intuition and not by
formula. In this respect *noh* acting resembles the classical Japanese art of swordsmanship. Both were informed by Zen; both, in
their higher manifestations, relied on the quality of inspiration,
the moment of truth; both were spiritual as well as physical disciplines. The *samurai*, like the actor, must master an elaborate
technique, but if he cannot see beyond it, he will never attain the
full mastery of his art. But when the divine frenzy seizes him;
when he becomes indifferent to life and death; when his sword
becomes a part of himself, and he is not using the sword, but *is*
the sword; then he is irresistible. Zeami could have given to his
actors the Chinese master's advice to young painters: 'Draw
bamboos for ten years, become a bamboo, then forget all about
bamboos when you are drawing. In possession of an infallible
technique, the individual places himself at the mercy of inspiration.' In its content, philosophy and form *noh* represents a constant inward progression: from the temporal to the transcendant,
from the material to the essence, from the real to the super-real.

In their stage positioning, as in their movement, *noh* actors
are guided by fixed conventions which are meaningful only in the
context of their theatre. A modern director moves his actors
according to the logic of the play and the requirements of the
immediate dramatic situation. This has not always been the case.
Until quite recently the actor's position was dictated by his importance not in the scene but in the company. The best positions
fell to the leading actor by right, and the supporting cast was kept
firmly on the fringes. *Noh* remains the supreme example of this
pattern of stage movement. In positioning the actors and musicians the four pillars have an important conventional significance.

They define the limits of the main stage proper; the stage assistants, who sit at the back, and the Chorus, at the left, are thus by convention 'off-stage'. The *hashigakari* provides a subsidiary acting area, which may also, by convention, represent the far distance. Actors enter up the *hashigakari* and take their stand before the nearest pillar to announce their names and functions. Their subsequent positions are governed by the pillars. That on upstage right, next to the *hashigakari*, is known as the *sh'te*'s pillar; the principal actor holds position here when he is not dancing. Downstage left, diagonally opposite, is the *waki*'s pillar. The effect of this conventional grouping is that the *waki* is automatically upstaged, since to converse with the *sh'te* he must turn away from the audience. The other pillars have their own names and functions. Upstage left is the flute-player's pillar, marking his position in the orchestra. Downstage right is the 'guide' or 'eye-fixing' pillar. In a sense all four are guide pillars so far as the *sh'te* is concerned. His mask has tiny eye-holes which allow him only to see straight ahead. In his movements and dances he orientates himself on the pillars around the stage. As the orchestra is at the rear and the *waki*, Chorus and supernumeraries at stage left, his dances are chiefly plotted from stage centre to downstage right, so that the pillar in the latter position is the most useful to him.

The Western spectator may be troubled by the apparent lack of focus in *noh*. He is told that the *sh'te* must be the centre of attention – and certainly the magnificence of the costume seems to justify this – but there still seem to be unnecessary and eye-catching distractions. His eye tends to wander to upstage centre, one of the prime positions in the Western theatre, and view, with alarm, things going on there which have nothing to do with the drama; for this is where the musicians sit, and when not playing they may be busy with their own affairs. One may often see a drummer, during a dialogue passage, restringing the framework of his drum – with vivid orange thread – unconscious of the fact that he is committing the Western theatre's cardinal sin of upstaging an actor. But these things are, to an extent, accidents of the indoor performance. When *noh* is played outdoors as it was meant to be, the stage assumes a different quality, and the relative importance of the characters is more immediately obvious. The stage and *hashigakari* are shadowed by their canopies. Against this obscurity the mask and brilliant costume of the *sh'te* stand out in sharp relief. One perceives that the costumes have a graduated brightness in accordance with the status of the wearer; the less important the character, the more his costume merges into the shadows of the stage. The *sh'te* wears the brightest colours and a mask. The *waki* is less vivid and has no mask. *Kyogen* costumes are still less obtrusive, and the musicians, Chorus and assistants wear a simple uniform consisting of a robe with stiffened shoulders in muted blue, brown or green over black. Under artificial light (nowadays usually fluorescent) the whole stage is washed with the same illumination, and the distinctions are minimized.

This, however, is not the whole answer. There are problems of focus, by Western standards, because *noh* has never admitted the concept of ensemble playing. In *Hagoromo* (*The Robe of Feathers*) three fishermen (*waki* and *waki-tsure*) find a beautiful robe caught in the branches of a pine-tree. They are about to carry it off as a national treasure when they are interrupted by the angel who owns it. She tells them that without it she cannot return to heaven, and the *waki*, moved by her distress, promises to give it back if she will dance for them. Some haggling ensues. The angel wants the robe before she dances, but the fishermen fear she may cheat them and fly away. She replies that such may be the ways of men, but not of angels, and the *waki*, ashamed, yields up his treasure. The culmination of the play is the hoped-for dance – a long dance – at the end of which the angel calls down blessings of mankind and disappears. But in production the fishermen pay no attention to what they have sacrificed so much to see. As the angel dances they are turned away from her, looking impassively into the middle distance. It is incidents of this sort that bring home so strongly the difference between the modern Western and the traditional Eastern stage: the theatre of ensemble playing, where 'there are no small parts, only small actors' and the theatre in which interest is concentrated on the individual performer. The *waki*'s duty, in this play as in others, is to act as 'feed' to the *sh'te* and introduce the dance. When the *sh'te* takes over, his work is done, and the only thing left for him to do is to make himself as inconspicuous as possible. When his lines are finished, he drops out of the picture, for all that he is still on stage. His behaviour is conditioned not by the demands of the scene, but by the etiquette of the theatre. Informed spectators accept the pattern, and what may be problems for us are not so for them. There is no need for the stage grouping to guide the eye to the significant point, for the audience is familiar with the ritual. It knows already what the significant point is, and where it is supposed to look.

We have now seen the elements of *noh*; it remains to consider them in combination. No description can adequately convey the flavour of a stage performance – particularly here, where words, music and subtle movement are so intimately related – but the following account may give at least a rough idea.

The play is Zeami's *Kagekiyo*, based on an episode in the *Heike Monogatari*. The leading character, who gives the play its name, was a general of the Taira family who distinguished himself in the wars against Yoritomo and Yoshitsune. Defeated, old, blind and destitute, he now lives like a hermit in his hovel, chanting the lays of dead warriors to the accompaniment of his lute. Such *Heike-biwa* recitations were a familiar art-form in the early fifteenth century, with their own school of performers who rivalled *noh* and influenced the dramatic form in several ways. What the Chorus in Aeschylus's *Agamemnon* say of themselves is true of him: 'When we are old, it is of others' valour we must sing.' He is an Achilles who has outlived his prime or, rather, an Achilles turned Homer. Renouncing the illusory and fleeting world, he sees his former triumphs as vanity. Found by his daughter after a long pilgrimage, he at first refuses to admit his identity, but yields when pressed and tells the story of one of his most famous exploits. But he still refuses to be drawn back into the world. He asks only for rites to be performed for him when he is dead, to smooth his path into the afterlife.

On this slender thread of plot the play is built. It takes the familiar form of the inquirer and the provoked reminiscence, which in this case gains pathos from the special relationship of the searcher and the sought. *Kagekiyo* has some resemblance to Sophocles' *Oedipus at Colonus*. In each a man who has known triumph and suffering transcends both to die in the odour of sanctity. But the story, such as it is, is of minimal importance. Our attention is directed to Kagekiyo himself and the contradictions of his character. He is headstrong, but keenly sensitive to the forces of nature. He craves for company in his loneliness, but shuns it when it comes. His blindness has cut him off, like Oedipus, from the sensory world, but allows him to perceive other, stronger forces at work. He is independent, but prone to self-pity. He clings in memory to a world he has abandoned in fact. Yet there is some hope for him. In his growing sense of his one-ness with nature, he foreshadows his ultimate emancipation from the tyranny of self.

In the outline that follows, the dialogue is only a synopsis of what is said.

CHARACTERS. Kagekiyo is, of course, played by the *sh'te*. Hitomaru, his daughter, has a closer relationship to him than is normally given to the *waki*: the part is therefore played by a *sh'te-tsure*. The *waki* plays the Villager.

INTRODUCTION. The stage has no drop-curtain, and the house lights remain up throughout. The beginning of the performance is signified by the lifting of the curtain over the dressing-room door. The musicians file down the *hashigakari* and take their customary places; the flautist by the upstage left pillar, the *kotsuzumi* player on his right, and the *otsuzumi* at the end. One stage assistant sits behind them. At the same time the Chorus-members enter through their sliding door and sit at stage left.

Two other assistants bring in the 'hovel', a bamboo structure with a thatched roof, draped for the present in purple. It is set upstage centre, in front of the musicians, with Kagekiyo already inside. He will remain there concealed until he enters the action. A stool is pushed under the drapery for him, and the assistants carefully adjust the folds.

D

The drums begin their rhythm, punctuated by the shouts which are essential to the tempo of the play and the actor's rapport with the music. Ideally, movement and music are in complete harmony, and take their tempo from each other, but a strong orchestra can dominate a weak actor and force him to conform to their beat.

Hitomaru and her servant come slowly down the *hashigakari*. She wears a flesh-coloured mask and rich brocade robe; the Servant is maskless. Advancing downstage, they face each other and chant to the beat of the drums:

BOTH. We are told that Kagekiyo is living in exile in Kyushu. But we do not know whether to believe this story. (*The* SERVANT *kneels.*)

HITOMARU (*solo, turning to the audience*). My name is Hitomaru. I live in Kamakura, and we are starting on a long journey to find my father. There are many hardships in store for us, but my longing will overcome them.

The Servant rises, and they face each other again. Together and individually they chant of the long journey they have already made. The Servant indicates this by his movements: three steps towards the audience, one step back to face Hitomaru. This is an excellent example of how *noh* compresses space and time; though they have been on the stage only a few minutes and have hardly moved, they talk of already having traversed several hundred miles. During this recitative the flute begins to pick up the melodic line. At its conclusion the actors cross downstage left and sit by the *waki* pillar, signifying that they have temporarily left the scene.

DEVELOPMENT. Meanwhile the stage assistants have come forward unobtrusively to the hovel. One reaches through the curtain and adjusts the *sh'te*'s robes. Kagekiyo, still unseen, begins his soliloquy. There is no movement on the stage, no sound of music. The theatre is dominated by his voice.

KAGEKIYO. I have lived here for years. . . . I took my own sight and now I cannot see. How many years? I cannot tell. I live in this dark hovel; I sleep when I am tired; I have the clothes I wear; I have grown thin from want.

The assistants take the curtain by the upper corners and lower it gently to the floor. Kagekiyo is revealed inside the hovel in a robe of brown and white, a cap of cloth of gold, and a brown wrinkled mask with the eyes closed to simulate blindness. Taking up his monody, the Chorus sings in his person as the drums return to pick up the beat.

CHORUS. I should have become a monk, or died. Now I am ashamed of myself. How can I hope for company here?

Hitomaru and the Servant rise and turn towards the hovel, attracted by the sound of the voice. Kagekiyo, oblivious of their presence, continues his soliloquy:

KAGEKIYO. I am blind, but when the breeze blows, I know that autumn comes. Whence does it come, I wonder?

HITOMARU. I have wandered here as in a dream. We have travelled far, through strange countries. Here there is no place for us to rest.

KAGEKIYO. No one has a place to rest, except in his own mind. All is vanity: all human beings, too. No one can tell me where I may rest.

These lines are the kernel of *noh* philosophy, and of the Zen doctrine on which it is based. The world is meaningless and empty of comfort. We seek eternally for happiness and peace, but it will not be discovered in this world.

The Servant asks where Kagekiyo may be found, and the old man feigns ignorance. Hitomaru and the Servant retreat to the pine-tree, sitting with their backs to the audience to indicate that they have left the scene. Still motionless, and without music,

Kagekiyo admits that he has recognized his daughter's voice. Drums and Chorus take up his unspoken thoughts.

CHORUS. I knew her, though I could not see her. I kept silent
   for fear of hurting her. My daughter, do not blame me!

Hitomaru and her servant walk from the stage along the *hashi-gakari*. Hitomaru stops at the first pine-tree. The Servant goes further and faces the curtain, which opens to reveal the Villager. On inquiry, he informs them that the old man they have just met is really Kagekiyo. Hearing this, Hitomaru makes the exquisitely simple gesture of weeping: the left hand moves slowly up to the eyes, the head bows. All three return to the stage. Hitomaru and her servant to the *waki* pillar, the Villager to the hovel. Rapping twice on the framework with his fan, he calls Kagekiyo by name. As the old man replies angrily, the Villager crosses half-way down to the 'guide' pillar and kneels; the centre stage is thus left free for Kagekiyo's soliloquy. (The stage movement at this point departs from the usual pattern, as the regular *waki* position is occupied by Hitomaru; but the *waki*'s move is still dictated by the necessity of leaving a clear field for the principal.)

The Chorus continues Kagekiyo's angry theme, and then, speaking for him, shows a change of mind. He emphasizes this by a single sharp stroke with his fan – his only movement since the play began.

CHORUS. I am wrong. I must not be angry and rebuff those who
   have helped me. My friend, forgive me.
      I am blind but I can see men's hearts. I know the change
   of seasons. I know when it is snowing, and can write it in my
   mind. But how quickly the scene passes. I hear the waves
   lapping on the beach, and know the tide is rising [the transitory image again]. Now I am a lutist; and to make amends
   for my rudeness, I will chant a passage from the *Tales of the
   Heike*.

He stands, and the stage assistant removes his stool. Picking up a stick, he gropes his way out of the hovel downstage. The Villager forces him to acknowledge his daughter's presence. Hitomaru rises and crosses to him; with arm outstretched she kneels at his feet, repeating the weeping gesture. Softened, the old man admits his identity. The Chorus, speaking for him, reminisces about the great days, and the Villager begs to hear his story. Kagekiyo agrees, on condition thay they leave when it is finished. Hitomaru goes back to the *waki* pillar, and the Villager sits in front of the Chorus.

CLIMAX. The stage assistant replaces Kagekiyo's stool and takes away his stick. He begins his lay, sitting at first, and motionless; the Chorus then takes up the chant while he dances out the story.

KAGEKIYO. Our army was losing to the enemy. I resolved that our only safety lay in killing Yoshitsune, their general. Taking this upon myself, I landed with a few men. We were immediately surrounded.

CHORUS. Kagekiyo killed several of them, and they began to retreat. He called one prominent among them by name — Mio-no-ya, a famous warrior, who avoided the challenge. Kagekiyo caught him by the backplate of his helmet, and in the struggle pulled it from his head. Mio-no-ya ran away, and shouted from a distance 'How strong your arm is!' Kagekiyo replied 'How strong your neck is!' And they parted amid laughter.

This Homeric episode, in which two warriors acknowledge each other's qualities and a kinship that transcends their political differences, epitomizes the spirit of the *samurai*. Kagekiyo dances the principal events, portraying himself and his enemy at the same time. We see the tug at the helmet, and the stagger backwards as the strap breaks.

With the dance the play ends. Its closure seems almost infinitely protracted, like the dying reverberations of a shout of triumph or, to use a favourite image of Japanese poetry, the diminishing ripples of a stone in water. Kagekiyo subsides into passivity and kneels. Hitomaru turns to face him. The assistant returns the old man's stick; all rise. Hitomaru crosses to her father. Hand on her shoulder, he bids her go. The Servant leaves first, then Hitomaru, in the same solemn procession by which they arrived. Kagekiyo looks after them, makes the weeping gesture, and follows. When he has reached the *sh'te* pillar, the Villager brings up the rear. The musicians are putting up their drums and turn to face each other in their own farewell ritual. Attendants carry off the hovel, and the musicians follow them out as the Chorus chants the closing lines.

What this bald description, like most descriptions, completely fails to convey is the hypnotic quality of *noh*. Writers have not dwelt on this, perhaps through fear of being thought subjective and unscholarly; but it must be mentioned, for it dominates the performance. The grouping of the Chorus and musicians about the central figure recalls that of the acolytes around their priest in Buddhist ceremony. The throbbing of the drums, the ritual gravity of the performers, and the measured choral recitation – which has been compared to recitative, or *sprechstimme*, or Gregorian chant, and is all of these but none, having no precise Western analogue – induce a hallucinatory sense to which the stage, existing in a void beyond time and space, contributes. At every performance one may see several of the audience asleep. Not from boredom: you do not attend *noh* without knowing what to expect. They have succumbed to the atmosphere; they are in a trance. An American friend, making her first visit to a *noh* play in my company, remarked that *noh* must be the Japanese equivalent of LSD. This sums up, quite accurately, the mood that is engendered by the performance, and the frame of reference in which the happenings on the stage must be appreciated. We have seen how, on the bare and uncommitted platform, the dramatist may control space and time at will. The characters similarly merge with each other. *Sh'te* and Chorus interchange personalities. The Chorus may speak the *sh'te*'s lines or give voice to his unspoken thoughts; the *sh'te* may act as his own Chorus and speak of himself as of a being apart.

But this is to say no more than that *noh* is, simply, ritual. Its aim is to illuminate something that is already almost completely known. The plots are all basically the same, and all familiar. There are no surprises or unexpected twists, any more than there are surprises in the Mass – which is, like *noh*, a dramatic presentation of an act of faith and a state of mind. In Japan a society which already operated largely in terms of ritual and ceremony evolved another ritual in its drama.

It is the *sh'te*'s performance by which the play stands, and the plays are classified according to his character in them. Zeami recognized three basic divisions: Old Man, Woman and Battle plays. The earlier cycles appear to have included one of each type, corresponding to the tripartite division of the individual play (the number three has always had a particular symbolic significance in Japanese thought) with *kyogen* between. Later, the number of categories was changed to five – God, Battle, Woman, Madman and Devil – and the length of the programme was correspondingly increased to five plays, again with intervening *kyogen*. The latter have the same function in *noh* as the satyr plays of the classical Greek theatre: to provide relief and relaxation for the audience after the drama.

The origins of *kyogen*, like those of any popular comedy, are obscure. Traditions that they were first performed by prisoners of war impressed as actors may be discounted. Such stories probably derive from the snobbish conviction that the lower art forms must have base origins. Later *kyogen* performers countered these charges – and compounded the obscurity – by fabricating their own histories of their art. Conscious of their own inferior social status, they sought to increase their importance by inventing a genealogy as illustrious as that of *noh*. In fact *kyogen* ('mad words') probably developed, like *noh*, out of *sarugaku*, and retained some of the earthy characteristics that the more refined form had shed. There are considerable problems, also, of text and authorship. The first authors were actors, concerned more with assembly than with originality, who put various pieces of comic business together and gave them a rudimentary plot, and the plays were for some time transmitted orally. In this they resemble the *kyogen* monologues in the *noh* play proper. In 1638 two hundred and three *kyogen* texts were written down and

classified, with strict instuctions that they were to be kept secret.
A new transcription was made in 1792; the manuscripts are still
in the hands of private families, which preserve the traditions of
their art as the Kanze and other schools do those of *noh*.

*Kyogen* plays vary in length – from ten minutes to three-
quarters of an hour or more – and draw their material from
various sources. Some are vignettes of everyday life, often in the
form of humorous dialogues with a bare minimum of action.
Their closest Western equivalents are the Greek 'mimes' of
Herodas, which clothe domestic conversation in dramatic and
poetic form. Older and younger brothers are familiar characters.
One, for instance, show the elder trying to persuade his junior
to go fishing in his place. He has hurt his leg, he claims, and 'the
circulation is stopping'. A comparable and still highly popular
form exists in the comic dialogue known as *manzai*, an Osaka
favourite, and by tradition born there; in its present state it is
indistinguishable from a music-hall cross-talk act.

Other *kyogen* have literary sources in Buddhist parables, or such
works as the *Tale of Genji*. Some are parodies of *noh*, as the satyr
plays parodied the themes and characters of Greek tragedy. They
resemble the medieval mime-farces still seen at the Mibu Shrine
in Kyoto, though with the addition of a text, and like them may
be compared to the early Italian popular comedy which preceded
the work of Plautus and Terence. These plays (the *fabulae
Atellanae*, or Atellan farces) drew both on their native folklore
and mythic-tragic material; the development in both countries
runs on parallel lines, though the Roman precedes the Japanese
by several centuries. *Kyogen* makes no claims to be a literary form.
Its humour is broad and largely visual. The following are some of
the best-known titles and subjects:

*Bo Shibari* (*Tied to a Pole*). One of the most popular. A master
has two servants who love to break into his *sake* cellar. When he
has to leave the house he ties them up, one with hands behind his
back, the other with his arms strapped to a long pole. Their
resourcefulness is equal to the situation. They mime the action
of opening the cellar door, going downstairs and removing a keg

of *sake*. The stage assistant brings on a bowl. Their problem now is how to get the *sake* to their lips. They solve this by co-operation, each holding the bowl for the other. They soon become staggering drunk, sing and perform a burlesque *noh* dance. The master comes home and drives them out.

*Fuzumo*. A lord has acquired a new servant, and tests his ability by challenging him to a bout of *sumo* wrestling. The servant wins easily. Humiliated, the master produces an enormous scroll and reads up on the subject. He is now confident of winning, and expresses his pleasure by leaping high in the air and coming down with his legs crossed. But he loses the second bout also. Tearing the scroll in a slow pantomime of disgust, he seizes a second servant, whom he knows he can beat, and drags him off the stage, shouting, 'In future, I'll only wrestle with you!'

*Utsubozaru* (*The Monkey and the Quiver*). A *daimyo*, going hunting, meets a travelling entertainer with a performing monkey, and demands its skin to make a quiver. The trainer reluctantly prepares to kill his pet, but the monkey thinks it is just another rehearsal and begins to perform its tricks. At this the trainer bursts into tears. The *daimyo* too is moved, spares the monkey's life, and gives it lavish presents – his fan, his sword and even his ceremonial outer robes. This play is particularly interesting for several reasons. One of the monkey's tricks is to mimic a sacred dance, with a *gohei* (a prayer-stick hung with cut paper) in its paw. This may hark back to an early function of *sarugaku*, the parody of religious ritual to provide relief. The play illustrates, alos, how even *kyogen* observes the Buddhist precepts. In sparing the monkey and divesting himself of his cloak of authority, the *daimyo* demonstrates that temporal power is as nothing beside the sanctity of life. The monkey is a traditional beginner's role. Four living members of the Nomura family, the leading *kyogen* actors in Japan today, chose it for their debut. In the performance that I saw, the monkey was played by a small girl (a sign of the times): Nomura Hatsue, a six-year-old, making her first appearance on the stage.

D 2

*Roku Jizo* (*The Six Stone Images*). A man wants to purchase images of the gods. His friend and two accomplices, in masks, try to fool him by pretending to be statues. As there are only three of them, and the man wants six, they have to double repeatedly across the stage and take up new positions, until the masks slip and their imposture is discovered. A variation of this for smaller companies involves only two actors, with one man pretending to be several deities at once.

*Shido-Hogaku* (*A Spell to Stop a Horse*). A *daimyo* intends to enter a tea-making contest, and sends his servant to his uncle to borrow tea-leaves, swords and a horse. The uncle lends them grudgingly, but warns that the horse has a peculiar vice; it bucks when anyone clears his throat, and can be calmed only by a certain formula, which the servant learns. Master and servant start off for the ceremony, and the servant, who feels he has been bullied enough, amuses himself by making the horse rear. When the master has been thrown several times he chases the servant off the stage. The chief attraction here is the *kyogen* horse, which looks like no animal that ever was; it is played by a man in skin-tight costume, on all fours, with a human mask and a shaggy mane.

*Naki Ama* (*The Crying Nun*). A priest covers up his bad preaching by always taking with him a senile nun who can be relied on to cry at the sermon. Ordered to preach before the abbot, he summons his accomplice to help him. The nun is a wonderful character. She hobbles onto the stage bent almost double, like a walking corpse. Her mask is green and wizened, and a yellow shawl covers her bald head. But the sermon is so bad that even she cannot stand it. The rattling of her beads grows slower and slower, her head droops, and she dozes off. The priest coughs indignantly, and she twitches into wakefulness. This process is repeated frequently as the dreary sermon (appropriately, on death) drones on. At the end the priest is coughing like a machine-gun and hammering on the lectern with his fan; the nun, oblivious, curls into a ball and sleeps. The only thing that wakes her is the bell signifying the end of the sermon, at which she sits up and demands part of the priest's fee for services rendered. They go off in angry argument.

*Futari Daimyo* (*Two Lords*). Two noblemen setting out on a journey and feeling disgraced because they have no-one to carry their swords press a passer-by into service. As soon as he has the swords, he threatens them, makes them perform animal imitations and runs off with the sword and their clothes.

The recurring theme of the humiliation of the *daimyo* by the lower orders may seem unlikely material for humour in a feudal society. In fact the aristocracy was so strongly entrenched, and so secure in its prestige, that it could permit itself to be mocked on the stage. Such violations of the social system were discounted as fantasy, impossible and therefore tolerable. Modern social satirists have encountered similar reactions. London's satirical theatre, The Establishment, created to attack the *mores* of the upper classes, found with dismay that those classes provided its best audience. They came to see their prerogatives mocked on the stage in the happy confidence that such things could never happen in real life. *Kyogen* enjoyed the same licence. It is the closest that the Japanese theatre, or indeed the whole of Japanese literature, comes to social satire. Many of the plays were taken into the later *kabuki* repertoire, which, like *kyogen*, claimed the right, within reasonable limits, of mocking the upper classes.

Both *noh* and *kyogen* derive from popular entertainment, but *kyogen* is clearly much closer to its sources. Its movements are less stately, its manner less refined. Nevertheless *kyogen*, as now performed, has become more dignified through centuries of association with its prestigious neighbour. It lacks the explosive vitality of the traditional Chinese farces – a vitality which it too must have had at its origin. *Utsobozaru*, for instance, is slowed down immeasurably by the protocol that governs conversation between a high-born *daimyo* and a lowly monkey-trainer. Everything has to be said twice, and relayed through the retainer who acts as intermediary. Today's *kyogen* is baggy-trousered farce which has put on a Sunday suit and a stiff collar. Its rare acrobatic moments now seem as incongruous, in context, as a belch at a vicarage tea-party. Many aspects of the physical performance have been borrowed from *noh*. The comic characters make the same slow, dignified entrance up the *hashigakari*, and the action often stops dead while we wait for the next character to reach the stage. Their movements, however, though stereotyped, are less restricted than in *noh*. The stage picture is still pivoted about the traditional positions – the *sh'te* and *waki* pillars – but the immediate needs of the scene dictate who shall occupy them. For example, *Futari Daimyo* begins with a grumbling conversation between the two lords. The chief speaker takes the *sh'te* pillar, and his companion the inferior position. When the passer-by seizes their swords and bullies them, he takes the *sh'te* pillar and both lords move to the *waki* side. Exits are faster than in *noh*, often taken at a run along the *hashigakari*, and the sliding Chorus-door is used more frequently. Masks are used only for special characters, like the Crying Nun, and the actors are less restricted in their facial expressions, though these are still limited in comparison with Western acting, and the actor communicates chiefly through physical gesture. There are no musicians or Chorus. Dialogue, though still chanted, is closer to the vernacular in language and delivery. The stage assistants, whose work is less demanding than in *noh*, are often young boys at the beginning of their training.

The full cycle of five serious and four comic plays was developed for an age and a class whose audiences could afford to spend the better part of a day at the theatres. Programmes of this length are still occasionally given, and are physically and emotionally demanding, though less so than one would at first suppose; it must be said, in all fairness, that the timelessness of the *noh* stage communicates itself to the auditorium, and one ceases to be aware of the passing of the hours. Modern practice, however, usually adapts itself to new habits and working conditions. The usual cycle now consists of three *noh* plays and one *kyogen*, and may be curtailed still further by presenting only two complete *noh* and the *shimai* of the third. There are an increasing number of programmes devoted to *kyogen*, which has become a cult in its own right and is enjoying something of a revival in present-day Tokyo.

It is likely, also, that the earlier cycles took considerably less time than they do now. The average length of a single *noh* play

now is about an hour and a quarter (though the shortest is twenty
minutes, and the longest two hours and a half). As originally conceived, they may have lasted about half this time. By dividing the
length of known historical festivals by the number of plays performed, scholars have calculated that the average *noh* may have
lasted no more than forty minutes. Complete accuracy is impossible – even now the same play may vary by as much as fifteen
minutes, depending on the school performing it – but it seems
certain that the gradual formulation of movements and music was
accompanied by a lengthening of the time of performance. As
*noh* became fixed, it grew slower. Part of this is unquestionably
due to the increasing veneration in which the art was held. A
play that becomes a 'classic' automatically loses some of its
vitality. Subsequent generations feel that they should treat it with
the respect due to its age, and that brisk handling would slight it.
We still suffer from this in our productions of Shakespeare.
His 'two hours' traffic of our stage' may be an understatement, but a four-and-a-half-hour *Hamlet* goes brutally to the other
extreme. The slow tempo of present *noh*, like the refinement
of *kyogen*, may simply represent the dignity of advanced old
age.

Any consideration of *noh* as living theatre art must admit, at
the outset, the enormous barriers that time and changing custom
have erected between the play and the audience. If the business
of a play is to communicate, *noh* seems determined to make such
communication as difficult as possible. It is profoundly oblique,
working most typically by indirection; it prefers the allusion to
the statement, the gesture to the act, the hint to the developed
idea. It avoids the actual and the direct. The report or memory of
an action is preferred to its presentation. This obliquity is reflected, as we have seen, in the furnishings of the stage. The setting exists only in language. Properties give the mere skeleton of
the object to be represented. Costumes and masks are notably
unrealistic; they form a stage shorthand, a code which conveys to
the initiated audience the wearer's character and social position.
The *sh'te* in mask and full costume – particularly when the hands
are concealed within the sleeves – gives the uncanny effect of an

impressionist sketch of a human being, an attenuated figure in which only the vital characteristics are reproduced and the rest left obscure. Stage gesture, like stage costume, forms its own code and reduces physical action to a few stylized movements.

In the texts a similar allusiveness reveals itself. *Noh* scripts, at first sight, are barren, monotonous and repetitive. Their deep and complex meaning reveals itself only with study. They are loaded with allusions to other stories and to traditional Chinese texts with which the audience could be expected to be familiar. Such allusiveness is, of course, familiar in other drama. Greek tragedy is similarly prone to illustrate an event by relevant example. When Antigone is imprisoned by Creon, the Chorus compares her fate to that of several mythic heroines incarcerated through no fault of their own. When Medea kills her children, the women of Corinth recall the similar atrocity committed by Ino and her subsequent fate. But in the Greek such illustrations are set out at sufficient length for even an ignorant audience to appreciate their relevance. *Noh* makes no such concessions. The allusions are confined to a phrase, a title, or a brief quotation; the audience is assumed to have the necessary knowledge and mental agility to supply the rest for itself. In *Shunkan* the exiled protagonist is left mourning on a barren rock, while a ship carries his companions back to shore. The Chorus chants that 'in his heart there is a grief whose depths surpass the Lady Sayo's sorrow at Matsura'. It is left to the audience to make the correct identification, and perceive the analogy between Shunkan's predicament and an incident of the fourth century A.D. The Lady Sayo's lover had abandoned her by sea. Unable to follow his ship, she remained desolate upon the shore and was transformed into a stone pillar. This, it might be added, is unusually explicit for a *noh* play. Often the references are far more esoteric, turning on one word – the 'pivot' or 'hinge' – which has one immediate meaning in its context but also contains an ambiguity which, correctly interpreted, will induce a whole new train of reflection. It is for this reason that *noh* has been the despair of translators.

By what right does any drama assume so cryptic a posture? Any play, other than the most trivial, exacts a contribution from the audience. Communication is a two-way business, and demands a fruitful meeting of minds. But *noh* seems to demand a contribution beyond all reason, to remain wilfully obscure, and to place a disproportionate onus on its spectators. The remoteness of *noh* stems from two causes, the social framework into which it was adopted, and the philosophy it was designed to expound. We can best illustrate the first of these by reverting to the history of the physical theatre.

In the final phase of its development, the *noh* stage was taken indoors, and though al fresco performances may still be given, it is as an indoor entertainment that it has chiefly survived. Often in the history of the theatre the stage serves as an architectural metaphor of the social conditions that produced it. The Greek theatre, in its pure form, perfectly embodies the idea of a communal performance. The Chorus dances in the *orchestra*, with the spectators on every side. As the performance evolves in the centre of the audience, so the drama springs from the mass of the people. The players are the people; the distinction between amateur and professional does not yet exist, nor is there any physical barrier between the actor and his audience. Theatre is group activity. Even the later Greek theatre attests to this by the frequency with which the audience may be drawn implicitly or explicitly into the action and function as a part of it, lit by the same sun and caught up by the same mood.

If the structure of the Greek theatre symbolizes a communal activity, the indoor *noh* stage represents its antithesis. We see a construction which is, from the first glance, artificial; a building within a building, a roof over a roof; a theatre which has literally been taken in out of the rain. The canopy remains, though it is now redundant, and the path of pebbles still surrounds the stage. The indoor *noh* theatre takes to its logical conclusion the process that began when the real pine-tree was replaced by its painted replica.

The theatre symbolizes the status which *noh* came to assume in Japanese society. Born among the people, it was extracted from its natural habitat and refined for the enjoyment of the élite. It became, like *gagaku*, a protected art, a hothouse flower, to be kept carefully apart from any influences that might corrupt it, for in Japanese eyes to change was to destroy. This protectiveness extended to the theatre, the players and the plays. Actors, patronized and idolized by the Shogunate, enjoyed a privileged status. They were given the distinctions of *samurai*, and the heads of each school were protected by hereditary succession. In effect the patronage of the Shogunate created a national system of financial support, and Ieasu, who created the feudal state, was one of *noh*'s keenest supporters and an occasional actor himself. Actors prospered and grew extravagant. Under Tsunayoshi, at the end of the seventeenth century, they enjoyed particular esteem, and performers from the Five Families were honoured with official positions. They made up an artificial social class, removed from their true origins to form a pampered group. The artificiality of their position is seen in their panic when the last Shogun resigned, and they felt the cold wind of the Meiji Restoration.

The plays were similarly cherished. Removed from the public domain and cultivated by an élite group, the scripts were immune to change. Any lingering impulse to develop the art was effectively choked. *Noh* developed to a certain point, and then stopped dead; after this the sole concern was to preserve what had already been accomplished. Although over three thousand *noh* plays are estimated to have been written since the second quarter of the fourteenth century, of which about a quarter survive, the practical repertory was limited to fewer than two hundred and fifty, the bulk of them by Kwanami and Zeami, the two earliest authors of note. Both before and after the Meiji Restoration, authors continued to compose in *noh* style, but the later plays were never given official recognition. The last major author, Kojiro, of the Kanze family, died in 1516. Kojiro was born about the time Zeami died. Like his predecessor he was accomplished in the practical stage arts, being a master *otsuzumi* player who seems to have performed *waki* roles. His work suggests the way in which *noh* might have developed, had it not been first interrupted by war (from 1467 to 1477), when Kyoto was reduced to ashes and the art neglected, and later constrained by its social cir-

1  *Kagura* invokes the sun

2 Religious pageantry: shrine festival, Asakusa, Tokyo

3 *Geisha* with rice seedlings, Sumiyoshi, Osaka

4 and 5 Dance as benediction and as entertainment: labourers, dancers and
audience, Sumiyoshi, Osaka

6  *Above*: Grace of ceremonial: *bugaku* dancers, Yasaka, Kyoto

7  *Top right*: Old Imperial Palace, Kyoto, protector of the courtly arts

8  *Lower right*: Osaka Castle, symbol of the feudal state

9  The beauty of
   simplicity: tea
   ceremony

10  The landscape of
    Zen: dry garden,
    Nanzenji, Kyoto

11 *Sumo* wrestlers, indoor training ring

12 Stage for torchlight *noh* performance, Heian Shrine, Kyoto

13 *Noh* stage, Yasukuni Shrine, Tokyo

14 Indoor *noh*: *Funa-Benkei (Benkei in the Boat)*

cumstances. He was the author of, among others, *Funa Benkei* (*Benkei in the Boat*) and *Rashomon*, a title which has won Western fame for other reasons. Kojiro endeavoured to heighten the dramatic effect of *noh* by enlarging the *waki* role. In *Funa Benkei* the *waki* plays the name part, not only speaking the prologue, but taking a major part in the action. In the second Act he engages in combat with a vengeful ghost (the *sh'te*) and subdues him by the power of his incantations. In *Rashomon* (whose only connection with the modern play and film of that name is the site) the *sh'te* does not appear at all until the second Act, and then in a mute role.

*Ataka* introduces a conflict situation in which *sh'te* and *waki* have roles of almost equal importance. Benkei and Yoshitsune, with a band of retainers, are escaping from the enemy disguised as wandering priests. Arriving at the Ataka barrier, they are challenged by Togashi, who suspects that they are not what they seem. Benkei tries to convince him, first by reading from a supposed list of charitable donations, and then by striking Yoshitsune, who is masquerading as a servant. Togashi is not deceived, but sympathizes with enemies who are compelled to such an alarming breach of etiquette, and lets them pass. Yoshitsune pardons Benkei for striking him, and they celebrate with a gift of *sake* that Togashi has sent after them. This play not only offers the dramatic excitement of the battle of wits, but comes, for *noh*, very close to spectacle: Benkei and his master are accompanied by eight or ten retainers. From plays like these, one can see what *noh* might have become if given scope.

The earlier tradition has thus been preserved unbroken; and it is a proud and venerable one. A Japanese scholar remarked that, when the Western world was preparing to celebrate the Shakespeare quatercentenary, his own country could look back on six hundred years of Zeami. But at what cost? Shakespeare's plays have survived on their merits. Flung into the arena, at the mercy of any hack who believed his style to be superior to the original, distorted by stars who wished to enlarge their parts, they have kept their integrity and their reputation. Even the French classical repertory, preserved by the *Comédie française* as a sacred trust, has been accessible to any other group who wished to stage the plays and experiment with them. But for *noh* there has only been one way, and that the original way. It is tantalizing to speculate on what would have happened to *noh* if it had not been so quickly and completely adopted by a restricted body of performers and an exclusive social group.

In his analysis of *noh*, the first important study of its kind in English, Arthur Waley stresses that the drama did not separate itself immediately, or ever completely, from the public. For a long time *noh* was the only sort of theatre that there was, and the people continued to attend it until they had evolved their own. Although the *samurai* reserved it for themselves by edict, the public could still see *kanjin* performances. A frequent source of eighteenth- and nineteenth-century humour was the boor who made uncultivated remarks at a *noh* performance, somewhat like the merchant and his wife in *The Knight of the Burning Pestle*. Waley argues also that the literary references which are now so obscure were originally part of the popular language as songs or ballads, and that the more erudite Buddhist allusions are not strictly necessary to the understanding of the play.

We might add that the ritualistic nature of the performance was initially no barrier to understanding. Ritual is inclusive, not exclusive, in its function. As Yeats was later to argue when he adapted *noh* plays for the Irish stage, it makes every spectator a participant by exacting a personal contribution from him. Ritual, in other words, is group art. It becomes exclusive only when the group is limited. The modern Japanese watching *noh* is in the same predicament as Yeats's audience watching his First and Second Musicians sitting crosslegged on the drawing-room floor. It is not his ritual. Understanding is no longer instinctive. It has to be acquired, and must always, with the best will in the world, remain partially foreign.

References which may once have been meaningful soon ceased to be so. Popular taste moved on, but *noh* did not: it kept the old forms unbroken. It preserved a language which had elsewhere become archaic, and allusions which required scholarship to be understood. In a sense this obscurity was demanded by *noh*'s new patrons. Any play asks some intellectual contribution from the audience; the drama of the élite is permitted to ask more, because appreciation has become a status symbol. Its audiences come not so much to enjoy the play as to prove their right to be there. Opera in the Western world, and particularly in the United States, has acquired a similar social significance, distinct from its artistic status. *Noh* became another badge of class, a new ritual among many to set the *samurai* apart from the despised lower orders. Appreciation was a mark of breeding; it was not the plays that were on trial, but the audience.

*Noh*'s closest Western parallel, on this level, is Senecan tragedy, which took Greek plays, purged them of their popular associations, and offered them to a limited and highly erudite audience. The parallel is not an exact one, for Seneca flatters only the literary pretensions of his clique, not their social esteem; but the same intellectual equipment is demanded of the audience. Seneca, like *noh*, makes no concessions. He does not need to enlighten an already knowledgeable coterie. What they are exploring is the depth of their own reading and the breadth of their perceptions. The more obscure the reference, the more flattered they will be at catching it. As in *noh*, the range of possible material is strictly circumscribed, and there is no room for novelty. The drama can only feed upon itself. There can be no variety, only increasingly recondite complication.

*Noh*, however, was more than an intelligence test. Its obscurity, though it served an immediate social purpose, rests on a more profound philosophical basis. *Noh*'s Buddhist affinities have already been touched on at several points in this chapter. It is time now to consider the relationship in greater detail, for it is a vital one, and affects both form and content.

Buddhism was officially introduced to Japan in A.D. 552. It came through Korea, and was adopted, in the first instance, as a political expedient, to foster alliances through a common religion. Overcoming initial hostility, the new faith became part of the Japanese way of life, sometimes merging with the earlier Shinto deities, sometimes propagating new sects of its own. Its priests and monks became guardians of literature and the arts, ensuring cultural continuity in an age of political chaos. It was in the sixth century also that Japan first became acquainted with the form of Buddhism known as Zen. The word derives from the Sanskrit *dhyana*, 'meditation', and its school differed markedly from the other manifestations of Buddhist thought to be found in Japan. It taught that enlightenment was not to be attained by reciting mystic formulas, or even by the study of the *sutras*, but only by direct intuitive perception. The individual must not hope for a saviour to show him the way, but make his own effort to grasp the meaning of the universe. Zen formulates elaborate rules to encourage the required mental discipline, but only as aids to the search. In its main tenets Zen distrusts the verbalizing of philosophical concepts. The successful student will receive sudden, overwhelming enlightenment, and perceive the true nature of the universe behind its meaningless temporal and material appearance.

Zen, though known so early, did not take hold until a travelling priest, Eisai, founded a school in Kyoto in 1191. Eisai had travelled widely in China and been profoundly influenced by what he saw there, for it was at this period that Zen was proving so fruitful in its relationship with the arts. The new sect flourished in Japan, and particularly among the *samurai* class, who found its insistence on austerity and self-reliance sympathetic to their own empirical philosophy. In the fourteenth and fifteenth centuries it became virtually the state religion. As this was also the formative period of *noh*, the two went hand in hand; it is impossible to consider one without the other. *Noh* plays in performance offer a practical illustration of Zen doctrine.

Zen teaches that the phenomenal world, the world we can see and touch, is a meaningless mask concealing the inner truth. It was remarked earlier in this chapter that the plays sometimes embody sermons: when they do, it is this sentiment that they chiefly expound, particularly through the mouths of *revenants*, who first recount their past glories and then expatiate on their transitory nature. But even where there is no explicit exposition, the thought is fundamental. The discrepancy between the real and the apparent is the core of many plots. It occurs conspicuously in those plays where the inquirer meets someone he assumes to be a local person, and who tells him a story; a change of mask and costume then reveals his informant in his true shape, as god, spirit or demon, eternal truth masquerading in earthly guise. This appears more clearly in a play already briefly discussed, *Aoi no Ue* (*The Lady Aoi*). When first the priestess draws the spirit from the sick body, it appears in kindly shape, with tranquil white mask (the familiar 'sympathetic feminine' type) and orange robe. A priest is then summoned to exorcise it. While he is conversing, the spirit's costume is changed, on stage. Assistants remove the orange robe and hold it before her like a screen. The priest turns to confront her, the robe is dropped and the spirit stands revealed in her true shape: the mask is now that of a devil. Holding the orange robe over her like a canopy, she engages him in dance-combat. The symbolism is obvious. The first costume was the beautiful husk, which has now cracked open to reveal the evil within. What once seemed pathetic is now seen as demonic, and we are shown the true face of jealousy. In *Aoi no Ue*, Zen builds on animistic foundations. It does so also in *Funa Benkei* (*Benkei in the Boat*) where the warrior priest accompanies his master, Prince Yoshitsune, on a journey by sea. A storm blows up and reveals itself as the spirit of a warrior Yoshitsune had once killed, perpetuating his animosity through natural forces. The metamorphoses of *noh* may be baneful as well as divine; the true nature of evil, like that of good, may not always be immediately perceptible.

Zen's influence on *noh* staging has already been discussed. A philosophy which disparages the material and temporal cannot countenance representational art. *Noh*'s setting, properties and movements transcend the phenomenal to convey the ideal. Nature, in Zen, is purged and refined; the irrelevant surface detail is discarded to concentrate on the essential pattern. What happens on the stage is paralleled by the activity in other Zen-influenced arts. The tea ceremony, which has strong affinities with *noh*, takes domestic objects, simple in design and sparsely decorated, and, by surrounding them with ritual usage, transforms them into a medium for assisting contemplation. A com-

mon habit and a natural need are turned into a rite; an everyday
activity acquires a deeper meaning. Similar aesthetic principles
control the landscape gardens of the period. The Japanese *niwa*,
unlike Western gardens, has never been a place where people
grow flowers or play. It is intended to express an idea and to
create another world – an ideal world, an approximation of
Nirvana. From early times its principal components were a lake,
an islet and a bridge, representing the Buddhist belief that such
a bridge conducted the believer to paradise. (This idea is also
embodied in *Shakkyo*, see p. 43). With the passing of the years,
and particularly under Zen influence, the natural and therefore
ephemeral beauty of trees, flowers, and water submits to greater
order and refinement. The lake assumes the shape of a Chinese
character and a more subtle meaning, and the materials become
increasingly austere. Water, believed to hold magical powers of
purification, is always present, at least by suggestion; but real
water is replaced by stones, moss or sand. Surviving gardens at
Kyoto show how this concept gradually took hold. The moss
garden of Saihoji Temple, laid out in its present form in 1339, contains probably the earliest attempt to reproduce natural scenery
in miniature, or with more austere materials: rocks are used to
depict the waterfall in a mountain and its downhill stream. The
*karesansui* ('dry gardens') of Nanzenji (see Plate 10) and Ryoanji
represent the logical culmination of this process. They are bare of
trees and water; the only natural elements are selected stones in
an expanse of neatly raked white sand, laid out according to Zen
principles. By abandoning conventional pictorial associations,
they invite the viewer to make his own interpretation. The rocks
of Ryoanji, laid out in 1450, have been variously seen as stones
rising above the rapids, tigers fording a stream with their cubs,
islands in a vast expanse of ocean, or mountain peaks soaring
through the clouds; they admit infinite interpretation by insisting
on none. Their primary purpose is to induce contemplation and
evoke the boundlessness of the Zen spirit. The austerity of the
Zen garden, and the chaste trappings of the *noh* stage, are products of the same philosophy.

To this philosophy, Plato's Theory of Forms provides an

approximate Western parallel. His concept of an Ideal World, perceptible through an enlightenment which is itself the product of rigid mental discipline, is analogous to the Zen doctrine of intuitive perception and produces a similar aesthetic theory – though Plato inspired no plays, but was, on the contrary, antagonistic to the theatre. For Plato, as for Zen, the phenomenal world is transitory and deceptive. He postulates an Ideal World, a world of Forms, of which our own is an inferior copy. This is not located in the mind: Plato conceives it as having a real and independent existence, over and above the material world, and as accessible to those whose mental discipline permits them to see beyond the evidence of their senses. For every material object in this world there is a perfect exemplar in the world of Forms. Plato argues that the individual may attain to a perception of these Forms by systematic progress through increasingly abstract disciplines, and this doctrine affects his theory of the fine arts. If the material world is no more than a base copy of a finer reality, representational art is doubly inferior, for it is a copy of a copy, two removes from truth. Thus the representational should be avoided, and the artist should concentrate on the essential form of things, not their material substance. Mere imitation is trivial, and ultimately corrupting.

Plato makes severe strictures on the drama of his time, which he feels to be preoccupied with the morbid, the sensational and the mundane. Here, several of his recommendations strikingly foreshadow Zeami's own advice. The actor should seek noble models and confine himself to them, not debase himself by copying the inferior or mean to give the audience a cheap thrill. Zeami similarly warns against sensationalism. *Noh* is full of ghosts and demons, but it is not their purpose to horrify. They are vehicles to expound the spiritual solace of Buddhism and give assurance of man's ultimate salvation; they are projections of the past into the present, and the present into the future, and give relief from temporal reality. Even a devil in *noh* must be a thing of beauty.

Plato disregards the fact that Greek tragedy had been anticipating some of his precepts for the best part of a century. Although its plots dealt with historical events or myths, which to the Greek mind passed as history, the stories themselves were comparatively unimportant. The play was judged by its interpretation of familiar material, and by the skill of its author in using a known plot to convey a new truth. In this respect the action of Greek tragedy was timeless, and the theatre emphasized this abstraction, as *noh* does, by its avoidance of realistic setting, costume and movement. There is thus a certain spiritual kinship between Greek tragedy and *noh* which carries through into the staging of the plays. Although the characters of *noh* may have a precise historical origin, like Benkei, Shunkan and Yoshitsune, the performance liberates them from the confines of their period. The setting is neutral, and the costumes eclectic: developed from several historical periods, they represent none. The pre-performance ritual and the formal stances of the actor continually insist that the play is to be taken on its own terms and not as a historical record; the undefined surroundings allow the spectator to concentrate on the timelessness of the story and its universal application. In many ways *noh* and Greek tragedy arrived, by separate routes, at identical theatrical conventions. Some of these, particularly those involving the use of the mask, will be examined at greater length in Chapter 5.

This spiritual kinship, however, is qualified. Greek tragedy was exploratory, *noh* intellectually static. Its purpose was not to reveal new truths, but to re-illuminate the old. Like the biblical plays of the European Middle Ages, they were bound to dogma and a sacred text, as the Greek plays never were. Originality was limited to the re-ordering of familiar material and the establishment of a definitive form.

Zen, which urges the transcendency of self, holds the artist and the warrior in particular esteem. Both professions demand the most exacting mental and physical discipline, and both, in their highest manifestations, rely on intuitive perception. The artist creating a masterpiece and the warrior fighting a battle break through to a higher level of consciousness. It is for this reason that the warrior-priest figures, like Benkei, assume such great symbolic importance; it is this philosophy, too, that underlies the system of training laid down by Zeami for the actor. The play *Kokaji* uses the mystique of the sword, at once a work of art and a weapon of destruction, to illustrate how the artist may enter into direct communion with the divine. An envoy is sent to the swordsmith Kokaji Munechika to order him to make a blade for the Emperor. Lacking a skilled assistant, Munechika goes to his shrine and prays there to the god Inari. A mystic Child appears, gives an account of famous swords in Chinese and Japanese history, promises aid and vanishes from sight. A forge is brought on, the swordsmith prepares for the ceremonial working of the blade, and the god Inari himself descends to help him in his task. Hammering together, they forge a miraculous blade which is presented to the envoy for conveyance to the Emperor.

In this frame of reference we may re-examine in greater detail a play previously cited as a typical example of 'actionless' *noh*, *Yamamba* (*The Old Woman of the Hills*). Like many plays, this re-interprets ancient folklore in the light of Zen. The Old Woman of the title is an animistic figure, a spirit who was believed to wander from mountain to mountain, caring for the hillsides and their people. The role is played by the *sh'te*.

The play begins with the entrance of the dancer (*waki*) and her retinue. Her name is Hyakuma, but she has come to be known as Hyakuma-Yamamba for her fame in the Mountain Spirit dance. Asking for shelter, they meet Yamamba herself, who appears first in the guise of an old woman, hobbling up the *hashigakari* with her stick. She offers hospitality on the condition that the dancer will perform her famous dance for her. When Hyakuma is unwilling, the woman reveals that she is the Mountain Hag in person: 'Though you have sung the song of the Mountain Hag for years, when have you given thought to the Mountain Hag herself?' This performance, she says, will be a service to her; presented with the appropriate rites, it will assist her escape from the cycle of transmigration and allow her to attain Nirvana. She promises that if the dance is performed she will appear in her true shape. After a brief interlude Hyakuma agrees. The Old Woman keeps her promise, and when the dance begins appears as herself. Her mask is now red and ugly, with long white hair falling in great tufts to her waist. Taking up the dance, she sings of her lonely wanderings from place to place. At her exit, the Chorus see her vanishing into the distance, until she is lost to sight.

This apparently simple, but in reality highly complex, plot embodies, first, the confrontation of art and reality. The dancer has spent her life imitating Yamamba, and has, she thinks, understood her nature. Confronted with Yamamba in person, she is at first sceptical, then frightened. It is the familiar discrepancy between truth and illusion. Hyakuma's apparently perfected art is still earthbound, and has not yet made the vital intuitive contact with transcendent reality. But when Yamamba herself takes up the dance the contact is made and the final step taken. *Yamamba*, in this light, is an allegory of the function of the arts in general, and of *noh* in particular: to arrive through art, which is itself limited and temporal, to a true perception of reality.

Like the stones of Ryoanji, *Yamamba* is capable of several interpretations. The Old Woman herself has been held by some to typify what Zen calls 'ignorant attachment' – the force that ties us to life and to the familiar round, because we know no better. The Old Woman recognizes this and hopes for ultimate escape; she has faith that the Buddhist rites will liberate her and break the chains that bind her to her mountains. This, too, illuminates the function of *noh*; dramatic dance has religious potency. Yamamba asks for Hyakuma's performance as a liberating rite.

The play has also been interpreted as an allegory of the true meaning of love. Love is a force working constantly in nature for our good. We tend to romanticize it and give it a kind, smiling face. But its true face may be ugly, careworn, wrinkled; love may be drudgery. Yamamba appears in two manifestations, as the dancer would like to imagine her, and as she really is, and the true face of love is so strange that the wanderers call her a demon. It is the familiar theme; we may be so blinded by our preconceptions that we cannot recognize the truth when we see it.

This contradiction is the heart of *noh* and governs both the play and the performance. In the theatre, as in life, superficial appearances are deceptive. A play apparently actionless reveals itself as full of action, though only in the mind. The quietude is only apparent; behind the surface tranquillity there is conflict and progression. Things are not what they seem. In this context *noh*'s apparently wilful obscurity has a deeper purpose. In the deceptive simplicity of its form and the allusiveness and ambiguity of its language, it is a living re-creation of its own philosophy, continually prompting the spectator, by all the technical means at its disposal, to penetrate the temporal expression of the art to find its inner meaning.

*Noh* achieves its dramatic power because of, not in spite of, its restrictions. Zeami and his followers discovered, like Racine after them, that by paring dramatic action to a minimum the play gains in intensity and gives the simplest movement force. Kagekiyo's snapping of his fan, like Phèdre's seizure of Hippolyte's sword, assumes momentous importance because it is the first dynamic gesture of a play which has already run for some forty-five minutes. As a later French dramatist, Jules Supervielle, was to argue, theatrical sophistication eventually returns, by a circular process, to a simplicity of statement which might easily pass for naïveté: the difference lies in an audience that is prepared to take much for granted and from their own store of memories and emotive associations give body to the outline presented on the stage. It is an argument of which Zeami would thoroughly have approved. In this connection it is worth quoting Oswald Sickert's letter to Arthur Waley, published in the latter's *The Noh Plays of Japan*:

> The best single moment I have seen was the dance of thanks to the fisherman who returns to the divine lady the Hagoromo, the robe without which even an angel cannot fly. It seemed to me an example of the excellent rule in art, that, if a right thing is perhaps rather dull or monotonous lasting five minutes, you will not cure the defect by cutting the performance to two and a half minutes; rather, give it ten minutes. If it's still rather dull, try twenty minutes or an hour. This presupposes that your limitations are right and that you are exploiting them. The thing may seem dull at first because at first it is the limitations the spectator feels; but the more these are ex-

ploited, the less they are felt to be limitations, and the more they become a medium. The divine lady returned on her steps at great length and fully six times after I had thought I could not bear it another moment. She went on for fully twenty minutes perhaps, or an hour or a night; I lost count of time: but I shall not recover from the longing she left when at last she floated backwards and under the fatal uplifted curtain.

*Noh*, as we have seen, had long since ceased to be a public art. Under the patronage of the Shogunate it had for centuries enjoyed a prosperous and secluded existence behind the high walls of class distinction. In 1867, when the Shogun resigned and power reverted to the Emperor, these walls were abruptly overthrown. With the disappearance of its patrons and the evolution of a new society, *noh* lost both its support and its public. Of all the traditional arts, it suffered most from the change; it was *gagaku*, as the distinctive art of the Imperial Household, that suffered least, for when the Emperor came into his own its traditions were preserved unchanged. The retiring Shogun announced, with brutal practicality, that the players now had three alternatives. They could seek the protection of the Imperial Court, continue to follow the Shogunate – without pay – or return to their homes as *ronin*. The players tried for some time to struggle on independently, performing on improvised stages wherever they could, but it was obvious that, if the art was to survive, a new patron had to be found.

In the end they turned, inevitably, to the Emperor, whom they found not only willing but enthusiastic. He gave the actors his favour, made a habit of organizing performances on visits to his ministers and the nobility, and used them to entertain distinguished guests. The Prince of Wales, later Edward VII, attended such a performance in 1869. In 1878 the Emperor had a private stage constructed in the Palace; one of the pictures in the Meiji Memorial Gallery shows him watching a play with his Empress. Other bodies, mostly scholarly, offered their support. *Noh*, in fact, survived the change largely because of the interest of antiquarians, who were anxious to preserve this living relic from the past. *Noh* scholarship had a long history – the texts first appear in 1601, the oldest commentary in 1595, and the first criticism sixty years later – and received new impetus in the Meiji Era; the Emperor was personally concerned for the survival of the traditional arts, fearing their disappearance in the confrontation with the West, and compiled a long account of Japanese traditions to be circulated through the country and remind the people of their heritage. Here again we may draw a parallel with Greek drama; it was the Alexandrian scholars who preserved the plays when they were disappearing from the theatrical repertoire, recognizing them as valuable repositories of vanishing language, history and tradition.

A *noh* society was formed, with much encouragement from other countries, particularly from ex-President Grant of the United States. This support was most strongly resisted, paradoxically enough, by the actors themselves, who believed that public assistance would deprive the Five Families of their individual autonomy, and destroy the 'school' tradition which had been fundamental to the creation and transmission of the art. These objections were eventually overcome, and the *Noh* Association, formed in 1896, made performances available, for the first time in centuries on a regular basis, to the general public. Individual subscriptions were invited, and joint performances given by actors from all schools. Up to the Second World War, however, this public was still, on the whole, limited to the wealthier classes. Performances were expensive, as they still are (the price varies according to the length of the cycle, but may be as much as 3000 yen), but *noh* retained its snob value; the new-rich attended to demonstrate their good taste.

It is difficult to assess the state of *noh* today. The schools continue in existence, have preserved their individuality and are self-supporting. There is no state subsidy, though there are private patrons and paying pupils. Performances are not given regularly. It is often hard to find out what is playing and when; harder, sometimes, to find where the theatres are. People in the next street may be oblivious of their existence. *Noh* still plays to a limited audience, through force of circumstances rather than from choice. Its patrons are those who have the time and patience to acquire the taste. Many Japanese now find the language of the plays completely incomprehensible; the traditional intonations augment the difficulties of an archaic language, and many of the audience sit through the performance with librettos in their laps. The atmosphere is scholarly, and strongly reminiscent of the triennial performance of the Greek play at Cambridge, where most of the spectators come fortified with texts. Televised *noh*, by the same token, uses subtitles, an admission that the scripts are in what is virtually a foreign language.

It is noticeable, too, that most of the audience are middle-aged or over. Many Japanese now claim that the art is dying, and that the younger, Americanized generation has no patience with its slow tempo. This impression is reinforced by the younger people themselves, most of whom cheerfully admit that they have never seen *noh* – or, for that matter, *kabuki* – and never intend to. For all that the theatres, at least in Tokyo, are full, and there is always a hard core of students who buy tickets at reduced rates. They cannot all be there on class assignments. But the future remains uncertain. It may well be that, having at last had to face the challenge to which the classic dramas of other cultures were exposed from their inception, and to compete for the attention of the general public, *noh* may build a new audience – though it will always be a small one – and continue to justify its existence on its own merits.

# IV

## The Theatre Suspected

Though Westerners go charily to *noh* plays, most of them pay at least a token visit to the theatre advertising itself widely, and in English, as 'the Mecca of Kabuki' – the Kabuki-za. It is impossible to avoid; together with the Meiji Shrine and Tokyo Tower it has become one of the sights, and travel agencies include it with the Queen Bee cabaret on their night tours. This association is unfortunate. It prompts the casual visitor to dismiss *kabuki* as simply another spectacular entertainment, and to ignore its significance in Japanese cultural tradition. The present Kabuki-za is one of the last remaining homes of a historic art.

It stands, appropriately, on the edge of the Ginza, Tokyo's central pleasure district, a bulging edifice in Japanese rococo, festooned with columns, canopies and curlicues; amid the lamps and streamers, a huge sign, again in English, welcomes visitors to 'the home of *kabuki*'. There is an English-speaking information desk and a lavishly illustrated English programme. What happens on the stage is entirely Japanese, but the performers feel, with some accuracy, that their art transcends the language barrier.

To reach the auditorium one must first pass through a shopping centre. A succession of lobbies reveals souvenir stalls, displays of artwork, trade exhibits, tea-rooms, a television lounge and three restaurants. Packed meals in gay boxes are in brisk demand: the usual *kabuki* performance lasts five and a half hours. There are two programmes a day, seven days a week, making demands of time and stamina on the actor that would bring tears to the eyes of

Equity. The average Western actor, by comparison, lives a life of pampered ease.

At first sight the tourist feels at home. The theatre is built in Western style, though shallower and wider; even the back rows are not too far from the stage. The house-lights, shrouded in paper lanterns, remain lit for most of the performance. There is a proscenium arch, unusually wide – it stretches almost the whole width of the auditorium – with a curtain striped in black, rust and green, the traditional *kabuki* colours. This will be drawn by hand, to reveal a succession of more splendid curtains as the programme proceeds. The popular Japanese theatre loves curtains, as it does all forms of gaudy decoration; the Jido Kaikan in Shibuya has one covered with hundreds of plastic balls in all colours and sizes. At the Kabuki-za, however, the curtains must be enjoyed with caution. What first appears as an intricate formal design will reveal itself, by a trademark or a minute slogan, as a giant advertisement for Pan-Am Airways or Mitsuya Soap. One thing is clear; *kabuki* is not, like *noh*, a hothouse flower, but very much in touch with the world outside.

The most obviously unwestern feature is a long raised walkway, beginning at the back of the theatre and cutting through the audience to the stage. This is the *hanamichi*, used primarily for extended entrances and exits. A larger version of the *hashigakari* of *noh*, from which it probably derived, it takes up most of the left-hand aisle. The audience itself seems to be in a state of constant movement. People come and go as they please. They sit through the pieces they are interested in, go out for a meal or gossip and return. A typical *kabuki* programme may contain two substantial dramas (themselves only Acts of much longer plays, now only rarely performed in full), shorter comic pieces often derived from *kyogen* and several dances. There is something for all tastes.

The rattle of wooden clappers cuts across the chatter of the audience, though without imposing complete silence; the play may run for fifteen minutes before the house is still. Music sounds, the usherettes stand guard around the *hanamichi*, and the curtain opens on *Sukeroku*.

This is a bravura piece, a fitting introduction to *kabuki*. An *aragoto* play, born in eighteenth-century Edo, it displays the dash and flair that the townsmen of that city thought of as their distinctive qualities; the qualities, too, of *kabuki* showmanship. The scene is the forecourt of a *geisha* house. Its lattice walls are bright vermilion, curtained off with straw matting. At stage left is an archway, hung with strips of brown curtain; at stage right an enormous water-cask, bigger than a man. Red-draped couches for the *geisha* dot the forestage.

The play begins magnificently with a series of processions. *Geisha* file through the archway and down the *hanamichi* simultaneously, tottering on high black lacquered clogs, shaded by parasols, and supported by the shoulders of their footmen. Their costumes are of rich brocade, their elaborate *coiffures* stuck through with pins and combs; they re-create the 'courtesans' parade', a familiar spectacle in the gay quarters of the feudal cities. 'Invisible' property men are busy among them, taking off their clogs, adjusting the folds of their robes, and ensuring the perfection of the stage picture. At their feet sit child attendants, wearing crystal head-dresses that shimmer in the light. The whole stage is vibrant with colour.

Another procession follows Ikyu down the *hanamichi*. He is the villain of the piece, a former *samurai*, who has unsuccessfully courted the favours of one of the *geisha*, Agekami. His beard is long and white, his face made up in exaggerated, sweeping lines, his gown of gold brocade. Six servants, eight maids and two footmen escort him, carrying his sword, pipe and stool. Forestage and the *hanamichi* are both crowded; there are now fifty-two characters on view, most of them extras, but each one of them sumptuously dressed. Ikyu makes new advances, which Agekami contemptuously rejects. She already has a lover, the townsman Sukeroku. There is another ground of dispute between the two men; Ikyu has stolen a famous sword, which Sukeroku is trying to locate and reclaim.

Agekami and her retinue withdraw, leaving Ikyu sulking on the stage. A flute plays and Sukeroku enters, without attendants, but an impressive sight in black and scarlet. Flaunting his parasol like

E

a peacock's tail, he struts and swaggers down the *hanamichi*; the action is suspended while he postures to demonstrate his manly charms. This is the type of popular hero that Edo audiences adored – a self-made man owing nothing to birth or privilege and so continually contrasted with the *samurai*, who are represented (in this play and in others) as villainous, cowardly and decadent. The townsman hero is handsome and elegant, a virile lover and a redoubtable swordsman. A lone wolf in a caste-ridden society, his arrogance is self-defence and his pugnacity a continual reassurance. He embodies the qualities of the theatre that idolized him; resourceful and independent, he is Cyrano *sans* nose, a Byronic James Bond. *Kabuki* is largely an escapist art. Through roles like these the bourgeoisie asserted an independence it could never claim in real life, and worked off its resentment against the omnipotent *samurai*.

When he has stopped preening himself and reached the *geisha* house, Sukeroku is surrounded by the admiring girls, who offer him pipes. They give no thought to Ikyu, who is eventually forced to demand one for himself. Sukeroku, in a superb gesture, places a pipe between his toes, and extends a contemptuous foot towards his discomfited rival. He hopes to provoke Ikyu into drawing his sword, and find out for certain whether he has his stolen treasure. The trick almost works. Ikyu slaps his hand to the hilt, but checks himself in time.

Ikyu's henchman, Kampera Mombei, comes in to provide comic relief. He has his master's sour disposition and a habit of speaking out of the corner of his mouth. His quarrel with a passing noodle-seller is a self-contained scene, like the sub-plots of Elizabethan drama, and the other characters sit motionless while it is played. Sukeroku finally intervenes and ends the quarrel by slapping a dish of noodles on the servant's head. Going further, he balances a wooden clog on Ikyu's head and challenges him to fight. Once again Ikyu restrains himself from drawing just in time. Sukeroku goads him. Casually drawing up a stool, he strikes it with his sword. It falls apart, cut clean in two. Ikyu replies by summoning a pack of club-wielding servants, who set about Sukeroku. This is no problem to our superman hero. They come at him in double file. Parting their ranks with unruffled aplomb, he strikes to left and right; the blows never connect, but the men fall like ninepins. It is an animated-cartoon battle, Popeye demolishing the enemy. Ikyu leaves in disgust.

Shinbei, Sukeroku's brother, appears to lecture him on the folly of his ways. Sukeroku explains the reason for his provocative behaviour, accuses Shinbei of being too timid, and gives him lessons in bravado. This makes another self-contained comic interlude. The brothers pick quarrels with several passers-by and force them to abase themselves by crawling between their legs. Shinbei is just beginning to enjoy the game when the last comer reveals herself as Manko, their mother. She too has come to complain about Sukeroku's behaviour, but is satisfied when she hears his plan about the sword.

Ikyu and Agekami come out in conversation. He is still pressing his suit and making himself offensive. Sukeroku, hiding behind Agekami's voluminous robes, hears himself abused. Reaching underneath the bench, he pinches Ikyu hard on the leg. After several repetitions Ikyu realizes what is happening, despite Agekami's efforts to conceal it. Sukeroku leaps out of hiding, and in the violent quarrel that follows Ikyu is finally provoked beyond endurance and draws his sword. It is indeed the stolen treasure. The secret is out, and the curtain closes on a tableau.

The final scene is rarely performed, for reasons that will be obvious. During the intermission the huge water-cask is dragged forward and filled to the brim. The curtain opens on Sukeroku and Ikyu in savage combat. It is a duel turned into ballet: they sway, leap, duck and thrust, and though the swords never make contact, the effect is electric. Ikyu is wounded; clapping his hand to his shoulder, he fastens a bunch of red ribbons to stand for blood. Then Sukeroku is hit. He lies prostrate and motionless. Is he dead? Ikyu stands astride him, and raises his sword for the *coup de grâce*; at the crucial moment Sukeroku springs to life, lunges upwards and pierces him beneath the arm. As he retrieves his prized sword from the body, a clamour is heard offstage. Ikyu's men are coming to avenge their master. Quick as a thought, Sukeroku dives into the tub of water. The enemy pour on with swords and ladders. Running down the *hanamichi*, they climb into the first balcony, and search among the audience. Baffled, they return to the *geisha* house and hunt on the roof there. Sukeroku is nowhere to be seen, and they continue their pursuit offstage. With much wallowing and splashing, Sukeroku emerges triumphantly from the tub. He is wounded and drags himself painfully out. Kenneth Tynan once remarked that an English audience invariably applauds when it sees real water on a stage. So does a Japanese. Normally decorous and restrained (at least in the Kabuki-za) they unfold like paper flowers when exposed to water. *Kabuki* theorists insist that their art avoids realism for its own sake. This may be generally true, but I have never heard an audience applaud so hard as when Sukeroku made his precarious, sodden appearance.

The effort has been too much even for him, and he faints. Agekami comes out of the *geisha* house and discovers him just as his pursuers return. Hiding him beneath her flowing robe, she sends them off in the wrong direction and tries to bring him round. Running to the tub, she carries water – real water – in the folds of her sumptuous brocade. Again the audience applauds, even as it shudders at the delicious extravagance. If it is sacrilege to spoil so beautiful a costume, Cyrano's immortal rejoinder comes to mind: 'Mais quel geste!' It is an atmosphere in which the Gascon would have felt himself at home. Sukeroku stirs and revives. Brandishing his recaptured sword, he springs up the ladder that his enemies have left against the house. The spotlight catches his triumphant pose, and Agekami gazes up at him adoringly as the curtain closes.

We are, it is clear, in a very different world from that of Zeami. *Noh* is austere, *kabuki* flamboyant; *noh* ritual, *kabuki* spectacle; *noh* offers spiritual consolation, *kabuki* physical excitement; *noh* seeks chaste models, *kabuki* delights in the eccentric, the extravagant and the wilfully perverse; *noh* is gentle, *kabuki* cruel; *noh* is concerned with the hereafter, *kabuki* bound by the here-and-now. Not every play is as vigorous or spectacular as *Sukeroku*, but all have something of these qualities. *Kabuki* loves extravagant display and prizes action above thought. The intellectual content of *noh* is everything, but in *kabuki* it is virtually non-existent. The popular drama idolizes the warrior hero and creates an aura of fantasy and romance. These qualities developed in *kabuki* because of its social position, and may be seen in the very beginning of the art.

*Kabuki* history is short by the standards of the Oriental theatre, a mere three hundred and fifty years against the six hundred of *noh*. Many of its plots and dances derive from the senior form, and it often reproduces, on a larger scale, the setting and groupings of the *noh* stage. But where *noh* became almost from the beginning a diversion of the élite, *kabuki* retained its contact with the popular arts from which it sprang. It has always been the theatre of the people, or at least the middle classes – though this may soon cease to be true – and, like all popular forms, has been susceptible to changing fashion. It developed its own rules and conventions, partly out of dramatic convenience, partly out of self-protection, and its subject-matter, in its own way, is almost as limited as that of *noh*. Nevertheless a looser form permitted greater variation, and allowed more opportunity for experiment. Some characteristics were developed in conscious opposition to *noh*: the melodramatic versus the cerebral, and the love of scenic spectacle in contrast to its avoidance. As we shall see, *kabuki* itself became a badge of class, flaunted in the face of the aristocracy to show that the lower orders had their own tastes and a right to their special privileges and pleasures.

Peter Quennell, in his biography of Shakespeare, suggests that our appreciation of Elizabethan drama, based largely on its literary merits, differs from that of the original audience, and that the crowds who flocked to the English public playhouse had much in common with the first *kabuki* audiences, their historical contemporaries. They came to the theatre to see a rousing spectacle and stylish swordplay. The seventeenth-century public would have enjoyed Hamlet's duel with Laertes more than his philosophizing, and would have felt perfectly at home, given a chance to see it, with Ikyu's combat to the death with Sukeroku. The analogy between the two forms, often made by Japanese scholars, is valid within limits. Both have similar physical features. Men play women's roles; the use of stage space, and many of the conventions, are the same; Chikamatsu Monzaemon, the leading dramatist of his time, is frequently called the Japanese Shakespeare. In subject-matter there is no comparison. The English world was opening as the Japanese was closing. Elizabethan drama was critical and adventurous, free to explore the whole realm of European thought; *kabuki* was restricted by its milieu to a limited range of approved subjects. Criticism of the social order, where it exists at all, is mild and hedged with precautions; there is no intellectual freedom, and no room for the expansion of ideas. *Kabuki* could produce no *Doctor Faustus*, no *Hamlet* or *King Lear*. It is as if we had from the Elizabethan theatre only the chronicle plays (pushed back in time to avoid political offence) and such domestic dramas as *Arden of Faversham*, *The Two Angry Women of Abingdon* and *A New Way to Pay Old Debts*.

In its social reference, however, the parallel is still a striking one. The relationship of the two styles of theatre in Japan has much in common with contemporary developments in England. In the sixteenth century, English theatre existed on two levels. At court the favoured form was the masque, devised for an educated and aristocratic audience, drawing heavily on classical mythology and presupposing an appreciation of erudite allusion and subtle reference. A knowledge of the Latin classics was taken for granted, as *noh* assumed a knowledge of Chinese. Elegant, learned, formally decorative and extremely expensive, the masque catered for a limited public and a cultivated taste.

On another level the public playhouse attracted audiences who made up in enthusiasm what they lacked in refinement. The plays, like the spectators, were boisterous and bloodthirsty. They prized action above thought and were concerned not so much with preserving a dead past as with portraying the vitality of a living present. Though the learned thought them vulgar and diffuse and accused them of lacking artistic form (we see in Ben Jonson a writer continually torn between what the critics admired and what the public wanted), the people loved them. Nevertheless it was inevitable that the public theatre should absorb and use for its own purposes elements from its aristocratic counterpart. We are all snobs; we like to see our social superiors on the stage and identify ourselves, by association, with tastes and standards officially found admirable. The English theatre in many ways has been hardly less class-conscious than the Japanese: Frederick Lonsdale and Noel Coward found their best audiences among suburban housewives. Even the most popular Elizabethan playwrights tossed in their scraps of Latin. Marlowe, Kyd and Shakespeare delighted in the masque. The groundlings thrilled to the squabbles of the aristocracy, and kings and princes became popular heroes.

This is, in essence, the relationship between *noh* and *kabuki*, though in a more rigidly stratified society the cleavage widened. Queen Elizabeth could summon Shakespeare's company to her palace; that the Shogun could watch *kabuki* was unthinkable. The public could see *noh* only by invitation, and the *samurai* were eventually, by the rules of their own caste, barred from the popular theatre. This odium is reflected in scholarship; *kabuki* was originally ignored by Western scholars because it was held in such low academic esteem in its own country. It reciprocated by affecting to despise the upper classes, but still borrowed glory by edging as close to them as it could. Borrowing themes and plays from *noh* and *kyogen*, it embodied them in its own performances, reproducing on the stage the doings of the *samurai* whom its audiences watched in real life with a half-contemptuous fascination, or transferring ideal *samurai* qualities to its own heroes. Even the Buddhist doctrines fundamental to *noh* have their place in the aesthetics of *kabuki* presentation, though in less obvious ways. The hierarchic structure of the performing companies or families are modelled in *kabuki*, as in *noh*, on the prevailing social system.

*Kabuki* claimed its own founding figure, in this case a woman, Okuni, a ceremonial dancer from the Izumo Shrine. About the time the first public playhouse was being built in London, she gave a performance on the dry bed of the Kamo river in Kyoto. It consisted of a Buddhist ceremonial dance with original variations. The audience had seen Buddhist dances before. What impressed them were the variations. They were, by all accounts,

highly erotic. The eroticism perpetuated itself in the later
*kabuki* performances, and the site in the nickname given to the
actors – *kawara-mono*, 'things of the river-bed'. The performances were expanded, with flute and drum accompaniment. In
the tradition, Okuni was joined first by her lover (Kyoto still
preserves a plaque to the first male performer of *kabuki*) and then
by a group of pupils.

Other troupes were formed in imitation. Okuni died in about
1610, but had many successors, mostly prostitutes; their performances were known as *onna* ('women's') *kabuki*. The word
*kabuki* itself is older than the theatre it came to describe, deriving from the verb *kabuku*, 'to incline', 'to lean out from the
straight'; it has some of the connotations of sexual irregularity
that were later associated with the performance, and also implies
the perversity, the deliberate cultivation of the freakish and
bizarre, that is *kabuki*'s characteristic quality. We might nowadays translate it by 'off-beat'. It was at this period too that the
*samisen* was first used, as it still is, for accompaniment; always a
popular instrument, it has today taken on a new lease of life in
jazz. The shows attracted the baneful eye of the Shogunate,
which distrusted manifestations of popular feeling for any reason
whatsoever. Adopting a high moral tone it declared the women
to be a source of public danger and in 1629 prohibited their
appearance on the stage. The companies retorted by reversing
roles: men took over the women's parts, and the actresses the
men's; but the Shogun, unimpressed, repeated his edict a year
later.

The theatre has always found it easy to circumvent specific
prohibitions. Actresses bowed to the inevitable and left the stage,
not to reappear in *kabuki* until the present century, but were replaced by handsome boys, who organized *wakashu* ('young men's')
*kabuki*. Once again morality was invoked. The Shogunate
brought charges of homosexuality (undoubtedly justified) and
suppressed this new manifestation in 1652. Throughout its
history, *kabuki* was to suffer from petty prohibitions; in its formative years it was under constant official surveillance. In 1654
yet a third form was born, known as *yaro kabuki*. The name was

significant: *yaro*, 'man', 'fellow', often 'playboy', stresses that
the performers are now robust men of mature age, against whom
the previous charges could not feasibly be brought. With no
more reasonable pretext for intervening, the authorities reluctantly permitted the plays to go on, though they continued to
hamper them at every turn with all the bureaucratic machinery
at their command. It is clear from the examination of Japanese
society as a whole that the moral arguments against *kabuki* were
no more than pretexts. If the actresses were prostitutes, prosti-
tution was a licensed activity; if the *wakashu* were homosexuals,
homosexuality was at least tolerated, and has even been held to
explain the popularity of young boy actors in certain special roles
in *noh*. It was public assemblies that the Shogunate distrusted,
and particularly those of this kind, which, by the attractions that
they offered, might cut across existing social barriers. There was
also a possibility of rioting, if the *samurai* competed for the boys'
or women's favours. It was for these reasons that the Shogunate
denied *kabuki* official recognition and tolerated its existence only
on the outer fringes of respectability. The next bout with law
and order was to come when the companies started to build
themselves permanent houses.

With the formation of *yaro kabuki* the plays could no longer
rely on the sexual attractions of the performers. They had to stand
on their own feet, and the challenge was the making of the art.
Early scenarios had been in revue form, loose amalgamations of
acts, songs and dances. The performers were now forced to compensate for their lack of physical charm by improved technique
and stronger scripts. *Kabuki* began to produce works in strict
play form, divided into Acts, and to develop its own playwrights.
The loss of women was irrelevant. What must have seemed at
first to be a limitation of the art became one of its greatest
strengths. In pure *kabuki* the masculine tradition has continued
to the present day, though its modern derivatives have reverted
to the use of actresses, for women's parts alone or for the entire
cast: the currently highly popular Girls' Opera, based at Takarazuka, goes back, historically speaking, to first principles. At the
Kabuki-za, the National Theatre and several provincial houses,

E 2

women's parts are still played by men (*onnagata*) as they have
been for centuries. Some actors have played male and female roles
interchangeably, but some, including a number of the most
famous, have devoted themselves exclusively to *onnagata* parts.
In the eighteenth century some went so far as to wear women's
costume off-stage, feeling that they had to live their roles every
day if they were to play them convincingly in performance. This
did not mean that the actors were effeminate. On the contrary,
*onnagata* roles are physically highly demanding. Sitting close, one
is conscious of the strong masculine physique under the women's
costumes. The actors might well be married, though it used to
be considered gauche to refer to their wives in public. A recent
Japanese film, Ichikawa Kon's *Yukinojo Hengei* (*An Actor's
Revenge*), uses one of these *onnagata* as protagonist, and shows him
involved in a revenge murder: the story gains piquancy from the
contrast between his entirely masculine actions and emotions and
his feminine attire. The custom has now ceased. Baiko, one of
today's most famous *onnagata* players, looks offstage like a successful, and slightly portly, businessman. In performance he is the
essence of feminity. To see Baiko's son, Kikunosuke, in the role
of a courtesan, and then to meet him backstage burly and gruff-
voiced, brings home vividly the technical accomplishment that
*onnagata* roles demand.

The history of *kabuki* proper is usually divided into three main
phases. At the beginning the art grew up in several centres independently, and distinct local styles emerged. Kyoto preferred
its acting realistic; Osaka developed the delicate, almost effeminate *wagoto* style; while Edo delighted in *aragoto* playing, more
romantic and highly emotional (*Sukeroku* is a typical *aragoto* play).
When Edo was firmly established as the capital and communication with other cities improved, these styles tended to merge,
but later *kabuki* acting owes much to the brag and bluster of its
early Edo days. It was in the second phase also that *kabuki* felt the
impact of another art form which was to influence it at a critical
point in its development no less strongly than *noh* had at its beginning.

This was *ningyo shibai*, the puppet theatre, respected as a major art in its own right. Its history and character will be discussed at greater length in Chapter 5, but some of its principal features must be mentioned here, as they were taken over by *kabuki* virtually unchanged. A popular art long before Okuni's striptease on the river-bed, it had not yet acquired a fixed location. Its early stages were impermanent and its figures made of clay. Permanent stages and wooden puppets did not appear till 1624–43. Forty years later an important doll theatre, the Takemoto-za, was built in Osaka, taking its name from the *joruri* chanter Takemoto Gidayu. Two forms of art, the *joruri*, or chanted story, and the manipulation of the puppet had come together to create a new form, which was, and is, highly distinctive and peculiarly Japanese, with no similarity to puppet art as presented in the Western world. Chanter and manipulator, voice and movement, were distinct. The silent manipulators confined themselves to controlling the figures – which itself developed into an art of great delicacy and refinement – while the chanter, isolated on a tiny platform at the side, doubled as narrator and Chorus, as well as providing the dialogue in an appropriate range of voices. His art has some affinities with that of the *noh* Chorus: both represent a transitional step from pure narrative to drama proper. In *noh* the Chorus may speak both of and for the characters, in the first person as well as the third. In the puppet play the responsibility belongs wholly to the chanter, and the puppets illustrate his recitation in action.

Doll plays became the fashion, and attracted the attention of serious playwrights, notably Chikamatsu Monzaemon, one of the greatest literary figures of Japan. This combination of talents temporarily eclipsed *kabuki*'s popularity. The live theatre, in self-defence, assimilated many of the features of its rival, and eventually regained its old position at the cost of important modifications to its character. On the actors the influence of the doll-theatre was enormous. In the repertoire, too, the puppets made their mark. Plays originally conceived for puppets were adapted for *kabuki*, and a large proportion of the present repertoire derives from this source. *Kabuki* capitalized on its rival's successes almost as fast as they were written: *Ehon Taiko Ki* (*The Taiko Picture Book*), for example, first performed by puppets in 1799, was played by actors in the following year. The *joruri* technique accompanied the plays and continues to be used. In works adapted from the puppet theatre and their later imitations, the chanter, accompanied by *samisen*, sits in a special alcove on one side of the stage. In *kabuki* the chanter shares the recitation with the actors: they normally speak their own lines, though for long passages only the chanter's voice may be heard. Sometimes there are two chanters, one on each side of the stage, if the scene represents two separate households. If they are not needed for a particular scene, or if the personnel must be changed (*joruri* chanting is arduous work), they are whisked out of sight on a small revolve and their replacements appear on the reverse; or, if the setting is too complex to allow this, they may be temporarily screened by drapes held by stage assistants while the change is effected. In these ways the puppet theatre continued to be a vital influence on *kabuki*, even when it had lost some of its own popularity; as late as 1831 players could honour this close association by presenting 'operated *kabuki*', in which the actors moved like puppets, uttering no word of dialogue.

One other important technical innovation of this period, which owed nothing to the puppets, was the revolving stage, a device which did not appear in the European theatre until the late nineteenth century. Hand operated, but nonetheless efficient, it covered most of the performing area and existed in simple or complex form: some theatres had concentric revolves, operating independently or in opposite directions. This new toy was seized on by the Japanese with the delight with which they have always greeted mechanical ingenuity. It gave the opportunity for even more lavish use of stage settings, which had become increasingly elaborate and were now considered as an art in their own right.

The third period (1781–1850) is regarded by some as *kabuki*'s golden age, by others as the beginning of its decadence. The fusion of symbolic puppets and realistic actors had created a unique style, ornate, magical and fantastic. Edo was now the acknowledged *kabuki* centre. Technically assured, the theatre captivated a continually growing audience. Actors, no longer 'creatures of the river-bed', lived on a hitherto unimagined scale of luxury and magnificence. They were immortalized in popular prints, had coteries of fans, became public idols and set new fashions. This success was not entirely due to the actors' merits. It came in part from the changing nature of Japanese society, in which the theatre secured a more central and more profitable place, and of which the actors were as much a symbol as a part.

Japanese feudal society, as we have seen, recognized three principle divisions. At the top, exalted and remote, were the Imperial Family and the nobles of the court, whose largely honorific duties were restricted to the distribution of rank and the ordering of ceremony. Next came the *samurai*, embracing the Shogun, the *daimyo* and their retainers. Beneath them were the workers: farmers, artisans and, at the very bottom, the lowest of the low, the merchants. Japan's economy was founded on a dangerously simple basis. The peasants farmed the land, and their overlords received part of the income in the form of taxation rice. When the ruling classes needed more support, larger taxes were exacted from the farmers. It was a system that ignored the middlemen. Buying and selling was considered a mean and filthy trade, and the merchants, officially beneath contempt, profited from the class consciousness of their superiors. Largely over-looked by the growing tax demands, they became increasingly necessary as intermediaries. The taxation rice was stored in Edo and doled out to the retainers of the Shogunate three times a year. At first the *samurai* used to draw their allowances in person. As this took time, many fell into the habit of deputing merchants and tea-house masters to do it for them, and, with the gradual impoverishment of their class, were forced to sell their allow-ances to the middlemen or ask for credit. In this way the mer-chants prospered while *samurai* and farmers alike suffered from the inflexibility of the system. Out of the transition from an agrarian to a monetary economy, in which money replaced rice as currency, rose a new and forceful class, the prosperous bour-geoisie. They had money to spend freely on their pleasures, and *kabuki*, the distinctive art form of the middle classes, grew rich with its patrons.

The Shogunate perceived the dangers. Like any authoritarian

government it was apprehensive of a large segment of the populace which had suddenly acquired too much wealth and leisure. Combined with this was the old distrust of assemblies, for any purpose; for when men congregate too freely, the seeds of insurrection may be sown. Seeking to confine and thus control the pleasure-seeking impulse, the authorities designated certain quarters as amusement centres, and suppressed the spread of theatres and other places of entertainment beyond the approved limits. As early as the beginning of the seventeenth century a segregated pleasure quarter had been established at Edo. It was known as Yoshiwara, 'the reed land', the poorest part of the city, a levelled hill unfit for other purposes. The reed land became the Nightless City. In the interests of public order the quarter was walled off and carefully policed. Visitors were limited to one day's stay and paid a tax on their pleasure. *Samurai* were forbidden to enter. If they defined the prohibition, as many did, they had to go in disguise. Copies of the huge straw hats they wore to hide their faces can still be bought in the costume shops in Asakusa, one of modern Tokyo's several pleasure districts. The disguised *samurai* is a familiar figure in *kabuki* plays, for the audience were delighted to see their rulers come down to their level. As the years passed, this segregation was more rigidly enforced.

These 'Gay Quarters' or 'Floating Cities', as the Japanese picturesquely called them, are still depicted for us in the plays and dances. *Mitsu Ningyo* (*Three Dolls*), a particularly colourful example, sets three representative characters – a courtesan, a playboy and his no less extravagant lackey – against a background of flowering cherry-trees, painted lanterns and rows of *geisha* houses, open and inviting. The familiar *ukiyoe* genre paintings have also immortalized this exotic and escapist sub-world. In their time they served the purpose of the modern film-fan magazine, showing popular idols – *kabuki* actors, famous *geisha*, *sumo* wrestlers – in characteristic attitudes and with a wealth of detail. We can see how lavish this tinsel paradise must have been, and how tempting a respite it offered from the drudgery of daily life. The Floating Cities, socially irregular, housed a population that was largely a displaced class, itself as 'off-beat' as the *kabuki* which it cherished. They became famous – and notorious – and inspired a tradition in Japanese literature which has continued to the present day. Their modern equivalents may be seen in the pleasure districts of the larger cities, which still exist within well-defined, though now intangible, boundaries, and preserve their individuality. Osaka has its Dotonbori and Sennichimae, Kyoto its Kawamarachi and Gion. Most famous of all is Tokyo's Ginza, known to every tourist and serviceman on leave. Properly speaking, the name belongs to only one street, running due north and south near Tokyo Station and housing several of the city's largest banks and department stores. But it has been appropriated for the whole surrounding district. The Ginza proudly announces its identity in signs erected across the streets. It has its limits and its barriers, though these are now largely invisible. Within it, innumerable shops, theatres, restaurants of every nationality, cinemas blue and otherwise, dance-halls, clubs and brothels jostle for space. By day it is comparatively quiet. At night, when the theatres are out, it jumps to life. It is a city within a city, brilliant with light, throbbing with life, and packed with merchandise.

Crowded into the Ginza's eighteenth-century equivalent, side by side with pedlars, prostitutes and other undesirables, the *kabuki* players gained in money what they lost in moral reputation. Another pretext for keeping the theatres apart – and one, indeed, in which there were serious grounds for concern – was the ever-present risk of fire. The whole city was burnt in 1659. Between 1804 and 1844 there were thirteen fires in major Edo theatres. This continues to be a hazard, demanding the most rigid precautions. In the Heian Shrine at Kyoto, where *noh* plays are given in the open air by torchlight, one can easily imagine oneself back in the fifteenth century, except for one thing, a shiny, red and very modern fire engine, poised for action just behind the Chorus tent. The non-smoking laws in Japanese theatres are enforced more rigidly than anywhere else in the world, though the cinemas, at least, defeat their purpose by persistently overselling well past the danger point. It is no uncommon thing to see a popular film in a Tokyo cinema and find the aisles so crowded that it is impossible to get in or out. (In Taiwan the Chinese carry this foolhardiness one stage further by locking the doors during the show; in a recent fire a whole cinema was burnt to the ground with most of the audience still trapped inside.)

Here again *kabuki* history runs parallel with that of the English public playhouse. Forced out of the city by continuing magisterial hostility, the London theatres moved into the red-light districts on the outskirts, which did nothing to enhance their prestige in the eyes of the law. The English authorities used plague, not fire, as their pretext for persecution, but the results were the same. In both countries the popular theatre was forced in upon itself and took defensive measures. Elizabethan players sought security in protective coloration. Their chief offence in the eyes of the law was that they had no recognized profession. Respectable trades were organized by guilds; the actors, standing outside this system, were irregular. The companies therefore borrowed respectability by organizing themselves on guild lines, with a system of masters and apprentices and agreed periods of training. By thus conforming with established practices they hoped to be tolerated, if not approved.

*Kabuki* players were forced to use a similar expedient. Conscious of their unorthodoxy, they attempted to redeem themselves by stabilizing their own organization on traditionally acceptable lines. From the earliest times the crafts and professions in Japan had adopted the clan system. The popular theatre, by necessity, accepted the same pattern. Within their own groups actors ape the society around them. A democratic society produces democratic actors. It is only comparatively recently, and particularly in the United States, that the actor has asserted his rights, as an individual, to determine the lines of his own performance, rather than accepting traditional modes of stage behaviour or the instructions of his actor-manager. The modern actor can say, 'I don't feel it that way', and expect to be taken seriously – something that would have been unthinkable in the time of Irving. The modern director is only rarely a tyrant; he functions more often as a combination of psychiatrist and father-confessor, working by suggestion and compromise to unify individual view-points and interpretations into an artistic whole. By the same token, hierarchical societies have traditionally produced hierarchical actors. To this the *kabuki* theatre was no exception.

Japanese tradition, reinforced by Confucianism, encouraged the concept of the family as the nucleus of social life. The actors, though considered untouchables by polite society, accepted the pattern which society approved, and thought of themselves as families, bound often by actual blood-ties, but if not, by the equally strong bonds of professional association, adoption, and the hereditary transmission of their art. Both *noh* and *kabuki* actors existed in unnatural social situations, though at opposite poles of respectability, and both formed themselves into family associations, known by the family name and admitting likely heirs by adoption if no suitable blood-descendant presented himself: the actors took no less care to preserve their line than the Imperial Family did with theirs. This system continues in *kabuki* today. If an actor is adopted into the family from outside his personal name is no longer relevant. He takes the family name, and in addition, a new personal name which is traditional within the company and has been borne by several actors before him. This changes as his career progresses; each marks a new grade in the accomplishment of his art and a higher level of professional recognition. Thus the actor Nakamura Utaemon, one of the most respected *kabuki* actors in Japan, was formerly known as Nakamura Fukusuka – Nakamura being the family name, and according to Japanese practice given first. The new Nakamura Fukusuka is a younger disciple of Utaemon, acceding to the new name because he is judged worthy by his peers. Utaemon himself is the sixth to bear that name in his family.

The organization of the *kabuki* company is as rigidly stratified as the feudal society in which it was created. Actors born into the illustrious stage families are automatically privileged. Pushed onto the stage almost as soon as they can walk, they learn the techniques of their art early; steeped in the family tradition, they are expected to continue it and carry it to new heights. Honoured off-stage as well as on, they have the privilege of private dressing-rooms (the Kabuki-za backstage area is a warren of cubicles, each hung with a family crest) and constitute the *kabuki* aristocracy. The best roles are theirs by hereditary right. Actors who come in from outside belong to the lower social stratum. They use the common dressing-room (*obeya*, 'big room') and must content themselves, even after years of experience, with minor roles. Skill, for them, is not enough. *Obeya* actors have to work as disciples of a recognized master, whose recommendation controls their slow and painful advancement up the hierarchy. It is, moreover, an expensive business, and requires the backing of wealthy patrons. Under this system few have risen from the *obeya* to the top rank. One of the exceptions was Nakamura Nakazo (1736–90); another was Ichikawa Kodanji IV (1812–66). Both became the leaders of their troupes. But such cases have been as unusual in the theatre as that of Hideyoshi was in politics; there was little room at the top. One considerable advantage of the system is that the minor roles are always superbly played, often by actors who have more experience than the principals: the latter may, through family prestige, often be pushed into roles beyond their current capabilities. The disadvantages are sufficiently obvious and present a particular hindrance to the popularization of the traditional Japanese theatre arts in the West. Entrepreneurs would like to take *kabuki* more widely overseas, but realize that this would mean some modification of the form; lacking the traditional background, Western audiences find pure *kabuki* difficult. But the older actors, who would be free to travel, refuse to accept the changes demanded in their programmes; the younger ones, more agreeable to compromise, dare not absent themselves from the parent company for the length of a tour, as they would lose their place in line and all their chances of advancement.

An actor takes his new name in a public ceremony (*kojo*) held as part of the performance. The curtain opens to reveal the whole company in line, kneeling formally on mats along the forestage. Each master introduces his disciple, and announces the change of name; Utaemon, a noted *onnagata* player, retains his 'female' voice, even for this extra-dramatic activity. Each member of the company then makes a short speech, varying in length according to the speaker's eminence, and the ceremony ends with a general obeisance towards the audience and a rhythmic pep-clap in which the whole theatre joins. Leading members of other families often honour these occasions, and the accompanying performances, with their presence. This successive assumption of traditional names is, in essence, ancestor-worship in a highly professional sphere, and has had a marked effect on the history of *kabuki* acting. Techniques as well as names are passed down through the generations. The actors regard themselves as heirs to the legacy of the past and as duty-bound to keep it alive. Acting styles and traditional business have been preserved virtually unchanged for centuries. As so many *kabuki* plays were originally written to display the merits of a particular actor, later generations feel an obligation to imitate their predecessors when the work is revived, and to model their style as closely as they can on that of the original performers. This is the restrictive factor in the *kabuki* performance, which tends to inhibit free response to contemporary influence though it has never operated as strongly as in *noh*.

The *kabuki* theatre, as has already been noted, adapted its stage and much of its ritual from the senior form. In the theatres as they now exist the extent of this debt is not immediately perceptible; the process of Westernization that accompanied the Meiji Era has given the stage a form more similar to our own. What we see at the Kabuki-za, however, is the result of a long and continuous process of adaptation. The earliest *kabuki* players found what accommodation they could – usually, on existing *noh* and *kagura* stages – and, as they became more settled, evolved a form more suited to their needs. Earle Ernst has shown in considerable detail the successive ways in which the elements of the *noh* stage were rearranged. In building, the companies were continually hampered by governmental regulations. The size of theatres came under official scrutiny; access from auditorium to backstage was prohibited, to prevent morally reprehensible contacts; sumptuary laws controlled expenditure on costumes; and the authorities were, for some time, adamant in refusing the theatres a permanent roof, which might be construed as an official admission that the new theatre had come to stay. In the end they were defeated by their own conflict of interest. Prejudice forbade a roof, but prudence insisted on it, if the ever-present danger of fire was to be minimized. (The brave Edo fireman, incidentally, is a recurring character in the *kabuki* plays.)

The most obvious survival from the *noh* theatre is now the long runway, a re-orientated *hashigakari* leading from the back of the auditorium to the stage. Its *kabuki* name, *hanamichi*, or 'flower path', has given rise to the tradition, supported by official *kabuki* publicists, that it derived from the *sumo* pathway up which fans carried presents to their favourite wrestlers. It seems more likely, however, that it is simply the familiar *hashigakari* in a new position, but still serving the same purpose: to allow extended entrances and exits. The *hanamichi* has its own conventions. Its length allows the actor to establish his individual character before entering the stage picture. It may serve as a neutral area, virtually a separate stage; or it may represent a road or riverbank leading to the main scene, as in Act VI of *Kanadehon Chushingura*, when it becomes a narrow path on which a pedestrian and a sedan chair jostle for right of way. Its prime value, however, is that it takes the actor into the centre of its audience, as the *hashigakari* does not. Reverting to the idea of the theatre as an architectural metaphor of its society, we see the *hanamichi* as restoring the contact with the audience that *noh* in its perfected form abandoned. The *hashigakari* is set apart from the audience, and railed off; the actor is kept within his private world. In *kabuki* the actors are presenting a drama which, both literally and metaphorically, evolves out of the audience. There is no rail, no barrier; the actor comes within touching distance. It is the drama of the élite that sets up barriers; in the Western world it was the aristocratic theatre, the masque, that created the proscenium arch, while its popular counterpart was still performing on an open stage.

In its early days *kabuki*, with a characteristically grandiose gesture, duplicated the *hanamichi*, taking advantage of the raised walkways that cut through the auditorium. Leading to the stage at left and right, they were linked by another walkway near the back, so that a large section of the audience was enclosed and the action, if necessary, could encompass them. Low walls divided the seating area into compartments holding about six people, who sat on *tatami* on the floor. Unrestricted by chairs, they could turn to follow the action in any direction. It was not until the 1870s that chairs began to appear, and then only for the convenience of foreign visitors. The Kabuki-za preserves a vestige of the old arrangement in the tier of ground-floor boxes, divided by half-walls, rather like the *loges* of the *Comédie française*. Each holds four people sitting on a raised dais or on the legless chair which is Japan's compromise between the old ways and the new.

Some modern theatres still enclose part of the audience in this way, though in the West the device is considered somewhat old-fashioned and reserved for musicals and cabaret. The Mogador in Paris has an elliptical runway enclosing the first half-dozen rows of stalls; the Casino du Liban, in Beirut, has an enormous one which cuts the audience in two, and is used at one point for a train which puffs its way among the diners – an effect of which *kabuki* would entirely have approved. The Takarazuka Theatre in Tokyo, home of mixed *kabuki* and the Girls' Opera, has the same device. But these are poor truncated versions of the double *hanamichi*; the Western theatre, in fact, has no real equivalent of the *hanamichi* at all.

The double *hanamichi* did not survive as a permanent feature. Reconstructions at the Waseda University Museum of Theatre History show how it atrophied to one runway with a platform half-way down its length, from which the actor could announce himself: eventually even this extension was lost. In theatres constructed to the Western plan a double *hanamichi* takes up too much aisle-space, and the modern theatres retain only one as a permanent feature, with recessed lighting down most of its length, and a trap near the stage for sudden apparitions. When a second one is needed, a temporary *hanamichi* is laid down the right aisle in the course of the performance.

This arrangement can still be very effective. *Yoshinogawa* (*The Yoshino River*) has a Romeo and Juliet plot of rival households confronting each other across a river. The river itself begins upstage centre and runs straight down towards the audience; its upper reaches are represented by revolving drums painted in a ripple design and turning slowly to give the effect of running water. The houses stand at left and right, the two *hanamichi* represent the banks, and the audience is, as it were, sitting in the river. (See Fig. 9.) The father of one household and the mother

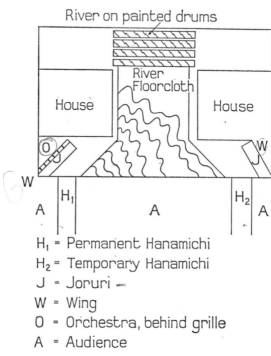

H₁ = Permanent Hanamichi
H₂ = Temporary Hanamichi
J = Joruri
W = Wing
O = Orchestra, behind grille
A = Audience

Fig. 9  *Kabuki* stage as laid out for *Yoshinogawa*, with two *joruri* and double *hanamichi*

of the other enter slowly up their respective *hanamichi*, speaking unrelated yet parallel phrases until, as they reach the stage, they perceive each other and their lines merge as dialogue. This use of the split stage continues throughout the play, in parallel action. Defying parental edict, the son of one house loves the daughter of the other. Threatened by the reigning tyrant and ordered to be brought to him as hostages, they choose death before dishonour. By their suffering and double suicide the parents are at last united.

In a closing scene of macabre beauty the girl's severed head is floated across the river to her lover's side, to touch his dead lips with her own in a posthumous ceremony of marriage. The houses open alternately to reveal successive scenes, and each side has its own *joruri* and *samisen*.

*Nozaki Mura* (*Nozaki Village*) ends with the parting of living lovers, though with a happier prospect. When they have survived several misunderstandings and entanglements to announce their love, it is decided for discretion's sake to send them home by separate ways. Most of the action has taken place indoors, but for the closing scene the stage revolves to show a river bank and a boat in the water. The girl embarks, and the boat, aided by a complicated arrangement of ropes and pulleys, is rowed straight off the stage and down the stage right *hanamichi*, representing the river. The young man is carried in a palanquin down the other, representing the bank. *Kabuki* likes to wring its spectacle dry. Boat and palanquin run parallel until they are half-way through the audience. There they pause; the bearers and the ferryman are hot. The former strip off their clothes, and elaborately pantomime exhaustion. On the other side the ferryman props his feet on the prow, ties a sweat-band round his head and lights up a pipe. All this is conducted in ballet movement, to music.

Other derivations from the *noh* stage had a shorter life. The earlier theatres retained the canopy above the stage and hung boards from it, giving the name of the play and the actors' titles. There is an echo of this practice in the technical vocabulary: actors of the highest grade are known as 'first plate' actors, from the place in which their names appeared in the lists. One may still see something of the sort at special *noh* and *kagura* performances, in the long strips of paper posted by the stage to list the programme and the artists' names. But as the scenery grew more realistic and elaborate, the canopy and its supporting pillars were found to be a hindrance. They were first disguised with strings of paper cherry blossoms, which still survive in some *kabuki* plays as conventional decorations hung inside the proscenium arch, and in the end removed altogether. The *kabuki* stage is now most reminiscent of its ancestor in its staging of the dances drawn from *noh* and its adaptations of *kyogen*, which provide a number of popular items in the repertoire. *Bo Shibari*, for instance, appears in dance form in *kabuki*; *Sannin Katawa* (*Three Cripples*) adapts the well-known *kyogen* story of three impostors who assume different physical handicaps to deceive a noble benefactor, get drunk on *sake*, and, when the lord returns, imitate the wrong infirmities in their confusion. As for *noh* dances, we have already noted the Okina-Sambaso dance, retained in several versions in *kabuki*, and the ever-popular *shishimai*. The staging of these adaptations usually presents a glossier version, on a larger scale, of the conventional *noh* setting, with painted pine-tree and bamboo expanded to fill the much wider stage, and an augmented orchestra, including *samisen* and chanters, ranged behind the performers. *Kanjincho* adapted from the *noh Ataka* (see p. 113), shows how faithful *kabuki* could be to its originals when it chose. It employs a chorus of ten, an equal number of *samisen*, six drums and a flute; the acting style is similarly expanded, being basically *noh* touched with *kabuki* flamboyance. Benkei sneers and roars magnificently at the inquisitive officer, and demonstrates his drinking prowess in the final celebration. Scorning the tiny *sake* cup, he empties both gourds into the lid of a tub, gulps down the wine with relish, and performs a drunken dance. In other adaptations, like *Dojo-ji*, the story of the serpent and the bell, and *Shunkan*, the plays are completely restaged, with all the scenic spectacle that *kabuki* is so well equipped to provide.

The present *kabuki* stage has its own permanent architectural features, though these may often be disguised with scenery. Downstage right is a grille behind which the musicians sit. Any scenery set in front of it is, almost invariably, similarly pierced, so that even in the most realistic set the musicians' place is obvious. Downstage left is the small alcove with its miniature revolve, the usual place for the *joruri* chanter. If the setting makes this impossible, there is another, higher alcove he can use; and when the set is really complicated, he may be driven out upon the forestage. Most of the stage space is occupied by the large revolve, and studded with trapdoors, some large enough for whole buildings or bridges to rise into sight. Stage settings are unfailingly magnificent, and utilize the full width of the stage to show several buildings, or rooms in the same building, side by side. As the subject-matter is largely domestic, interior settings are the most familiar. The rooms may be shut off by screens or blinds and successively disclosed as the action demands, thus giving the effect of a series of small stages within the larger one, not unlike the 'simultaneous staging' of the medieval morality plays, where all the required locations were on view at the same time and opened and used as appropriate.

By Western standards these settings show a curious combination of styles. The buildings themselves are usually solidly constructed and realistic in every detail (the time needed to erect such sets accounts for the many intermissions in a *kabuki* programme and contributes not a little to its length). Surrounding details tend to be realistic also – real hedges, real trees, solid fences and gates. But these may be set within a framework of other trees painted on canvas flats, like the exteriors of the mid-nineteenth-century Western theatre, and invariably cut off short below the sight-line; these in turn are backed not by a cyclorama, but by neutrally painted flats butted together at angles, like a folding screen. Most of these peripheral units must be mobile; when the revolve turns, wings slide in and out, new groundrows appear, and branches fold out of sight. This sort of *kabuki* scenery, in its elegant, flimsy, painted artificiality, is reminiscent of the cardboard delicacy of the Victorian toy theatre and operates in much the same way. It is as mobile as the actors – sometimes more so.

Act VIII of the famous *Kanadehon Chushingura* (*The Forty-Seven Ronin*) shows the journey of a mother and her daughter to a far estate to enforce a neglected marriage contract. On their way they pass a wedding procession, which occasions mournful reflections on the contrast between their present undignified journey and the lavish ceremony which ought to have been theirs. The scenery makes the journey for them. We first see cut-out trees against a black backdrop. These fold into the wings, and the curtain drops from sight to reveal a panorama of Mount Fuji behind a groundrow of low hills. The wedding procession is shown as in the middle distance by small cut-out figures moving up the hillside. As the women come nearer to their goal, Mount Fuji is replaced by a view of clouds, distant houses and a castle, and, in the final transformation, by a handsome pavilion standing in a lake. This is scenery as the theatres of the English Restoration used it, in their first discovery of stage mechanics; it has its own life and its own moments of glory, independent of the contributions of the actors. Thanks to elaborate and flawlessly operated stage machinery, this mobility is not confined to flat pieces. Huge built settings rise and spread themselves, fold up and sink from sight. The set becomes another actor, and frequently receives its own well-justified applause. Much of the joy lies in watching these stage mechanics, which Japanese audiences have always loved. In the early days of the cinema many were more interested in the projector than in the screen.

*Kabuki* makes no attempt to baffle the audience. On the contrary, the mechanics are usually patent. We applaud the artifice, not the illusion. Add to this the full resources of modern stage lighting, and you have a stage which is a pictorial pastiche, in part anachronistic, but never inharmonious, a combination of elements from every period since the art began. The lighting, in fact, reveals the same inconsistencies as the set. Special effects are usually handled with the utmost realism, but the mainstage lighting is flat and unselective. The auditorium lighting is keyed to that of the stage. Normally, as in *noh*, the house-lights stay at least half up. For night scenes, however, when any spill from the auditorium would ruin the stage picture, the house is plunged in darkness. But *kabuki* prefers its actors brightly lit. Scenes of darkness are kept to a minimum, and at the first convenient pretext the lights are brought full up again. Thus a single tiny lantern brought upon the stage can have an amusingly disproportionate effect; as soon as it appears the stage is once more radiant. Properties are impeccably constructed, perfect in every detail, and often at great expense, though the budget has been curtailed in recent years. It is often these tiny details of a production that stick in the mind when the rest has faded. In *Saigo to Butahime*, one of the more modern *kabuki* plays, the action takes place in a *geisha* house, and involves the hopeless love of a fat and ugly *geisha* for a fugitive revolutionary. In mutual despair they decide on suicide. The *geisha* throws open the windows, the wind blows out the lantern and moonlight floods the room. They are interrupted by two of the revolutionary's followers, who run in with lamps; by their light the lantern is seen still swinging gently where the wind had caught it. It is a minute detail; no one would have missed it if it had not been there. But it is this perfection of realistic detail within the framework of a generally stylized performance that characterizes *kabuki*. Sometimes, as in the settings, there must be a compromise between the formal and the naturalistic. We have already seen the *kyogen* horse, which owes its shape solely to dramatic convention, and not at all to nature. The *kabuki* horse is half nature, half convention: a detailed head and body supported by four very human limbs. Act v of *Kanadehon Chushingura* presents a wild boar in the same manner, impersonated by a man on all fours inside a hollow body. Comparison of these conventions illuminates the aesthetic theories that produce them.

Amid all this scenic splendour the floor is usually left bare. There is no attempt to cover its naked boards with painted soil, grass or masonry. Trees, rocks and hills emerge from it abruptly, not blended with a groundcloth. In *kabuki* theory, as in *noh*, tension is assumed between the moving vertical line of the actor and the horizontal of the stage, and in both forms this contact is essential to the dance. The characteristic *noh* walk, with gliding step and knees slightly bent, suggests this tension; it is as if the actor were fighting a force stronger than gravity, so that he can raise his feet only with an effort, and the resulting stamp assumes particular significance. This is no less true in *kabuki*, though the movements are more realistically conceived. The bare plank floor emphasizes the essential artificiality of the setting; it is no illusionistic picture, but, frankly and admittedly, a stage contrivance.

*Kabuki* acting, at first acquaintance, seems as eclectic as its settings and to change its style not merely from play to play, but from moment to moment. It is, in fact, made up of patterned movement and based on a rigidly preserved traditional choreography. The actor receives extensive training in movement and gesture, which he then applies, guided by the interpretations of the past, to the role he is playing. This tradition is no less strong for being preserved largely without written records; there is no Japanese equivalent of Laban Notation. In consequence the actor is an imitator rather than an innovator. Improvisation is not easy, nor does the complexity of movement lend itself to experiment or free interpretation. Actors perpetuate their predecessors' styles with their names: in their way the gestures of *kabuki* have become as stereotyped as *noh* and the actors try to follow the form established as most suitable to each occasion. Like *noh*, too, they have their basis in the movements and gestures of everyday life, but sublimate them into dance.

Within its self-imposed limits, however, *kabuki* is much more flexible. In performance the technique may produce what looks like almost total naturalism, something in the manner of the D'Oyly Carte operetta style, where, though we know that the acting is rigidly traditional and every small move is prescribed, this is not always easily apparent on the stage. At the other end of the scale it may turn into highly formal pantomime and dance. The musical-comedy form, in fact, may be the best analogy. In *My Fair Lady* we do not take it amiss when Higgins, Pickering and Eliza suddenly break from a naturalistic scene into a dance, or when a heterogeneous collection of bystanders, without warning, forms into a line and sings. This gives some idea of the range permissible to *kabuki*. There is something of the ritual of *noh* here, and something, too, of the freedom of the street performer. *Kabuki* actors may suddenly freeze into an elaborate tableau at moments of high tension; they may stiffen into a fantastic pose, arms outstretched, eyes crossed (a *mie*); they may perform violent acrobatics to indicate a state of mind.

The costumes, even for the smallest roles, are sumptuous. More realistic than those of *noh*, they are still far from completely so. Masks are not worn, but the make-up is often so elaborate as to constitute a mask, and is controlled by no less rigid conventions. Young women and handsome and sympathetic young men have dead-white faces, like the 'sympathetic female' masks of *noh*, and derived from accepted social custom. In a sunbaked society, pale skin denotes the upper classes, privileged to sit at home in the shade while others go to work. In the conventions of classical Mediterranean art, women were usually shown white and men brick-red; the well-born Roman women wore white make-up, and *leukos*, 'white', is a familiar term in Greek tragedy to describe the ideal of feminine beauty. Conversely, in modern society, where the masses wear an urban pallor, the aristocracy affects an out-door look: it signifies that they are rich enough to spend their winters on the Riviera. The women of *kabuki*, like their feudal prototypes, paint out their eyebrows and wear new ones higher up the forehead; their wigs are faithful copies of historical exemplars. White make-up is also worn by thieves – perhaps because *kabuki*, with its customary perversity, conceives them as an underworld aristocracy; perhaps because, like the genuine aristocracy, they spent most of their lives hiding from the sun; perhaps for technical reasons, the white face being favoured because it showed up better by candlelight. Rustic or villainous characters are made up in various shades of red. Generally speaking, the more evil a character, the redder he becomes. (It may or may not be relevant that the Japanese turn bright red when drunk.) *Kabuki* make-up at its most exaggerated is seen in the *aragoto* style, which uses broad bands of colour to throw the muscular structure into high relief.

*Kabuki* speech, though closer to the vernacular than *noh*, is still far from colloquial. Based on old forms, it has survived as a special stage language; it is the spoken Japanese of three centuries ago, and may be hardly more comprehensible to the average member of the audience than the archaic High Court style of *noh*. Diction (which is, by Western standards, appalling, though this is hardly relevant: the Japanese have always preferred the visual image to the word) employs a rhythmic intonation, which at one end of the scale may approach naturalistic speech-patterns and at the other produce a highly formal sing-song chant; as with the gestures, there is a wide range of variation possible between these two extremes. 'Women' speak in a falsetto, which, though it may not much resemble a real woman's voice, certainly comes far closer than the women of *noh*, who may often be basses. *Onnagata* acting, in fact, reveals most clearly the distinctive features of the *kabuki* style. It is certainly not naturalistic acting; though here again we must enter a proviso and remember that its models, Japanese feudal womanhood, themselves owed more to art than to nature. In the studied precision of their footwork, the handling of the robe and the sinuous movements of the head and neck, the *onnagata* players present a convincing and highly accept-able impression of a woman, compared to which the actresses of new *kabuki* seem strangely limp and colourless.

The *kabuki* actor, then, reveals himself to the audience by a code of gestures more or less abstracted from real life, and balletically conceived. They do not exactly reproduce the gestures of real life, but are usually close enough for their meaning to be apparent (as in the *kabuki* battles, where swords never actually touch, and a thrust aimed in the general direction of the oppo-nent's body indicates a death-blow). But every move is important. There is no such thing as a meaningless gesture. Each must be given its full weight in time, and the more important gestures must be artificially prolonged. (Oswald Sickert's remarks on the time-extension techniques of *noh*, quoted in Chapter 3, are no less pertinent here.) This accounts for the apparently erratic and generally slow tempo of *kabuki*, and for the complaint heard often from Western visitors that it is hard to tell where the climaxes are meant to be. It is a performance built around the individual actor, who in turn builds his performance around the individual movements. And this means that what we should call trivial gestures may be given as much importance, seemingly, as large ones; by the same token, small-part players from time to time may dominate the stage while the principals stand motionless to wait their turn.

Examples are essential here. The play *Honcho Nijushi Ko* (*Twenty-four Examples of Filial Piety*) is based, like so many, on family rivalry. The scene is the house of Nagao Kenshin, where Katsuyori, the son of his enemy, has contrived to get himself em-ployed as a gardener to spy out his plans. Kenshin penetrates the disguise, but does not reveal his knowledge. To rid himself of the enemy within his gates, he sends the youth to deliver a letter, and immediately orders his warriors to follow and kill him. It is a scene we have seen many times in gangster films. As handled by a Western author and director it would probably go something like this: Kenshin gives Katsuyori the letter, with many protestations of trust and affection; Katsuyori departs; Kenshin immediately turns to his henchmen, who have been waiting sinister and impassive near by, and says, 'Kill him'; blackout. (A close Western classical example is, in fact, the murder of Banquo in *Macbeth*.) The director would work for the contrast between the false amiability and the curt brutality of the last command; an elaborate discussion of how he was going to be killed, with what or by whom, would seem to be an anticlimax. The scene would end on a desirable note of tension.

This is not what happens in *kabuki*. Here Kenshin gives Katsuyori his instructions and sends him off down the *hanamichi*. He then summons his warriors. First comes a swordsman, who performs a martial dance to demonstrate his prowess, and runs down the *hanamichi* at accelerating speed. Then comes a spearman, who does a similar dance of exactly equal length, and departs in the same fashion. The curtain closes.

By our standards this is anticlimactic. Most Western directors would, I suspect, feel that if one were going to show the warriors at all, two are either too many or not enough. But by *kabuki* standards the warriors have their individual statements to make, and, like politicians on television, demand equal time. Another example is found in *Sannin Katawa*, which has already been briefly noted as farce derived from *kyogen*. A wealthy lord offers employment to the handicapped, and three applicants arrive: a cripple, a mute and a blind man. Each enters up the *hanamichi*, with a long and elaborate pantomime of his particular affliction. Each presents himself in the same way, in the same amount of time. A Western director would feel the compulsion to vary the pattern by bringing them on in different ways, or at least to work to a climax by increasing the tempo, with the second entrance faster than the first, and the third fastest of all. *Kabuki* sees them as separate 'turns', in which three actors, of equal importance, have their individual statements to make, which are relished by the audience each on its own merits. Each exists in its own right, not as one component of a larger whole, and responsive to the pattern of that whole. *Kabuki* in its traditional form has no director. This is actor-centred drama.

*Kabuki* is very much the drama of the individual moment. We see this first of all in the settings. The scenery is allowed its individual moments of glory. Earle Ernst insists that it is never permitted to dominate the actors. I find, on the contrary, that there are many moments when it clearly does so; the action freezes while we watch an elaborate change or a vast building rise into place, and when we have enjoyed this sufficiently, the actors' movement resumes. It would be fairer to say that the scenery interacts with the players as they interact with each other, each one being dominant in turn. The division of the stage space follows the same pattern. Although the sets are vast and lavish, they are rarely used in full for any length of time. Parts are used in isolation from the rest; rooms not required by the immediate action may be shuttered off, or, if they remain occupied, the characters in them group into a silent tableau till they are called upon to speak. This technique is seen most obviously in the 'parallel-action' plays (of which *Yoshinogawa* is only one of several examples), where the wide stage becomes to all intents and purposes two, used alternately. And the actors usually act against the setting, not within it; they resign no part of their individuality to their surroundings. Setting and action are, to this extent, independent; the setting is permitted to make its own statement, and then yields the stage to the actors. This represents a conception of the scenic function which has now largely vanished from the Western world. The modern directorial concept seeks for a unity, and sees actor, set and lighting as working together in a larger whole. One may, however, still find traces of the older attitude. I recall, in Athens, a production of *Macbeth* by the Greek National Theatre. The setting was exceedingly beautiful and striking: baronial Gothic seen through Greek eyes, refined to pure economy of line, with a perfect sense of period that was at the same time modern. The acting, by contrast, was Victorian.

Alexis Minotis, as Macbeth, and his wife, Katina Paxinou, as his
lady, virtually ignored the possibilities that the setting offered;
they played firmly in front of it, obliterating it from the audience's
mind, and taking centre stage as if by divine right; it was like
seeing John Philip Kemble on a stage designed by Loudon Saint-
hill. *Kabuki* has something of the same effect. Its movements and
groupings are dictated by a company etiquette and a traditional
conception of stage behaviour which does not necessarily arise
from the logic of the play-structure.

We have spoken of the players as 'interacting'; this term must
now be severely qualified, *Kabuki* admits no concept of ensemble
playing. Crowd scenes, for this reason, are lackadaisical affairs
that would make the Duke of Saxe-Meiningen turn in his grave.
Their members are still individuals; there is no unity of purpose
or group sense, and important crowd lines are lost in the shuffle.
Directed *kabuki* (as at the National Theatre) handles its crowds
balletically, spacing the members with geometrical precision and
letting them move, turn, and even sometimes speak as one. A
crowd scene which is effective in naturalistic terms lies outside
the compass of *kabuki*; the conditions of the art reject it.

The relationship between two actors in dialogue is the same
as that between two groups of actors on the split stage: when one
is busy, the other is still. Or, to put this in *noh* terminology, two
actors playing a scene together alternate the roles of *sh'te* and
*waki*. They act as 'feeds' for each other in turn, and do their best
not to detract from the individuality of the other's performance.
They stand together, but do not work together; as Ernst puts it
'the almost complete absence of physical contact in the *kabuki*. . .
appears to be the result of the unwillingness of the actor to forfeit
any part of his expressiveness to another actor'. In dialogue this
may be seen by watching the actor who is *not* speaking (though
this is difficult; the combination of sing-song recitative and
stylized gesture has the same hypnotic attraction as *noh*). He
either does not react at all, or deliberately delays his reaction
until his partner's lines have finished and his own begun. Even
the word 'dialogue' must be qualified. The lines do not truly
interact, but exist as a series of separate though related state-

F

ments, marked off and denying any sense of progression by the convention of dropping the voice at the end of each line. In this they closely resemble the structure of much of the *stichomythia* of Greek tragedy, which is not so much 'dialogue' in our sense of the word as two independent and alternating lines of thought.

This analogy may perhaps be taken a little further. The structure of the *kabuki* dance recalls Plutarch's description of its Greek counterpart as an enchainment of separate, isolated mimetic gestures, steps punctuated by attitudes. This pattern is substantially followed in the structure of Greek tragedy, conceived as a series of independent scenes, which, though they all relate to the central story line, do not necessarily relate in detail to each other. This produces certain inconsistencies, in character as in plot, which are seen even more obviously in Greek comedy, where the characterization may shift radically between the beginning of the play and its end; Greek drama, too, is responsive to the dictates of the individual moment. These inconsistencies have been seized upon by the more pedantic scholars with the same enthusiasm the Baker Street Irregulars display in proving Dr Watson a bigamist – and with as little point. They are inconsistencies only by our standards. Greek tragedy and comedy, like *kabuki*, adhere to a different conception of theatrical performance. *Kabuki* is seen as a succession of individual moments. In this it responds, hardly less than *noh*, to the essential Buddhist doctrine that the world around us is impermanent, and exists only in a series of fleeting, unrelated and accidental phenomena. We see this in literary form in Japanese nature-poetry: where Wordsworth defined his art as emotion recollected in tranquillity, the *haiku* represents emotion taken on the wing, a fleeting moment frozen in verse like a moth in amber. The same attitude explains the modern passion for snapshot photography, and the balanced perfection of each individual frame in the Japanese film. But where *noh* attempts to transcend the momentary world, *kabuki* reproduces it. It does not try to build in time or to bring the action to a climax. On the contrary, *kabuki* philosophy insists that the play should be seen as a succession of impressive visual moments, and that the action could be stopped at any time to show a perfectly balanced tableau. This explains the apparent incivility of the audience. Knowing what *kabuki* is, and the sort of continuity they may expect, they assume that they can wander into the theatre at any point and still see something that will immediately interest them and draw them into the action. Unfortunately many carry over their *kabuki* habits to modern plays. The stragglers may still be arriving half-way through the first Act, as if Giraudoux constructed his plays on the same pattern as Chikamatsu Monzaemon. Western directors working with Japanese actors in modern plays have found that their greatest difficulty lies in persuading the cast to accept a concept of play structure so radically different from their own; they still insist on playing only from scene to scene, and cannot grasp the necessity of subordinating one scene to another, or sustaining a progression of interest throughout the play.

One further example, and a particularly striking one, may serve to illustrate the difference between the traditional Japanese concept and our own. The dead who litter the stage after a *kabuki* sword-fight normally get up and walk away when the battle is over. This happens even in 'new *kabuki*', which is much closer to our naturalism. Before condemning this practice as ridiculous, we should reflect that it is, *in itself*, no more ridiculous than our custom of resurrecting the dead for a curtain call, or, indeed, of permitting a curtain call at all. Its apparent oddity derives from our conception of stage time. The naturalistic theatre tends to equate stage time, at least approximately, with real time (though it may be divided arbitrarily into acts, and punctuated with intermissions, to accommodate the physical needs of the spectators), just as it tends to equate stage behaviour, at least approximately, with off-stage behaviour. Thus, the play is considered *in extenso*, and the effect of any action is considered to remain in force until the next convenient stopping place. The Japanese theatre, which, like the Greek, is not primarily interested in the literal reproduction of actuality, considers time to be expandable or compressible according to the dramatic exigencies of the moment, divides the play into a series of momentary impressions, and sees no compulsion to prolong the effects of an action beyond their dramatic utility. Just as the 'invisible' stage assistant removes properties that have no further purpose, the dead may rise again when they have made their point. To keep them lying there would be untidy, superfluous and dramatically irrelevant.

It might be argued, indeed, that the structure of the *kabuki* play reproduces the characteristic sentence-pattern of the Japanese language. This analogy certainly holds true for Greek, where the love of parallelism, syntactical symmetry and balanced clauses is reflected in the 'double structure' so beloved of Greek tragedy, where two stories are balanced against each other in the manner of debate, and the play takes its point from the opposition between them. Japanese is largely paratactic. It has no subordination and little inflection; the words and phrases are strung together in an unrelieved and undifferentiated continuum, with the sentence ending denoted by the principal verb. To use a textbook illustration: *Sono hito-ga motte-i-masu mono-wa handobagu-de su* (What she is holding is her handbag) is really a combination of two sentences: *Sono hito-ga aru mono-wa motte-i-masu; sono mono-wa handobagu-de su* (She is holding a certain thing; that thing is a handbag).

The function of the words in the sentence is indicated not by their own inflections, but by the addition of the appropriate suffixes, or postpositions; thus, *wa* normally indicates that the preceding word or phrase is the subject of the sentence, and *de* denotes the predicate complement. In the same way *kabuki* imposes on the continuum of the action certain arbitrary devices to indicate that a certain moment is of particular importance. The climax does not evolve obviously from the action itself; it is imposed on the action by external means.

The most obvious of these devices is the clapper-board, operated at stage left by a grave, black-robed stage assistant, which not only signals the opening of the play, but underlines significant moments within it. Several sharp beats draw attention to an important gesture, and a whole crescendo accompanies a sustained passage of critical action or an exit down the *hanamichi*. Alternatively, the unseen off-stage orchestra may mark selected passages with music, or the actors may apply their own emphasis by freezing into a *mie*. Earle Ernst happily compares these violent, limb-locked posturings to the taut, musclebound ferocity of 'temple guardians', the effigies of minor deities that flank the gateway of a Buddhist shrine. They surely owe at least as much to the puppet actors that inspired so many of the details of *kabuki*. Having suddenly fallen into a *mie*, the actors may just as rapidly walk away from it; the continuum is resumed. In *noh* we saw how the stage dynamics of Western practice could be ignored, for the audience already knows where to look and what the critical moments are. In *kabuki*, with its wider stage and more diffuse plots, the *mie* and its cognate devices provide the requisite additional emphasis. Each act customarily closes with a tableau, and it is interesting to see how this practice has been retained, half unconsciously, in productions of modern Japanese and Western plays. Actors will often hold position for what seems an interminable time before the curtain finally falls.

Among the actors, efficient and ubiquitous, robed and veiled in black like the *ninja* of the feudal war machine, move the stage assistants. Like their counterparts in *noh*, they are seen but yet invisible. They belong to the mechanics of the play, and like the ropes, pulleys, trapdoors and the stage revolve are apparent if one cares to look. Their chief function is to keep the stage tidy. Any discarded property is immediately removed – even the shoes which, by Japanese custom, are taken off before entering a house and treading on the cherished *tatami*. For all its spectacular nature, *kabuki* still retains this aspect of the dramatic economy of *noh*. Once its utility is over, a property becomes a useless distraction and merely clutters up the stage. The assistants may also take an open part in scene changes: one may even see them stroll on with hammers, in mid-performance, to make a minor repair to the set. A traditional function was to hold candles before a leading actor's face to give him prominence at moments of high intensity – a visual equivalent of the clapper-board, and analogous to a cinematic close-up. Modern lighting has made this function redundant, but they are still called upon to assist the actor physically in other ways. They help in the tricky on-stage costume changes, when two or three may gather round an actor at the same time (Japanese television has adapted this, not unwittily, for men's tailoring commercials). In *Shunkan* they have a more arduous duty. At one point a ship appears on stage, and warriors pour down the gang-plank to the shore. The warriors are heavy and the gang-plank flimsy. Underneath it sits the stage assistant, doggedly supporting it with his shoulders.

Their role may sometimes be more active. In a later scene of *Honcho Nijushi Ko*, Kenshin's daughter, who loves Katsuyori, although he is her father's sworn enemy, steals a sacred heirloom from her home on his behalf. It is a magnificent battle helmet, draped in fox fur. She intends to row secretly across the lake to meet her lover, but remembers, too late, that it is winter; the lake is covered by a sheet of ice, too thin to walk across, too solid to row through. As she stands in this Eliza-like predicament, irresolute on a bridge in her garden, she chances to glance into the pool beneath and sees the reflection of a fox beside her own. She is terrified, but after several experiments realizes that it comes from the fox-fur helmet in her hand. Remembering that the fox is an emissary of the gods, she assumes it came in answer to her prayers. According to an old legend, the fox was the first to cross the early winter ice, finding a safe path across the treacherous crust. If she follows the fox, she will be safe. At this point, as the helmet and the fox-divinity are identified in her mind, the heirloom with its swinging mane takes on a life of its own. Supported by a property man on a long pole, it moves ahead, inviting her to follow; it is operated by the *korumbo*, or 'black man', as *kabuki* calls the stage assistant, as though it were a puppet. As she runs after it she is encouraged by further signs of vulpine favour – 'fox fires', will-o'-the-wisps, floating in the darkness to reveal a supernatural agency at work. These too are held by the assistants, on long poles like fishing rods.

We have called the *korumbo* conventionally invisible, as in *noh*, but the convention is a different and in certain ways an uneasy one. A stage convention works only when both sides understand the rules and abide by them. As long as the audience accepts that a man in black, as in *kabuki*, or in an unobtrusive uniform, as in *noh*, is meant to be invisible, he is; his presence is neither disturbing nor embarrassing. The *kabuki* assistant, however, often seems reluctant to accept the convention himself. To begin with, his costume makes a greater attempt at real concealment. In addition, he appears self-conscious. His movements are furtive; he tries to be really invisible. He enters at a run, bent double, and makes himself as inconspicuous as he can behind the scenery. Sometimes he will spend a whole scene lying on the floor behind a bench, to be in position to remove when it is no longer needed. And, paradoxically, the more he tries to hide himself, the more obvious he is. To pretend that a man is invisible, as *noh* does, is the easiest thing in the world. But there is no way of making him really invisible, except by removing him from the stage altogether. The harder *kabuki* tries, the more distracting its failure becomes. In some plays the *korumbo* changes colour for more effective camouflage. In snow-bound scenes (one of the rare occasions when the stage is covered with a floor-cloth) he wears white, to blend into the scenery. The National Theatre production of *Shunkan* offers a new variation. Here the scene represents a barren island set against a background of stylized waves. At one point, several characters have discarded their sandals and left them lying by a rock. The stage assistant enters to remove them in the customary fashion. But he is not wearing black. His robe is decorated with a swirling pattern of blue and white, the sea-motif of the background against which he is seen. In isolation the effect is strangely beautiful; it is as if a stray wave had come in and washed the sandals out to sea. In context, however, it rings false. The disguise is so nearly successful that it attracts the wrong sort of attention. This may be a historical problem; there is not enough material for us to judge. The self-consciousness of the modern *korumbo* may stem from the insidious intrusions of more recent theatre concepts, in the light of which he is an anachronism. It is more likely, however, that the difference between the wholly successful *noh* convention and its only partially successful *kabuki* counterpart has always existed. *Kabuki*, as we have seen, in many ways effects a compromise between the formal and the naturalistic styles. This seems to be one compromise that did not completely succeed. In *noh* the stage assistant is of a piece with his formal surroundings; against the more elaborate stage pictures of *kabuki* he is occasionally incongruous.

The world of *kabuki* is that of its audience. It mirrors the hopes and fears, pleasures and privations, hard facts and fantasies, of a class which admitted and resented its inferiority and sought romance and temporary escape in the theatre. Its attitude towards the *samurai* is ambivalent, a love-hate relationship, cherishing what it affects to mock. With one half of its being it fawns upon the aristocracy and builds its plays around their lives and their philosophy. This offered material of great dramatic value. The *samurai* imposed upon himself a code no less strict than he enforced on others, and one which has been popularized under the later name of *bushido* 'the way of the warrior'. His life was dedicated to his immediate lord; the feudal system with its hierarchical structure and restriction of allegiance only made this loyalty fiercer. The *samurai* was pledged to preserve his lord's honour and his own. To this all else – his life, his family, his possessions – was subordinate. Insults could be wiped out only in blood. The vendetta was not merely tolerated but recognized by law, which with characteristic bureaucratic caution demanded notice in writing of attempted revenge-murder. For the defeated *samurai* there was only one way out: *seppuku*, suicide by disembowelment. Capture was the ultimate ignominy; warriors were trained and expected to fight to the death. This attitude has been held to explain, though not to condone, the inhumane treatment meted out to prisoners in the Second World War: an army conditioned to give their lives without question had no sympathy for opponents who surrendered.

*Kabuki* played fruitfully with these examples. The *samurai* code was one of the chief themes of popular literature. Romantic-historical fiction in cheap editions depicted the exploits of the *samurai* in war and familiarized the lower orders with the spirit that motivated their masters. This influence was not confined to art. Some tried to emulate the *samurai*, if not in their lives, at least in their deaths, and appropriated the forbidden privilege of *seppuku*. The plays capitalized on this popular interest. *Jidaimono*, or 'historical pieces', ransack the remote and recent past. The famous vendetta of the Soga brothers, who sought vengeance for their father's death, inspired a whole series of plays and dances; one of them was traditionally included in every New Year's programme. *Tengajaya no Katakiuchi* traces, through five long acts, the ramifications of a family feud in Osaka, based on an actual incident of 1609, and shows the picaresque adventures of a pair of brothers on their way to seek revenge. There are elaborate turns of fortune and comic as well as serious villains.

Other plays were based upon the great clan wars and the period of anarchy recorded in the *Heike Monogatari* and similar works; *kabuki*, like *noh*, found much material in epic. More recent political events were also treated, though with greater caution. The government prohibited the undisguised dramatization of contemporary events and the use of the real names of persons in authority, to prevent scandal. In consequence the plays were often moved back to an earlier period (as Verdi, after the initial fiasco of *La Traviata*, transposed it to a century before) and the names of the characters were slightly changed: the historical Mitsuhide Akechi became Mitsuhide Takechi, and Kenshin Uesugi became Kenshin Nagao.

The most famous vendetta play of all was *Kanadehon Chushingura* (*The Alphabet Book of the Forty-seven Exemplary Loyal Subjects*, but more familiar as *The Forty-seven Ronin*), based on a historical event of 1702. Dramatized in 1748 by three writers in collaboration (a familiar practice in *kabuki*, as in the Elizabethan theatre) it was one of over a hundred plays on a subject which continues to inspire a spate of films. Its principal interest here lies in the fact that it is a perfect illustration of the *samurai* code; its chief characters are loyal retainers who take upon themselves a vendetta bequeathed them by their master. He had died as a result of an insult and a quarrel, leaving them as *ronin*, masterless men. Forming an elaborate conspiracy, they took it on themselves to kill his enemy and offer his head on the grave of their lord. The law, as we have seen, demanded notice of such attempts in writing: this the *ronin* deliberately failed to give, as it would have warned the enemy of their intentions. Having accomplished their revenge, they notified the government of what they had done and

F 2

calmly awaited the consequences. It was a *cause célèbre*, and dragged on for some time. Enormous public sympathy had been aroused, and the authorities were forced to proceed with discretion. The *ronin* were treated more like honoured guests than prisoners, and, when the verdict was inevitably given against them, were permitted the honour of *seppuku*, as *samurai*, rather than a common beheading. They were buried beside the lord they had avenged.

*Kanadehon Chushingura*, though its modern fame is partly factitious (it was banned by the American Occupation as embodying dangerous aspects of the Japanese feudal spirit, and the protests lasted for years), well illustrates both the rigours of the *samurai* code and the emulation it inspired in others. The audience, no less than the *ronin*, sought to identify themselves with their masters. This attitude manifests itself in *kabuki* in other ways. Even those plays, such as *Sukeroku*, which construct their own popular heroes and are apparently anti-*samurai*, transfer to the bourgeoisie the qualities which the aristocracy found admirable. Sukeroku's braggadocio is motivated by family honour. He is prepared to face all odds and hazard his life to recover the treasured sword. *Kabuki* portrays an aristocracy of its own, drawn from the stratum of society in which it had its being, that has its own code, dignity and traditions no less importunate than those of the *samurai*. Both classical and modern novelists, exploring the sociology of the sub-world, have revealed a hierarchy within a hierarchy, and a meticulous code of social observance. Sukeroku's female counterpart is his mistress, Agekami. Like the *geisha* in so many plays she is no common prostitute, but an Edo Marie Duplessis, a high courtesan with a will and character of her own. She distributes her favours not haphazardly, but to men that she respects; she is loving, devoted and loyal. The husband-wife relationships of *jidaimono*, the fated marriages and doomed betrothals, and the conflicts of interest that they provoke, have their parallel in the liaisons between townsman and courtesan. *Kabuki* transfers to its world and its characters the standards of the other.

The ultimate extension of this attitude is the creation of plays dealing with an underworld aristocracy, thieves, highwaymen and other criminals who inhabit a realm outside the law, but still embody the *samurai* code. They are Macheaths without the surrounding squalor – or Mack the Knife with a *samurai* sword; robust, swaggering figures whose derring-do wins admiration, and whose peculations are on an enormous scale. In these plays *kabuki*'s ambivalent social attitude is most clearly revealed. While glorifying an anarchic demi-monde in which characters win wealth and prestige by crimes against society, it still upholds that society's supreme virtues; fantasy-escape from repression is, at the same time, a reaffirmation of faith. The values are the same, though the personnel and milieu have changed. Ishikawa Goemon, 'the best thief in Japan', an actual personage who flourished at the end of the sixteenth century, inspired more than ten *kabuki* scripts. Boiled to death in a cauldron, he left his own poetic epitaph: 'Even if the time should come when there is no more sand left on the beach, the world will have its complement of thieves.' One of the longest plays about him, *Sanmon Gosan no Hiri*, was the first produced in Osaka in 1778; the gorgeous showmanship of the opening scenes reveals the admiration with which such characters were regarded. Goemon has come from China to help a plot to overthrow the government. The play opens with a balletic duel between his followers and the army, in which the latter are robbed of the huge sum of 7000 *ryo*. An inner curtain falls to show one of *kabuki*'s most breathtaking scenic effects, a view of the upper story of the great gate (*sanmon*) of the Nanzenji Shrine in Kyoto. It towers above the blossoming cherry-trees, brilliantly lacquered in vermilion and gold. Goemon is a brilliant spectacle himself, with gold pipe and gold-embroidered Chinese coat. In spite of his perilous situation – he has taken this high refuge to avoid his enemies – his opening words are magnificently casual: 'What a lovely view!' As he struts and postures on the balcony, the cherry-trees are pulled away and the building rises, so that we now see the full height of the gate and the courtyard in front. The technical feat is even more impressive when one realizes that the supporting machinery was first built in the Edo period, without benefit of electricity or steel ropes. Goemon's enemy enters and spies his reflection in a pool of water. They challenge each other in poetic dialogue. Goemon hurls a dagger, which his opponent neatly parries on a water-dipper. The curtain closes on a defiant *mie*. This is the sort of entertainment that the *kabuki* audiences loved, thrilling to Goemon and his kind as other audiences have done to Robin Hood, Dick Turpin and Robert Macaire. They found in them a colourful individuality that refreshed the regulated drabness of their own lives and could appease their consciences and the censorious authorities by pointing out that Goemon paid his dues to society in the end.

With the death of the feudal system and the growth of a democratic spirit, the later drama, in turning back to historical sources, looked more critically upon the *samurai*. It tried to show the human being behind the social mask and to demonstrate that the aristocracy too had its mortal frailties. In classical *kabuki*, however, the critical spirit is confined within strict limits. Though the *samurai* may be parodied, there is no attack on the basis of their rule. The system is inflexible and impervious to assault. The effete and decadent *samurai* who sometimes mince and twitter across the stage are no more symptoms of a popular uprising than the commoners who abuse their lords in *kyogen* – or, for that matter, the slaves who abuse their masters in Roman comedy, or the precocious servants of Victorian novelists. A closed system begets a closed mind. Revolution was inconceivable – on both sides. The Shogunate was built into the Japanese way of life, and solid enough to tolerate occasional impertinences. The end came, not so much by a gradual process of disintegration from within, but by a strong blast from without; with a bang, and not a whimper.

Against this wall the individual passions beat in vain. *Kanadehon Chushingura* demonstrates, as well as the virtues of the *samurai*, the obduracy of the law that they upheld. The action of the *ronin* was admirable, but illegal. They were applauded as popular heroes, but all admitted the inevitability and the justice of their punishment. In all its manifestations the central issue of *kabuki* is essentially the same: the individual against the system, in which the system inevitably triumphs. *Kabuki* itself had come into being as an act of artistic revolt, distrusted by the Shogunate because it championed a world of individual passion contrary to social order. The subsequent position of the art, and the themes of its plays, show how the 'off-beat' impulse was tamed and confined.

The system, as represented in the plays, may appear in its legal or its moral aspects; there is no effective difference. Although the individual may assert himself against it, he ends by admitting its tabus and accepting its punishment. *Kabuki* distinguishes between *jidaimono* (historical) and *sewamono* (domestic) plays; but in a sense most plays are *sewamono*, illustrating the conflict between individual desires and passions and the rules laid down by society. The sense of duty – to lord, honour, father or family – is paramount and transcends personal inclination. *Kabuki* moves in a world which is, in its way, as ritualistic as that of *noh*. The conflicts are all essentially identical and the end is pre-ordained. It is a world with which we are more familiar in the French neo-classical theatre, where individual interests are subjugated to the demands of *gloire* and decorum; the rare individual who struggles and wins (like le Cid) does so only by divine or royal intervention, which itself embodies and transcends the system.

*Sewamono* plays therefore end, more often than not, unhappily; the protagonist acquiesces in the impossibility of change. Discussing Japanese food with a companion, I once remarked how much I disliked *tofu*, the bean-curd cake with the appearance and consistency of foam rubber. She replied, quite seriously, 'But how can you dislike it? It's quite tasteless.' It was the prototypical answer of a people who have traditionally preferred the negative to the positive virtues. It is the submissive hero, not the revolutionary, who is cherished. The *samurai* accepts his suicide. Lovers kill themselves rather than attempt illicit happiness. If *sewamono*, in synopsis, reads like the more lugubrious outpourings of the women's magazines, the impression is not far wrong. One of the more romantic Japanese festivals, the *Tanabata Matsuri* (Feast of the Weaver), on 7 July, typically celebrates two thwarted lovers turned into stars and condemned to see each other only one day each year across the Milky Way. The plays, similarly, prefer blighted to consummated love and a sad ending to a happy one.

One example will suffice here: a particularly interesting one, as it involves a couple who come into conflict with the code and go voluntarily to their deaths, although the youth is blameless and the woman guilty only in intention. This is *Yari no Gonza Kasana Katabira* (*Gonza the Spearman*) by the great Chikamatsu Monzaemon, based on a contemporary scandal. The wife of a master of the tea-ceremony is trapped by an unsuccessful admirer in an apparently adulterous situation with one of her husband's disciples. Although she is secretly in love with the youth, she has not revealed it; her guilt lies only in the mind. When the rival accuses them on manufactured evidence, they run away together, in the knowledge that they are doomed. The husband is bound by the social code to avenge his honour; they know their respite can be only temporary, and confront him in the end of their own volition. In the last scene of the play they go to meet their executioners. It is a summer evening in Osaka by the waterside. Music is playing, and a gay procession of dancers winds up the *hanamichi*. The avengers are watching the ferryboat, but miss the runaways; it would still be possible for them to escape. But they do not try. Leaving the boat, they wait for the inevitable on the shore. The avengers return; one engages the youth in a vicious duel, while the other pursues the wife, who hides herself among the dancers on the bridge. But when the youth is killed, she comes running to his side and is there struck down. The code has been fulfilled.

*Kabuki*'s preoccupation with the limited world of the *samurai*, the townsman and the courtesan arises from necessity. There was little else about which it could safely write. As long as it concerned itself with triviality and the exploration of the *status quo*, or clothed its satires in fantasy that made them acceptable, it escaped the worst of governmental interference. In the declining years of the Shogunate the first whispers of protest begin to be heard, and *kabuki*, sensitive to popular feeling, went as far as it dared. In 1851, Segawa Joko III wrote *Sakura Gimin 'Den*, which may be translated as *The Life and Martyrdom of a Public Hero of Sakura*. In seven Acts and twenty-eight scenes, it was adapted from a novel on the hitherto unmentionable subject of the proletarian revolt. The hero, in the play called Sogo, was in real life Kiuchi Sogoro, leader of a local peasant uprising after the failure of the rice crop in 1653. We see him first negotiating with his local overlords, the Hotta family, to lessen the crushing tax-burden on the farmers. The administrators are divided. Some are sympathetic, while others seek to conceal their own misappropriations. As presented at the National Theatre the opening scene effectively conveys the perils of the individual confronting the entrenched social order. The great gate of the Hotta mansion revolves, showing inside and outside in turn. We see, first, Sogo and a mass of farmers at the gate, presenting their petition to a single, nervous representative of the aristocracy. Inside, the balance is reversed. Once he has entered the *daimyo*'s world, Sogo is at his mercy. He is now the lonely figure, pleading with the robed, impassive lords who sit like idols on their carved stools, not even condescending to look at him.

A promised inquiry does not materialize, and Sogo, in desperation, determines to present his petition to the Shogun himself, though such a breach of protocol was punishable by death. Declared an outlaw, he makes a furtive farewell visit to his family. There is a moving scene on the snowbound river bank, where a ferryman insists on rowing him across in spite of the law. His boat has been padlocked for the night, but the ferryman takes an axe, severs the chain, and rows the fugitive home. His impulsive and decisive act foreshadows Sogo's own; he too is determined to cut chains and defy the law to help his people.

There follows a long scene in which Sogo takes leave of his family. To protect his wife, he has prepared a letter of divorce; by law a criminal's family had to share his punishment. His wife, in the self-sacrificial spirit that *kabuki* continually glorifies, refuses to accept it, and makes him tear it up. Breaking from his son's arms, Sogo trudges through the snow and down the *hanamichi* to his inevitable death.

At the Shogun's palace the court is arrayed in splendour on a bridge, while Sogo grovels on the ground beneath. He evades the guards for long enough to toss his petition to Matsudaira, a leading minister. Matsudaira announces that so irregular a petition cannot be received, and apparently throws it back; but Sogo sees that he has returned only the outer wrapping, and put the petition itself inside his robe, signifying that it will have his personal attention. Sogo is satisfied. It is the last we see of him. We learn later that he and his family have been crucified.

The final scene returns to Hotta's mansion, where the despot is increasingly terrified by apparitions. Strange fires appear, a sepulchral voice intones, and Hotta sees the accusing ghosts of Sogo's family. Finally, shown that his corruption has extended to his own household and that his lust for power has bred a corresponding lust in others, he repents. To appease the angry spirits he repeals the taxes and swears to live a better life hereafter.

Modern research has suggested that most of the events of this play are founded on fact. Sogoro's shrine is still revered in Sakura, where the local people commemorate him in their ballads. But such a play could not be presented while the Tokugawa Shogunate was at its height. In 1851 – ten years before Commodore Perry, seventeen before Meiji – the times were more propitious. *Sakura Gimin Den* appeared against a background of popular dissatisfaction with the Shogunate's agrarian policy. To this extent it was a protest play. It must be noticed, however, how long the protest took in coming, and how mild it eventually was. It does not condemn the system, any more than Racine's *Britannicus* attacks the idea of monarchical government. It points merely to individual abuses within this system, while respecting the authority under which such abuses become possible. Modern critics have complained that Hotta suffers too little for his crimes. They miss the point. In its historical context, the despot's repentance was enough. To have inflicted further punishment on Hotta might have implied that the system itself was rotten.

The first production of *Sakura Gimin Den* was a solid success and ran for three consecutive months. Subsequent revivals were less happy, and confirmed *kabuki*'s uneasiness in dealing with more cogent and realistic subjects. The showmanship of *kabuki* finds peasant drama, in particular, unattractive. Prizing beauty, gaiety and eroticism it despises the more realistic representation of working-class life as *momen shibai*, 'cotton plays'. *Kabuki* preferred 'silk plays' about the rich and high-born, which allowed more opportunity for display. For this reason, revivals of *Sakura Gimin Den* glossed over the social implications and concentrated on those moments where traditional *kabuki* felt more at home: the melodrama of the court scene and the pathos of the family leave taking.

As contemporary social unrest impinged, albeit slightly, on the *kabuki* world of the 1850s, the psychology of modern power politics has influenced some plays of the present century. *Yoritomo no Shi* (*Yoritomo's Death*), written in 1932, investigates feudal history from a modern standpoint. It deals with the rule of the Minamoto family at Kamakura, and in particular with the death of its greatest member, who had subdued the Taira clan and risen to supreme power. History states that Yoritomo died by falling from his horse, but there is reason to suspect this as official whitewash; the more sordid truth seems to be that he suffered a stroke while visiting one of his many mistresses. Mayamo Seika's play takes this as a basis for an investigation of the nature of power. It is set in 1201, during the third anniversary of Yoritomo's death. We see the uneasiness of the retainers, pledged to preserve the official account, and the personal embarrassment this causes them. Yoriie, Yoritomo's son and successor, is obsessed with finding out the truth. His investigations, using bribery and the threat of torture, only reveal the insecurity of his own position, Masako, his mother, emerges as the Agrippina of Minamoto politics. Holding a spear at her son's throat, she insists that the lie must be preserved at all costs, if family prestige is not to suffer. The interest of government demand that Yoriie continue to play his part. As the play ends, he realizes what the part is. Ostensibly the Shogun, in supreme power, he is really only a pawn in the game. Overcome by humiliation, he falls weeping to the floor.

In its acute psychological study of a neurotic ruler confronted with the facts of power, in its concern with propaganda and the noble lie, this play is very much of its time, and yet traditional in its use of historical events to study, at a safe remove, the workings of contemporary politics. Yet, like *Sakura Gimin Den*, it does not fit happily into the *kabuki* framework. The extrovert nature of *kabuki* is not well equipped to deal with psychology. Deprived of colour and action, it lapses too easily into dullness. *Kabuki* is limited by the circumstances of its evolution. Its elaborate techniques were developed to extract the maximum theatrical value from a narrowly restricted range of material. When it turns to more profound themes, these techniques are no longer appropriate, and there is nothing to take their place. To cope adequately with the newer themes which writers have tried to implant in it, it would have to change its nature radically; and then it would no longer be *kabuki*. Today's performers, conscious of this inherent difficulty, and of the growing status of their art as a 'classic', have tended to avoid the more recent plays, and draw increasingly on the vast seventeenth- and eighteenth-century repertoire. The writing of *kabuki* has never stopped, as *noh* did for all practical purposes; one may now see, in the same programme, one play written in 1799, another in 1848, a third in 1916. But the older plays are still preferred, though even these can only rarely be performed in full. *Kanadehon Chushingura*, given in its entirety a few years ago, ran for thirteen hours. Today's productions offer only excerpts, glittering slices of enormous, indigestible wholes.

Kabuki, like *noh*, faced some hazards after the Meiji Restoration, though as it had never been subsidized by the Shogunate its financial position was unchanged. Its content, however, was called into question. In the re-evaluation of the traditional arts that followed contact with the West, *kabuki* was criticized for its superficiality, extravagance and wantonness. The Tokyo Prefecture instructed the theatres not to offer anything which might demean Japan in foreign eyes; the traditional tendency towards the erotic must be curbed, and the theatres offer good, clean, family entertainment. Nor must they present a distorted picture of history. The habit of transposing periods and altering historical names – which had begun as a security measure – was now forbidden. This self-consciousness towards the West was *kabuki*'s greatest danger, though it produced new and often valuable technical advances. Gaslight was introduced in 1872 – an innovation that must have been regretted when eight years later one theatre was blacked out for non-payment of bills. The first proscenium stage in Japan, the Shintomi-za, was built in Tokyo in 1878, and followed by the first Kabuki-za, which opened in 1889 with the full glory of electric light. The present theatre is the fifth on the site. Of its predecessors, two were destroyed by the old enemy, fire, one in the great Tokyo earthquake of 1923, and the fourth in the bombing of 1945. The present building was restored in 1951.

Other compromises with the West were not so well received. A ticking clock was substituted for the traditional clappers (the Japanese equivalent of the French *trois coups*) at the beginning of one performance; new instruments – bugle, music box and xylophone – were heard in the orchestra, and Western fireworks contributed to the stage spectacles. Plays were written on topical themes. A dramatization of the Satsuma Rebellion (the last reactionary opposition to the Meiji Restoration) appeared in 1877, and in 1879 a unique play, *The Wanderer's Strange Story* (subtitled *A Foreign Kabuki*), attempted to combine the theatres of Europe and Japan. In the story a Japanese fisherman was shipwrecked, and in his travels visited the United States, England and France. It included a play within a play, as seen by the fisherman in Paris, performed by Western actors. The audiences roundly condemned it.

It is easy to be facetious about these experiments. The criticisms often levelled against them reflect our own rather condescending theatrical attitudes. One of the favourite legends of the Meiji theatre is of the Japanese Hamlet who entered on a bicycle down the *hanamichi*. It is almost impossible, now, to find out whether this is true or not. *Si non è vero, è ben trovato*; someone once described the Japanese theatre to me as 'a mythology within a mythology that has created its own mythology', and the myth in this case, if myth it is, is sufficiently like other things we know did happen. We laugh at it, and talk glibly about Japanese infatuation with Western technology; but when Puck rides a bicycle on the French stage, as he did at the *Comédie française* in 1965, we talk about theatricalism, biomechanics and the director's right to experiment. We may still be derisive, but for more respectable reasons. Many Japanese were alarmed by the modernization of *kabuki*, and formed societies to study and preserve the old traditions while encouraging a more meaningful content. To this the Meiji government was sympathetic. It saw *kabuki*'s value as a propaganda medium for keeping the public aware of their past. Modern *kabuki* has abandoned its more eccentric experiments and returned to a traditional posture, leaving innovations to the 'new' and 'mixed' forms.

In consequence the former lawless, popular entertainment has now come to be regarded by many as the 'classical' theatre of Japan, while *noh* has receded even further into the background. This attitude is reflected in contemporary scholarship. Faubion Bowers's *Japanese Theatre* belies its title by being concerned almost exclusively with *kabuki*, admitting *noh*, together with the earlier dance-forms, only as an 'influence'. There is some danger, indeed, that *kabuki* will become even more remote by pricing itself out of the popular market. Bowers remarks that in 1940 the price of tickets had risen from 8 yen (the best) to 200 or 300. In 1967 the best seats are 2500 yen and the cheapest 300. This is not entirely due to the devaluation of the currency. Theatregoers tend to be well-to-do; it is also obvious that most of the audiences at the Kabuki-za are middle-aged or over, and women. The poorer devotees crowd the upper balconies, from which they bellow their enthusiasm. These true *aficionados* contribute to the liveliness of the performance by shouting approval and the pet names of their favourite actors at crucial moments of the performance. They are as disciplined as the French *claque* and more genuine; the shouts must be perfectly timed, and require as much knowledge and precision as that displayed by the actors themselves.

One beneficial result of Meiji intervention was a rise in the actors' social status. The Emperor, determined to divest himself of the traditional exclusiveness of his caste, went out of his way to give attention to the popular arts, attending *sumo* wrestling in 1872 and a *kabuki* performance five years later. In 1887 the actor Ichikawa Danjuro IX had the unprecedented honour of a command performance, which did as much for the player in Japan as Queen Victoria's knighting of Henry Irving did for his English contemporary. The old segregation was abolished, and actors were admitted within the pale of respectable society. It is a mark of this new respect that a leading *kabuki* actor has been invited to play the present Emperor in a Japanese film about Pearl Harbour – a peculiarly sensitive role, since it marks the first portrayal of a living Emperor on the screen.

The latest innovation which *kabuki* has to face, seen variously as an asset and a threat, is the establishment of the National Theatre. It opened in 1966, amid controversy. Should it confine itself to native works, or admit Western classics also? At present it operates on a compromise basis. The large hall, since its opening, has been devoted to *kabuki*, and the smaller to occasional Western and modern Japanese plays. *Cyrano de Bergerac* was an almost inevitable choice. What causes chief concern, however, is the composition of the company and the function of the director. The latter is new to *kabuki*, first appearing in 1926 in imitation of Western practice. Traditionally, regulation of the performances was left to the actors themselves, supervised by the head of the 'family'; it is they who have handed down, largely by memory, the traditional gestures and blocking of scenes. The director is a new, and to some dangerous, element, who threatens to disrupt the traditional pattern. Further controversy was aroused when one revival of a play that had not been produced for over a century was entrusted to a university professor of theatre history. Some critics feel that the National Theatre is preoccupied with history at the expense of entertainment, and that the age of a play is no guarantee of its value.

The hand of the director certainly makes itself felt, by no means to the drama's disadvantage. There is a stronger sense of progression and of working towards a climax. The National Theatre productions may be seen as an example of the various attempts to work out a compromise between old techniques and modern attitudes that characterize the modern Japanese theatre at its best. Here, old plays are subtly remoulded by contemporary artistic influence; in the Nissei and other major commercial theatres modern plays are interpreted by traditional techniques. They work from different angles to a common meeting-ground. The National Theatre's most shocking innovation in the eyes of purists is that it cuts across the old family tradition. Actors are drawn from several companies and are no longer acting with their adoptive brothers. The National Theatre has had no time to build a 'family' of its own. This, in the end, may be all to the good; it makes possible the experiments that the older groups, with their instinctive conservatism, have rejected. Some of them are undoubtedly successful. In *Sakura Gimin Den*, for instance, the director takes advantage of the flexibility of *kabuki* speech to emphasize the distinction between two social groups. The court and aristocracy deliver their lines in formal recitative, the peasantry more naturalistically, and this distinction reinforces the sense of two worlds which can never meet. It is by such devices, perhaps, that the ideal combination may be reached: a *kabuki* theatre with modern appeal, but founded firmly on the traditions of the past; a venerable art shaped by a single, unifying hand.

# 5

## Puppet, Mask, Costume, Actor

When the Australian Marionette Theatre played in Tokyo on its
Far Eastern tour, the audience was to some extent predictable.
The *corps diplomatique* was out in force, and there was a substantial contingent of children. There was also something not com-
monly seen at such entertainments in the West: unaccompanied
adults, giving the performance their serious critical attention. In
Japan puppetry is an art for mature minds, demanding no less
creative ability, and no less sophisticated an audience, than its
human counterpart. *Bunraku*, with its traditional hand-operated
puppets, ranks as a major theatrical form. The marionette theatre
employs its own directors and choreographers. All concerned
recognize the dignity of their calling and their responsibility to
live up to the expectations of their public. The typical audience
of the West, which persists in regarding puppetry as children's
entertainment, gets the performances that it deserves.

The puppet theatre of Japan, in the form now known as
*bunraku*, came about from the fusion of two arts as ancient as they
were popular: that of the puppet itself and that of the story-teller.
Prints offer evidence of the steps by which the puppet stage
reached its present highly sophisticated shape. The simplest form
is a box carried by a single showman and revealing a succession of
painted scenes to accompany his narrative. This evolves into something like the 'penny plain, twopence coloured' theatre of
Victorian England, beloved of Robert Louis Stevenson; the
figures are cut out, mounted flat, and moved from the side of the

stage by wires. Articulated figures begin to make their appearance, both in sacred and secular uses. In fact the development
closely parallels the history of the puppet theatre in other cultures: the West, too, produced its religious automata. The
Orient, however, has traditionally preferred figures moved by
rods or trigger-controls, and operated from below or behind
(now best known to the West through Russia, and the tours of
the Moscow State Puppet Theatre), while the West has increasingly favoured the marionette, figures controlled by long strings
from above. It would be tempting to explore the symbolism of
this, particularly as regards the social status of the art in its respective spheres. The Japanese illustrations show the gradual
progression from street performances, with the unconcealed
showman working a puppet held above his head and supported by
a partner with a drum, to more permanent locales. We see
domestic performances, with the figures, each still worked by a
single operator, appearing over the top of a screen; performances
on shrine-stages, including a miniature version of *Funa Benkei*,
which is mechanically highly elaborate and supported by an
orchestra in the same position as for *kagura* and *noh*; and finally
the theatre acquiring its own premises, with the audience at first
seated haphazardly on the open ground before the stage, and later
corralled within partitions in the manner of *kabuki*. Awaji Island,
on the Inland Sea, is regarded as the cradle of the puppet art in its
classical form, with three operators to each figure. Performances
were first given on the island in the late sixteenth century, and
have flourished there in the Ningyo-za to this day.

The puppet theatre was originally a popular, and therefore
despised, entertainment. It rose to respectability, and became a
cult, through its association with the more prestigious art of
*joruri*. The public story-teller was an important figure in early
Japanese as in other cultures, particularly those of the East. The
concomitant of illiteracy is a thriving oral tradition. One may still
see in Japan, and particularly in Osaka, this tradition embodied
in the *rakugo*, or reciter of humorous monologues. He sits on a
*tatami* mat on the stage and entertains the audience with long
anecdotes, sometimes using simple properties, but usually relying

on the unaided power of his voice. His performance is now built into something like the British music-hall programme as it used to be, together with *manzai*, conjurers and musical acts. *Joruri* represents a similar, though more elaborate, tradition, aimed at a more sophisticated audience: the recitation of metrical romance to *samisen* accompaniment. The combination of *joruri* and puppets created a new kind of entertainment, which in turn inspired a mania that seriously threatened *kabuki*; the actors, as we have seen, were forced to fight back by appropriating many of the puppet techniques.

Osaka's first theatre in the new tradition, the Takemoto-za, was founded in 1685 by Takemoto Gidayu, the reciter, and Chikamatsu Monzaemon. The fame of the former was so great that only his immediate successor ventured to adopt his personal stage name: similar deference has been shown to some of the great names of *kabuki*. It received, however, the ultimate accolade of adoption as a common noun: *gidayu-bushi* (*gidayu-narrative*) is used as an alternative to *joruri*, and *kabuki*, which derives more than half its repertoire from this source, calls such plays *gidayu-mono*. In 1703 Gidayu's former disciple Toyotake Wakadayu founded his own theatre in the Dotombori district, still one of Osaka's major amusement centres. The tenth inheritor of his name has recently died. The stage family names of these two men have been perpetuated by all subsequent *joruri* chanters. Several smaller theatres were founded at the same time.

The sudden overwhelming popularity that the puppet theatre enjoyed in the early eighteenth century (a time when it was also particularly popular in England and there, too, rivalled the actors on their own ground) remains the most conspicuous historical example, in the performing arts, of the fads and crazes to which the Japanese temperament was susceptible. It was this tendency that the Shogunate so distrusted and did its best to curb, in its political applications; it has appeared again and again in modern times – notably in the Meiji craze for imitating all things Western, and in more specific manifestations. *Pachinko* parlours, containing row upon row of pin-ball machines, appeared some years ago, and are still part of the urban scene; the contemporary craze is for *discothèques* and coffee-bars which specialize in the music of one school or one composer. The enthusiasm for the puppet theatre attracted the attention of serious artists – Izumo, Sosuko, Kaion, Hanji, all illustrious names in Japanese literature, as well as Chikamatsu himself. Donald Keene has compared it to the Elizabethan public theatre as an essentially popular art ennobled by great poetry. It is at this point that the histories of the puppet theatre in East and West conspicuously diverge. *Bunraku*, for most of its history, has enjoyed the privileged and largely protected status accorded to high art, while the puppet theatre of the West, in general, has seen a systematic decline.

Overwhelmed in turn by a remodelled *kabuki*, the Osaka theatres closed their doors about seventy years later, and their personnel suffered considerable hardship. Some hired themselves out as domestic entertainers; there is an echo of this in the pseudo-*bunraku* offered at Gion, in Kyoto, as part of a cabaret. Many were scattered through the country districts, teaching their art to enthusiastic farmers. About a hundred villages are known to preserve puppet heads dating from this time and now regarded as national treasures. Some districts also evolved their own artistic variations: one of these, *koruma ningyo*, is described at the end of this chapter.

It was an outsider who restored the art to urban favour. Uemura Bunrakuken, an antique dealer and collector of curios, came to Osaka from Awaji Island, which had a long connection with puppetry. Impelled by his own fondness for *joruri*, he recovered the professionals from poverty, assembled a new company, and began performances in the city. Little information remains about the early programmes – his name first appears in connection with the art in 1811 – but in 1872 a new theatre, the Bunraku-za was formally opened, along with several imitators. Thus *bunraku*, originally a personal name, has now become the standard term for the puppet theatre. The other groups dissolved under the Meiji Restoration, but the Bunraku-za survives. Its company performs in Osaka for most of the year, supported by its local club of patrons, and tours at intervals, particularly to Kyoto and the National Theatre in Tokyo.

Although the *joruri* and the puppet-theatre have been spoken of as combining, the literary art preserved its superior status. This is immediately evident in the theatre, where the chanter and his *samisen* accompanist sit in a place apart and have their names announced before each performance – an honour not accorded to the manipulators. In *kabuki* the *joruri* element is often dominated by the size and scenic splendour of the stage. In *bunraku* the chanter, by virtue of his size, dominates the action more easily and more frequently. This distinction is also obvious in the social history of the art, where the chanters came to enjoy privileges that the manipulators were denied. It is important, too, in *bunraku* theory. The narrative element is of the utmost importance. Though the puppets are allowed their own display of individual virtuosity, they are regarded primarily as illustrating the recitation. The chanter does not put words into their mouths; they fit their actions to his words. The puppets are not independent performers, but an extension of the *joruri* into visual terms.

The *bunraku* stage, in the form to which it finally evolved, is much smaller than that for *kabuki*, but with its own complexity. Operators stand on the stage floor, wearing wooden clogs, which they stamp to provide appropriate sound effects, and often use in the manner of the clappers on the *kabuki* stage. They are partially concealed from sight by a permanent groundrow, rather lower than waist-high, and set as far as possible downstage, and by other successively higher partitions which form part of the set proper. In a complicated set there may be several of these, dividing the depth of the stage into distinct and parallel acting areas. The operators move from one to another – i.e. upstage or downstage – through small swinging doors, or a panel temporarily removed. These doors, in some cases, are kept shut tight when not in use by a device which seems astonishingly crude compared to the sophistication of the rest of the performance: a delicate scene is often interrupted by the appearance of a disembodied arm, which proceeds, obviously and noisily, to hammer the doors together with a large staple. However, one soon learns to ignore this, like the conventional devices of the larger theatres. Scenery is, of necessity, comparatively simple. A permanent door on each side, hung with a black curtain, gives access to the downstage area. If the setting involves a house – as it usually does – this is set upstage behind another, higher groundrow, and enclosed by hanging panels at the sides; these are removed bodily by one of the operators to allow entrances and exits. There may be other entrances along the rear wall. Most *bunraku* scenery is hung, its lower edges coming just below the audience's line of vision, to give the operators the minimum of obstruction on stage level. In exterior settings some set pieces may be used – walls, gateways and so

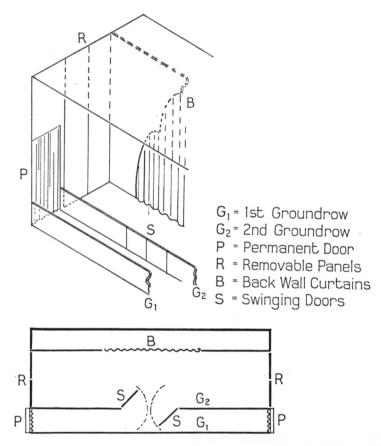

$G_1$ = 1st Groundrow
$G_2$ = 2nd Groundrow
P = Permanent Door
R = Removable Panels
B = Back Wall Curtains
S = Swinging Doors

Fig. 10. Typical *bunraku* interior scene and stage plan

forth – which cut across the acting area, but these are few in number. For the most part, settings are composed in a series of horizontal planes, running parallel to the footlights and ending in a canvas backdrop. (See Fig. 10.) *Kabuki* itself, largely under *bunraku* influence, has tended to follow the same pattern.

There is an obvious necessity for unimpeded movement. With three operators working each figure, even a simple dialogue scene must find room for six people besides the puppets. As the action becomes more complex and characters multiply, there may well be twenty operators or more on stage at the same time. In scenes of duel and battle, they must judge their movements and positions to a hair's-breadth to avoid chaos. Working *vis-à-vis* each other, they evolve their own precise choreography, of which the audience is rarely aware, but which is as demanding as any ballet. *Bunraku* is unique among the major puppet theatres of the world in leaving its operators largely unconcealed. They are in view from the waist up. The assistants wear black robes and pointed hoods with minute eyeholes, which give them conventional invisibility: they resemble to this extent the stage assistants of *kabuki* in their dress and function. But in most cases the principal operator for each figure, who ranks as a major artist and controls the most important movements, is unmasked, and his face is visible beside the puppet's head throughout. He may wear white or more resplendent colours, in contrast to his assistants' black, and in the bravura pieces (such as the final scene of *Honcho Nijushi Ko*, described below), which call for extreme technical virtuosity, all three operators may play barefaced and in lavish robes. On television, where the close-up imposes different demands, the master surrenders his privilege and wears a black hood like the others.

However, any description makes the operators seem more obtrusive than they are. Their presence does not dominate that of the puppets. On the contrary, they become part of the framework within which the puppets operate. As in the *noh* play the lavish costumes of the figures provide a focal point; from this the operators, in their various degrees of dress, shade off into the background. In the natural course of things the three operators are rarely visible at once. When the puppet is in profile, the two assistants are masked by their chief; when it turns full face, the puppet itself is large enough to mask one of them, or two if the costume is a full one. Sometimes the operators loom against the background like the puppets' shadows. In a duel or mêlée (like the forcible tattooing of Toza in *Kamakura Sandai Ki*, described below), when six or nine operators are working in a tight cluster, wheeling and turning with their characters, one has the uncanny impression of a black thundercloud from which lightning shoots forth – the lightning being the vivid costumes of the puppets as they poise and strike. But, as in *kabuki*, the mechanics are always obvious if one cares to look. It is this that frees *bunraku* from the awful coyness which is Western puppetry's besetting sin – the total concealment of the operator and the pretence that the characters are 'little people' with a life of their own. An audience whose intelligence is thus insulted can hardly be expected to take the puppet theatre seriously; and to this cause, perhaps more than any other, we may attribute the low esteem in which the art is usually held. *Bunraku* makes no such pretence. It admits that the puppet is only a means to an end, and asks for the audience's complicity in the enterprise, just as the *noh* and *kabuki* actors offer no illusion of being real people, but frankly and openly display the techniques of their art.

The puppets command attention for their mechanical ingenuity and the perfection of their dress and carriage. The principal figures are about four feet high, with fully articulated arms, legs and hands; the eyes open and close, the eyebrows move up and down. In manipulation the master puppeteer controls the head, trunk and right arm. His left hand, inserted into the puppet's body, grasps an elaborate trigger control which works the head and facial movements by whalebone springs. His right hand operates a similar control for the puppet's hand, though he may sometimes insert his arm into the puppet's sleeve and use his hand to substitute for its own. The first assistant operates the left arm in the same way, and the second the legs. Co-ordination with other operators is the hardest technical feat for any puppeteer to master. Here it is particularly difficult, for the conditions of the art demand that three men shall think, move and feel as one, and they rehearse meticulously until a perfect rapport is achieved. Ideally this demands years of training, and as long as *bunraku* was practised, like *kabuki*, as a hereditary art, this is what it had. The old masters spent years in apprenticeship, and learnt, often painfully (they were beaten if they made mistakes) to see the puppet as virtually another limb, an extension of themselves. Those days have gone. It once took twenty years to make a master puppeteer; it now takes five. This tends to be apparent in performance. One critic lamented to me that even old men, trained in the strict manner, could support a puppet's head for long periods without a tremor; even young operators cannot do this now.

The discipline of movement, however, is still extraordinary. Normally attention is concentrated, as in *kabuki*, on one figure at a time, while the others subside into quiescence; but in the duels and other scenes of concerted action there is no faltering. Again as in *kabuki* it would be possible to stop the play at any given moment and see a perfectly balanced tableau. The movements are not completely representational, and reproduction of the more prosaic gestures is avoided. With puppets of this sort there can be no floor for them to walk on. In theory they tread an imaginary floor, level with the top of the groundrow. In practice, even this is often ignored. The figures may be held some distance above it to give them prominence, or be moved from point to point in sitting position without an intervening walk. This sort of realism is not *bunraku*'s aim. Though there may be passages of perfectly reproduced naturalistic movement (as, for example, in the fingering of a *samisen*), these are seen as self-contained *tours de force* within a conventional framework. There is no overriding pretence that the puppets are really people and, consequently, no compulsion on them to obey the normal physical laws. Undressed, the figures are often deliberately grotesque. A warrior stripped down to his tattoo marks shows a distorted muscular development and a peasant woman has enormous pendulous breasts. Size is similarly determined by convention. Subsidiary figures are smaller than the principals; though this may be used occasionally to give

an illusion of diminishing perspective, it basically reflects a
pictorial convention at least as old as the Egyptians, whereby a
character's rank is indicated by his physical stature. The minor
figures, also, have fewer mechanics, and only one operator. In
the more complex characters, the eyebrows are the most expressive features. Something of this has permeated into modern
media; the Japanese animated cartoon primarily uses eyes and
eyebrows to establish mood and character, where its Western
counterpart animates the whole face.

The assistant operators function also as occasional property
men, aided by others who do nothing else. They help the puppet
to hold objects, unfold scrolls or fans for him, and remove things
he has discarded; they assist in costume changes, which are almost
as frequent and as ornate as in *kabuki*; they move screens, open
doors, and function as Master of Ceremonies to introduce the
chanter and his accompanist.

The chanter, as we have seen, is an artist in his own right. He
sits in a decorated alcove at stage left, with his script on a small
stand before him. Usually one man takes all the voices, shifting
pitch and tone as demanded, and narrating the intervening passages. He is a combination of Chorus and *raconteur*, who at the
same time holds dialogues with himself. Occasionally there may
be two chanters, taking individual parts in important dialogue
scenes. They are replaced frequently (by means of a revolve, as
in *kabuki*), for their performance is an exhausting one. They enter
completely into the emotions of the play, laughing, weeping,
shrieking, growling; here they contrast markedly with the
operators, who remain grave and impassive throughout, for any
flicker of emotion on their faces would upstage the puppets.
They finish their performance bathed in sweat.

Two of the great *joruri* chanters, both products of the Meiji
Era, have recently died: Toyotake Wakadayu at the age of seventy-
eight, and Yamashiro Shojo at seventy-six. Wakadayu, though
almost blind, remained active till the end; unable to see his
script, he would recite from memory, turning over a handful of
pages from time to time as a gesture. He had been in the profession from his early boyhood, and become a master-reciter at

the age of thirteen. The work of these two men shows the range of individual styles possible, even under so strict a discipline. Wakadayu was known for his more natural, unaffected delivery; Shojo was a romantic, particularly effective in the pathos of *sewamono* plays. With their passing, *bunraku* has lost an important link with its history.

The chanter continued to enjoy prestige even when the art as a whole had fallen into disrepute. In the first half of the nineteenth century, when the popularity of *bunraku* was once more high, the artists, like the *kabuki* players, became known for their extravagant living. The Shogunate included them in its sumptuary laws — the more strict, perhaps, because it saw its own power dwindling. From 1842 stringent regulations restricted the puppet theatre personnel to certain sectors of the city. Later amendments created a significant distinction. *Kabuki* actors and puppeteers were still confined, but *joruri* chanters were permitted to live where they liked. In the Meiji Era, *bunraku* suffered from the establishment of the capital, both *de jure* and *de facto*, in Tokyo. Its traditional stronghold was in Osaka, and when the Imperial Household moved from Kyoto, it came to be looked down upon as a provincial art. Tokyo audiences liked the plays, but not the puppets; they were traditionally inclined to favour *kabuki* or marionettes. Some chanters profited by this, acquiring large Tokyo followings by giving solo recitations and severing the play from the puppet action. Another consequence of the move may be seen in the sporadic attempts made by *bunraku* to modernize itself, and to conform with the Western tastes now so fashionable in the capital. In 1891 in Tokyo the *bunraku* produced *Nikko-zan*, a play set at Nikko and showing a love affair between a foreigner and a *geisha*; a further concession was the use of English words for comic effect. The play was a failure, closing after three days. *Bunraku* today, like *kabuki*, relies chiefly on the traditional repertoire.

There is, perhaps, no need to go into this repertoire in detail. Because of *bunraku*'s enormous influence on *kabuki*, what has been said about one can be taken as applying to the other. A brief description of two typical plays will suffice.

G

*Kamakura Sandai Ki* (*Kamakura Trilogy*), written by several playwrights in collaboration, was first staged on Osaka in 1748 under
a different title. It was banned shortly afterwards by the Tokugawa Shogunate because of the political relevance of its theme: it
dealt with the battle of Osaka Castle (1614–15) in which
Tokugawa Ieasu, the founder of the dynasty, took a prominent
part. After eleven years it was restaged in an altered version,
with the title and the names of the principal characters changed.
Tokugawa Ieasu became Tokimasa Hojo, and Yukimura Sanada,
his enemy, Takatsuna Sasaki. The involved plot shows the latter
engaged in guerrilla warfare against the Shogunate and confusing
his opponents by assuming different identities. Captured while
disguised as a farmer named Toza, he convinces the Shogun that
he is harmless by refusing to acknowledge his real wife and embracing Toza's. His impersonation is so successful that Hojo employs him as a retainer, though first forcibly tattooing him to ensure that there will be no more mistakes. The false Toza is sent
on a delicate mission to Hojo's daughter, Tokihime, who has run
away from her father to marry one of his enemies. He is instructed
to persuade her to turn against her new family and return.

Tokihime is living in reduced circumstances with her betrothed
Miuranosuke, and his old mother. This gives an opportunity for
one of the self-contained comic scenes that *kabuki* also enjoys.
Tokihime is one of the pampered aristocracy, a 'scarlet princess',
who cannot adjust to the demands of a humble domestic life. We
see her vainly engaged in household chores. An old servant, a
splendid comic character much addicted to *sake*, gives her a
vigorous demonstration of how things should be done; she tucks
a mixing-bowl between her feet and stirs with frantic energy and
washes rice with equal enthusiasm. It is at moments like this that
the operators come into their own; it is their technical virtuosity that is on display here, and not the literary art of *joruri*.
The false Toza enters the house on his commission and hides in a
well, from which, with one mighty spear-thrust, he impales one
of Hojo's spies; then, revealing himself in his true character, he
urges Miuranosuke back to the fight. The mother, who is dying,
throws herself on a spear, for fear that her son's affection for her

will keep him from his duty. The scene ends with Sasaki posturing in the branches of a pine-tree, and Miuranosuke in a martial attitude below, while, in the background, Tokihime weeps over the old woman's body.

*Tsubosaka Reigen Ki* (*Miracle at Tsubosaka*), though written in the Meiji Era, preserves the classical values in a fable of a wife's devotion to her blind husband. Noticing that she regularly leaves the house at the same time each morning, he accuses her of having a lover. She explains that she has been going to the Goddess of Mercy at the Tsubosaka temple to pray for his sight to be restored. Humbled and contrite, the husband accompanies her, and persuades her to leave him for three days fasting as a penance. As soon as she has gone he climbs with enormous difficulty to the cliff-top and throws himself down, so that he may be a burden to her no longer. Discovering the body and maddened with grief, she follows him to death. The scene changes to the valley where their crumpled bodies lie. A light glows from the rock; it is the goddess herself, so moved by their devotion that she restores them to life. As the rays of the morning sun appear symbolically above the mountains, the husband discovers that he also has his sight again. The play closes with their dance of joy.

These brief descriptions should make it obvious that *bunraku* and *kabuki* move in the same world, with the same observances and standards. Decorum is paramount. Individual desires and passions must be subordinated to the harsh requirements of the social code. Tragedy occurs when loyalties conflict. The death of an individual (as in the case of Miuranosuke's mother) is justified by larger necessities. We see, as in *kabuki*, the superman hero, supreme embodiment of the qualities of the *samurai*; we see, too, the fatalism which can lapse so easily into sentimentality. In many cases, of course, the plays are substantially the same. A large part of the *kabuki* repertoire consists of rewritten adaptations of *bunraku* predecessors. The two forms share the dangers of their material, as they share its possibilities. *Bunraku*, like *kabuki*, is prohibited from topicality, and must keep its social satire within tolerable limits. The scene between Tokihime and the maid-servant is a case in point. There can be no real satire of the princess herself, who belongs to the ruling classes. The attack is oblique, with the servant exploited as the comic figure. It might be noticed, incidentally, that *bunraku* employs the parallel divisions of the acting area much as *kabuki* uses different stage levels to depict a stratified society whose groups rarely, if ever, come into physical contact with each other.

In their technical means of expression, also, *kabuki* and *bunraku* have much in common. Some of the more obvious similarities have already been pointed out. Both theatres use the same striped curtains, in the same three colours. *Bunraku* puppeteers and *kabuki* property men perform largely similar functions. The *joruri* chanter has the same function and position in both. *Bunraku*, in one of its more recent innovations, has even acquired its own *hanamichi*, recessed so that the operators are still half concealed. *Kabuki*, in taking over the puppet plays, often copied the costumes to the last detail, together with much of the acting style. The actor may use bodily movement as a substitute for facial expression, but the puppet must; it is here that the *kabuki* actor most clearly shows his affiliations. This has been noted previously, in connection with the *mie*. When the *kabuki* protagonist, with his mask-like make-up, strikes his triumphant and contorted pose, eyes rolling and eyebrows working frantically, he is imitating his puppet counterpart. These affinities reveal themselves also in more subtle ways. We have seen *kabuki* drama as being concerned primarily with the conflict of self-interest and social obligation, in which the latter inevitably wins. *Bunraku*, by its staging, reinforces this doctrine. The characters are  literally, manipulated by forces larger than themselves – their operators; they have no independence, no volition of their own, but must conform to the pattern that has been laid down for them, and the lines that are prescribed for them to speak. The effect that *kabuki* accomplishes by the depersonalization of the actor is produced in *bunraku* by the conditions of its being.

There are, of course, substantial differences. The splendour and ingenuity of *kabuki* scenery are largely denied to *bunraku*, though  the  latter  has  its  own  mechanical  compensations. *Bunraku* has no revolve, but can use the slip-stage. At the end of

*Kamakura Sandai Ki,* the house which has occupied stage centre for most of the action is slid half-way into the wings, while trees are moved on simultaneously from the right. It is as if our point of vision has moved, so that we now see a corner of the house and the garden beyond. The scenery itself is operable, like a more elaborate puppet; it can be taken apart and reassembled to allow the movement of the operators and the characters they hold. When Takatsuna Sasaki climbs his tree, the branches move upwards on wires to give us a better view of him. Stage lifts allow the settings, operators and all, to rise and fall; thus, in *Tsubosaka Reigen Ki,* we see first the cliff-top and the shrine, and then the valley beneath. Doors open in walls, hedges and apparently solid rock. The principle is the same as in *kabuki* and in *noh.* The setting does not impose itself on the action, but adjusts to it, following the needs of the immediate dramatic moment.

In some ways *bunraku,* working on a smaller scale in a more intimate theatre, uses mechanics to convey what *kabuki* must do by suggestion. We have already seen the *kabuki* version of *Honcho Nijushi Ko* (pp. 158, 166), in which the girl steals the fox-plumed helmet, the famous heirloom, to give to her lover and her father's enemy, and is guided by the spirit of the fox across

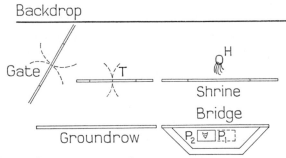

H = Helmet in niche
P₁ = Panel for trick reflections
P₂ = Pool
T = Trick door with painted bush and
    lantern used for costume changes

Fig. 11. *Honcho Nijushi Ko, bunraku* version

the frozen lake. In the original *bunraku* version things happen
rather differently. The set shows the girl's garden, with a gate
on the right, the shrine holding the helmet on the left, and a
bush and lantern painted flat on a set piece stage centre. Downstage left, forming part of the front groundrow, is a painted pool
spanned by a bridge (see Fig. 11). We see, first, the fox in person.
He is an endearing creation, snow-white, and worked by a single
operator. He scratches his ear ingratiatingly with his hindpaw,
trots over to the shrine, and makes friendly and protective gestures
towards the helmet. As the girl steals through the gate the fox
vanishes. Taking the helmet from its place she approaches the
bridge and sees the image of the fox reflected in the pool below.
In *kabuki* this is done entirely by suggestion. In *bunraku* we see the
magical reflection for ourselves. The pool is tilted towards us,
defying the laws of nature, and the reflection is painted on a
sliding panel worked on strings by a property man sitting in full
view at the corner of the stage. With a click the head appears;
another click and it has gone. The girl is possessed by the spirit
of the fox. Hanging the helmet on the wall, she dances. Her
movements grow vulpine, and there is a magnificent costume
change: swirling behind the bush at stage centre, she reappears
through it (by a trick door) almost instantaneously, dressed now
in snow white instead of flame red. She crawls, sniffs and scratches;
the helmet itself begins to dance, and two foxes, no less, come
out to join them. The curtain closes on an ecstatic tableau in
which girl, helmet and foxes have become one, animated by the
same spirit.

Mechanical considerations also determine the greater degree
of physical brutality to be found in *bunraku*. *Kabuki* is often brutal
enough, and ingenious in devising new and bloody means of
slaughter – a reflection of the philosophy that human suffering,
like human happiness, is ephemeral, so that death too can be
viewed as a passing spectacle. But *kabuki* is limited by working
with flesh and blood, so that it must often stop short of the extremes of violence. In practice, it is not as bloodthirsty as the
scripts make it sound, and works more often by suggestion. The
sword-thrusts never connect, red ribbons stand for blood, and

the severed heads are not only dummies, but obvious dummies. Climactic acts of violence are hidden from the audience, but foreshadowed by stage action. A girl who is about to commit suicide and then be beheaded predicts her fate by snapping the head off a doll. A man about to stab his enemy through a wall first plunges his spear through a paper lantern, extinguishing the light; the smaller action presages the larger, and we do not actually see the death. (It turns out, in true *kabuki* style, that he has really stabbed his own mother.) *Bunraku*, however, admits no such impediments, and takes advantage of its insensate actors to present scenes of violence which are protracted and horrifying. *Natsu Matsuri Naniwa Ki (Story of a Summer Festival)* contains a famous murder scene on an empty plot of ground in Osaka. It is a sultry summer evening with a festival going on near by. Danshichi meets his grasping father-in-law, Giheiji, argues with him, loses patience, and goes berserk. He repeatedly stabs, kicks and hacks his victim. The old man's body is tossed over the partition, the operators scrambling underneath to catch it; filthy, bedraggled and streaming with blood, the dying man clings to his murderer's foot; only after every drop of agony has been extracted from the scene is the writhing, screaming body given the *coup de grâce*. In *Tsubosaka Reigen Ki*, the scene of the blind man climbing the cliff is given the same treatment. He stumbles and falls, hurts his feet on the rock and his face on the branches of a tree; only after this has been exploited to the full is he allowed to jump. Yet puppetry, by its nature, depersonalizes. What would be revolting if portrayed by live actors, here assumes the quality of malevolent and tainted poetry, which no less reveals the darker side of the Japanese character.

Up to this point we have been considering *noh*, *kabuki* and *bunraku* as three distinct, though historically related, manifestations of the dramatic impulse, answering different needs and functioning, at least in the case of the first two, in widely different social milieux. We have seen, at the same time, how freely one could borrow from another. But this borrowing – not only of plays, but of stage techniques – is possible only because the three forms, for all their superficial differences, subscribe to a common concept of theatrical art. The relationship between the puppet theatre and its flesh-and-blood counterpart is indicative of what this concept is.

In the English-speaking world today the puppet theatre is barely tolerated. Relegated to the theatrical basement, it is viewed, if at all, with amused condescension, classed either as folk-art or as children's entertainment, and considered unworthy of serious critical notice. It is alarming to find how this attitude has even infiltrated Western writing on *bunraku*. Donald Keene prefaces an otherwise excellent book by comparing puppets to performing monkeys, a statement which infuriates because it so completely misses the point. The puppets, at least in this context, are not aping the live actors, but responding to the same artistic pressures which shape the actors' own performance.

This condescending view of puppet art has not always existed; it does not, even today, in many European countries. Yves Joly in Paris, Hermann Aicher in Salzburg, and numerous companies in Germany and Switzerland are devoted to the fostering of the puppet theatre as a mature and sensitive art, infinitely expressive and combining the flexibility of film with the immediacy of stage performance. Trnka in Czechoslovakia and Obratzov in Russia have used the medium to make serious statements about the human condition. Puppetry's satirical possibilities have been widely recognized in Europe. Its power of abstraction allows it to comment without offence. In Fascist Italy the puppet stage offered political satire which would never have been tolerated from live actors. In the communist countries it has been regularly used for propaganda purposes, and in India to publicize birth-control. Though the subjects may not be high art, they recognize the power of the medium. Subjects too elevated or too delicate for human handling have found a natural home on the puppet stage. One may, by choosing one's places well, see performances ranging from a complete realization of a Mozart opera to 'pure' puppetry, manipulated abstractions which bear the same relationship to the art of the stage as Norman McLaren's films to that of the cinema.

Even here, however, puppetry is normally considered a

separate art, responsive to its own rules and disciplines, and drawing on talents other than those of the live theatre. In Japan this has not been the case. From its inception *bunraku*'s affinities with its flesh-and-blood counterpart were recognized, and its overwhelming popularity attracted artists from other fields. From it *kabuki* borrowed plays, techniques and a new acting style. *Bunraku* and *kabuki* became inextricably merged and mutually influential. Though the puppets may have owed their early supremacy to a fad, they retained interest by their merits and by their uncontested right to be considered on the same terms as the actors. This position, despite economic problems and rival attractions, they still hold.

Why should this affinity have existed in Japan, when it so conspicuously has not done so in other countries? Most Western puppet theorists, now, would argue that the puppet theatre's prime function is to do what the live theatre cannot do, and explore areas denied to actors limited by their humanity. This view would countenance the abstractions practised by Yves Joly, and currently by Bil Baird in his new warehouse theatre in New York, as well as such forms as the 'space opera' offered by the Puppet Theatre of Danzig, which utilizes the puppeteer's ability to animate the normally inanimate and transcend the customary stage limitations of space and time in a way normally possible, at great expense, only to film. Japan exploits these possibilities too. I saw, on television, a flirtation between a businessman's umbrella and a frilly parasol, both invested with almost human characteristics, fluttering, spreading, waltzing and ending with an uncomfortably graphic seduction. The idea is not new, but the objects were handled with a precision and economy of movement characteristically Japanese. I watched, too, in the NHK television studios, the taping of a children's show in which puppets played an important part. It was one of a regular morning series involving a family of rabbits (played by children in enormous padded costumes) lost in a wood. The Queen of the Forest sent help in the form of echoes. These were what can only be called science-fiction marionettes. One was spherical, with bulging eyes rotating with a ratchet sound; the body opened like a clam

G 2

and a radio aerial rose from inside. Another had a body made of springs and eyes that lit up. A third was built like a pyramid of child's blocks, and could take himself apart and reassemble himself in various ways.

But these are modern forms. The traditional puppet theatre in Japan has confined itself to doing what, as its history shows, actors *could* do; and the reason for this lies in the approach of the classical actor to his art. It is therefore appropriate, at this point, to recapitulate briefly, and consider the live actor and the puppet not as separate phenomena, but as manifestations of the same dramatic impulse.

The art of the theatre, from the Greeks to the present day, has assumed innumerable particular manifestations; but all of these may be divided into two main groups, embodying diametrically opposed conceptions of the function of the stage and its relationship to the audience. These have gone by different names, more or less precise, from time to time – 'naturalistic' and 'conventional', 'realistic' and 'formal' and, in current terminology, 'representational' and 'presentational' theatre. Representational theatre aims at offering a slice of life. It puts the audience into the position of Ebenezer Scrooge in *A Christmas Carol*, who by supernatural means is conducted through other people's houses and allowed an intimate glimpse of their lives while remaining unobserved himself. In the theatre the audience is the unobserved observer. Behind the curtain lies a 'real' world of which it is permitted controlled glimpses. The scenic arts are dedicated to reproducing actuality as closely as they can. When the designer paints a house, he makes it look like a real house. The actor dresses, moves and speaks the way his character would do in real life. Representational theatre varies from period to period according to the technical resources available, prevailing artistic conventions and the current definition of realism; as we saw in connection with *noh* acting, what is realistic in one frame of reference may be formal in another. Restoration comedy, for instance, must be classed as representational theatre, though its techniques seem highly artificial to us now. Most of the theatre we now see is of the representational type. It has reached one peak in the productions of the Moscow Arts Theatre, where every move, every nuance of sound and lighting is devoted to reproducing the larger world outside, and where the actors investigate their characters as they would the case histories of living people, informing their impersonations with psychology. It has reached another on film and television. The camera has a wider range; instead of reproducing real locations on stage, it can bring their actuality to the screen. Television cultivates the feeling that we are looking through a peephole into someone else's home. The small screen, like the proscenium arch, becomes a one-way window.

Of course this reproduction of actuality must be controlled. There would be no artistic satisfaction in watching real characters playing themselves on the stage. Real life is diffuse, unco-ordinated and distressingly untidy. In the theatre, action must be manipulated to provide a climax and a resolution; movement must be patterned to be meaningful; dialogue must trim the random irrelevancies of normal conversation and progress towards an end. The theatre has occasionally experimented with taking real people off the streets and asking them to be themselves on the stage; the result is, almost inevitably, disastrous. The audience expects the performance to look real, not be real; the two are not necessarily the same thing. There is a famous story of David Belasco, high priest of American naturalism, painting the leaves of a plant a vivid, unnatural green, to make them look natural on the stage. The cinema may cast non-professionals – documentary films regularly do this, and the neo-realistic Italian directors have used them with conspicuous success – but here, though the performers' responses may be natural, untrained and uninhibited, they must be shaped into the finished product. Art is made on the cutting-room floor, where the director gives his raw material order and form. Representational theatre, then, may be very strictly controlled – in the Moscow Arts Theatre actors are rehearsed to the last flicker of an eyebrow – but the control is not permitted to be too apparent. The finished work preserves the surface illusion of actuality. If we become too aware of the control – if a climax, for instance, is too suddenly or obviously heightened, or if the character-motivation is too arbitrary – we grow uneasy and call the play artificial.

In such a theatre the audience has no part in the performance. It cannot have, for this would disturb the illusion of reality. It is assumed from the beginning that the actors are in one place, the audience in another, and that the two cannot merge. The actors must keep up an elaborate pretence of being unconscious of the audience's presence, though in fact they are keenly aware of it. They sense its mood and modulate their performances accordingly; they pause for laughs. But they must not show they are aware. When John Barrymore stalked down to the footlights and snarled at a boor reading a newspaper in the front row, he was breaking the fundamental rule of representational theatre.

Presentational theatre makes no such pretence, and imposes no such barrier. It admits from the beginning that the play is a play and the stage a stage. It does not try to delude the audience with scenery. Normally its stage represents no particular place or period. It may be decorated, like the Greek, with an architectural façade, or, as in *noh*, with a painted tree; but these serve as background merely, and set off the action without confining it. Even when some realistic elements are used, as in the elaborate constructions of *kabuki*, they are set within a formal frame, and admit the artifice by exposing the mechanics. *Kabuki* changes its sets in full or half light. The audience enjoys the machinery as much as the picture, and is constantly reminded that it is watching stage scenery, not the real thing. Costumes, though deriving from everyday life, show their essentially theatrical nature in their colour and design. They could not be worn in the street. Deliberately artificial elements, like the masks of *noh* and Greek tragedy, or the exaggerated make-up of *kabuki*, divorce the actor from real life.

The same is true of the characters: they exist only on the stage. Representational characters are presumed to have an off-stage life which has begun before the curtain rises and continues after it falls. Modern actors, particularly those trained in the Stanislavsky system (arrogantly canonized as The Method, as if there were only one), re-create this off-stage life to find the key to their own performances. Stanislavsky, in directing *Othello*, prepared a dossier on every character accounting for his on-stage presence by a series of incidents, which Shakespeare did not write, in his off-stage past. Actors are encouraged to select incidents from their own past, by 'emotional recall', suitable to the character they are playing, and to give his actions psychological continuity by identifying with him. Acting, to use a current catch-phrase, is being.

The presentational character, on the other hand, has no off-stage life at all. His costume, gestures and, usually, language label him 'performer'. His behaviour has meaning only on the stage, and can exist only within the established conventions of the performance. This attitude is symbolized by the *kabuki* habit of elevating characters through the stage floor, already posed in a striking tableau. It is perfectly appropriate. They come from nowhere, they go nowhere. Their life is contained within the proscenium arch. They are a phenomenologist's delight; they cease to exist when no-one is looking at them. The West offers few such examples of the pure presentational style. There is one striking analogy, however, and a famous one: the Cocteau-Stravinsky oratorio *Oedipus Rex*. For the libretto Cocteau used his own version of Latin, which was neither classical nor ecclesiastical, though it had affinities with both. It was stage Latin, deliberately formulated as a theatrical language, and valid only within the terms of the performance. The characters were larger-than-life puppets. Creon entered, like the *kabuki* players, from underground. It is this attitude that colours the traditional Japanese performance. The language of *noh* and *kabuki* is Japanese, but outmoded, surviving only on the stage, and its artificiality is emphasized by the delivery. Though the actors may be playing characters drawn from history or contemporary life, they make no attempt to reproduce the way they actually dressed, moved or spoke. In real life the general Yoshitsune was a commanding figure with a long drooping moustache. The stage Yoshitsune in *Funa Benkei* is a small boy in armour. Here, acting is conspicuously not being. The audience accepts the boy as Yoshitsune because it accepts the rules of the game, the theatrical convention evolved from tradition, formulated in performance and familiar to both sides of the house. Knowledge of these rules is a pre-requisite. Without it the performance becomes as meaningless as a cricket match to a Congolese, or a tribal rite to an urban cricketer.

By demolishing pretences the presentational theatre can admit the presence of the audience. There is no barrier, tangible or otherwise, which permanently divides the two. Action can evolve in the midst of the audience, as it does on the *hanamichi*, or in the *orchestra* of the Greek theatre; the audience may be directly addressed, as happens in *kabuki*, *noh*, and both Greek and Eliza-bethan drama. Actors and audience are regarded as co-operating in the presentation; the actors' costumes and stage behaviour serve only to give them emphasis, not to set them completely apart. In Chapter 3 much was said of the apparent remoteness of *noh*, but it was emphasized that the form is remote only to an uninitiated audience. For those who know the rules, communion with the players is strengthened, not weakened, by the complex conventions; they are all playing the same game. *Noh*, *kabuki* and *bunraku* assume an audience which is *au fait* and accepts the per-formance for what it is; which is conscious, always, of theatri-cality. One example of this frank communion is in the announce-ments which are dropped into the performance. In *kabuki* we have already seen the *kojo*, or formal naming ceremony, in which an actor accedes to the next title in rank. This is reserved for the more distinguished performers. For the lower grades and parti-cularly for children on the threshold of their stage careers, there is a more informal method, whereby introductions are inserted casually into the context of the play. A senior actor stops the scene, brings the child forward and presents him to the public. There is applause, and the scene proceeds. The same thing happens in *bunraku*. Often a scene opens with lower-grade chan-ters who declaim from an enclosed box on the stage itself. The masters reserve themselves for the main action. Before they appear on the revolve, the scene stops for an assistant to intro-duce them. Such incidents are not incongruous in this kind of theatre. They are made possible by the intimate rapport between the performer and his public from which the presentational theatre derives so much of its economy and its vitality.

The larger question of why any society should prefer one form of theatre to another is, properly speaking, outside the scope of this book; but, in outline, the history of drama suggests the following considerations. Generally speaking, the form of the theatre is conditioned by the subject-matter with which it deals. Presentational theatre emerges in an age which recognizes the existence of forces greater than the individual human being; forces which it cannot reproduce exactly, for they lie beyond human scope, but which it may hint at or allude to, and with which it tries to come to terms. The actor realizes that imitation, in its narrow sense, is not only impertinent, but impossible; the author that the arguments are more important than the individuals involved. By symbol and suggestion the theatre attempts to bring these higher issues within the limits of human comprehension. We have already used *noh*, *kabuki*, the Greek theatre of the fifth century B.C. and the Elizabethan public playhouse as examples of this sort of theatre; we might add to these the medieval drama of the Christian Church and the theatrical experiments of post-Revolutionary Russia. There are others, but these, the prime examples, suffice to show a pattern.

Greek drama was born at a time when man was still uncertain of his status in the universe. Observing all about him the working of powerful and inexplicable forces, he thought of himself rather in the terms with which geologists have dismissed the entire human race – 'a tiny irritation on earth's surface'. He was anxious to comprehend the forces that manipulated him, so far as was within his power, and define his relationship to them, but still admitted the existence of what he could not understand. When Man admits himself so dominated, the status of individual men is negligible. For this reason the Greek drama of the earlier fifth century is not concerned with the realistic portrayal of individuals. In Aeschylus the characters have little individual identity; they are not rounded portraits. The dramatist is concerned primarily with the forces that work above and through them, compared to which they are of small account. He brings the gods onto the stage or shows the operation of the divine will through characters who, puppet-like, are manipulated by forces outside their own control. The purely human interest of the *Oresteia* is slight. We may be moved temporarily by Cassandra or amused by Orestes' old nurse, but Orestes himself, the central figure, diminishes in importance as the action proceeds, and is finally edged off stage by divinities who make his case their battleground and continue the struggle when he is gone. In Sophocles the individual is elevated to a higher place, responsive to the quickening humanism of the age – we know a good deal more about Oedipus as a person than we know about Agamemnon – but here too, the conflict is not between one individual and another, but between the individual and the pressures which surround him. It has been argued that this confrontation of the individual with the *Zeitgeist*, the temporal with the transcendental, gives Sophoclean tragedy its unique power. The dichotomy is reflected in the increasingly ambiguous status of the Greek theatre, half sacred and half secular.

Drama cannot represent what it cannot formulate. It cannot bring these greater forces onto the stage as they are, for it does not know precisely what they are. It can only hint at them, and try to convey their power by symbols. Thus Greek tragedy at its greatest was not concerned with the literal reproduction of the world around it. Instead it sought symbols for the various forces involved and tried to perceive the underlying pattern of their relationship. Early Greek tragedy is stage algebra. We are told only so much of the individual nature of $X$ and $Y$ as will make a coherent and interesting story, on the basis of which the wider issues can be explored. Greek sculpture shows the same characteristics. It is concerned first with formal relationships, then with idealizations. It is a later age – the age that also produced Euripides – that concerns itself with the detailed reproduction of the individual human being and the portrait bust.

*Noh* is born out of a similar tension. Its immediate action is temporal, and often violent, though this violence is only hinted at by the actors' gestures. When Japanese propagandists asked why the theatre was producing no war plays, the scholars an-

15 The urban background of *kabuki*: old residential quarter, Kyoto

16 The Kamo River, site of the first *kabuki* performance

17  Actors on the *hanamichi*

18 Poster advertising *kojo* ceremony, Kabuki-za, Tokyo

19  *A mie*

21 Puppet head

20 Temple guardian, Shitennoji, Osaka

23  *Bunraku*

Actor applying *aragoto* makeup

24  *Noh* actors in the twilight of their art

swered that *noh* was full of war plays. In a sense it is; the plays reflect the warrior's chief concerns, the excitement of the battle and the inevitability of death. However, the legends and historical incidents are used only as a starting-point for the study of man's relationship with the Ultimate. *Noh* deals with the powers that override the trivia of human existence, and, therefore, in its stage manifestations, takes much the same shape as Greek tragedy. It is not concerned with representation, because the human concerns are too trivial and the transcendental forces too vast to be represented. It evolves its own symbolic language. *Kabuki*, similarly, admits the existence of forces greater than the individual, though its orientation is social rather than metaphysical. Conceived in a hierarchical society, it saw the pattern as more important than the individual. The latter had meaning only as he was defined within his family, his group and his professional and social class, and by the web of his own loyalties and connections. *Kabuki*, like Euripidean tragedy, permits the introduction of more realistic elements, because the forces it acknowledges are closer to home, but the pattern is still more important than the individual manifestations. To an extent, *kabuki* audiences constituted a classless society, but by their very rebellion admitted the supremacy of the order against which they rebelled and from the pressures of which in the theatre, they sought temporary easement. Though *kabuki* evolves its extrovert heroes who win glory by defying the traditions and conventions, its fantasies are kept within strict bounds. The pattern of *Kanadehon Chushingura* is the accepted one. We might adapt the Spanish proverb: take what you like and pay for it, says the Shogun.

The medieval Christian drama conspicuously recognized a controlling force more powerful for being formulated in Holy Writ. Doctrinal exposition combined with folk-art to produce plays in which the characters, though permitted their often freakish individuality, were responsive to the higher power. I recall vividly one moment of the Mermaid Theatre production of the Wakefield Cycle. God, having created the world, sat motionless upon an upper platform while the scenes of Genesis unfolded below. Although he was constantly present to our eyes, we forgot him for the tribulations of Adam, Eve and their descendants. But at the murder of Abel, God stretched out one hand and called, 'Cain!'; and I believe that at that one word, the most devout atheist in the audience trembled. The medieval players could not show God, but could suggest him, by a mask or by his position in a place conventionally identified as 'Heaven'. In dealing with the people of this world, particularly those whose biblical characters leave room for dramatic expansion, the medieval drama is often graphically realistic. In its presentation of the greater forces of Heaven and Hell it cannot be. Even the Renaissance championship of humanity is overlaid by the acknowledgement of higher powers, which cannot be reproduced and therefore must be presented by appropriate symbols; and, by the same token, the post-Revolutionary Russian theatre acknowledged the supremacy of the mass will, compared to which the individual is nothing. Constructivism returns, for different reasons, to an Aeschylean simplicity. The actor forfeits his individuality; the settings reduce the natural world to mere outline.

Representational theatre, on the other hand, tends to emerge in ages which, for one reason or another, have adopted a more limited frame of reference: which dismiss metaphysics as irrelevant to the human condition, and concentrate on the material world and its social organization. They tend to be smug ages, which think they know all the answers, or at least refuse to face the questions. If they inquire at all, their questions are limited to their immediate environment. We may adduce here, as prime examples, the Greek theatre of the fourth century B.C. and its Roman imitators; the English theatre for virtually the whole of the eighteenth and nineteenth centuries; the French *pièce bien faite*; and the social drama of Ibsen. These are all concerned with the world around us; either with the mirroring of that world, so that we may see ourselves and our friends to our delight, or, as in Ibsen's social investigations, with the probing of selected phenomena within it. As the representational theatre concerns itself with the world we know from our own experience, it can mirror that world as accurately as possible on the stage. The presentational theatre shows us something other.

This is, obviously, no more than a rough classification. There are countless variations and conflicting influences. This is obvious in the chequered history of *kabuki*; some of its later manifestations come very close to representational theatre, and could be taken as such by audiences who know nothing of the previous history of the form. It is for this reason that *kabuki*, on its Western tours, has won a readier acceptance than *noh*; it comes closer to the common meeting-ground of everyday experience. Both presentational and representational theatre embody conventions. In the latter it is a convention when the action is divided into three Acts, or when Bernard Shaw writes a play about Saint Joan in which the characters speak modern English instead of medieval French. And, as Hubert Heffner has said, we are never in our heart of hearts convinced that we are really watching Antony and Cleopatra, and not Richard Burton and Elizabeth Taylor. But in representational theatre conventions are admitted grudgingly and according to need. In presentational theatre conventions are the primary language, formulated by mutual agreement to express the otherwise inexpressible. In this way the presentational theatre comes near to magical or religious ritual where symbol and suggestion serve the same function, and to these forms, in its early history, it is closely connected. It may often borrow devices from the witchdoctor or the priest, though it soon establishes these as a separate theatrical language.

How do we know which character is which, and what their natures are? In representational theatre, we are allowed to eavesdrop on what purports to be a private conversation and make deductions about the speakers based on what we hear and see — as Sherlock Holmes reconstructed a client's history by observing his speech, dress and mannerisms, and as we ourselves, on a less exalted level, make everyday inferences about people from random observations and overheard conversations. If he knows his job, the playwright will plant clues for us, and plant them early, unless for some reason he wishes to be deliberately obscure. We know that Nora, in *A Doll's House*, is frivolous, immature and sentimental by watching her behaviour in company. In *Who's Afraid of Virginia Woolf?* we know that George is a professor, that

Martha is drunk, and that they have just come from a faculty
party, from the apparently casual remarks they address to each
other. Everything they say or do contributes to our store of information. Stage conversation, though it seems casual, must be
patterned as carefully as stage movement. The playwright's job
is to release the right information at the right moment while
keeping the illusion of ordinary conversation. We object when
his expository technique becomes too obvious. This sense of
strain is apparent, for instance, in the opening scene of Sheridan's
*The Rivals*. There is much important information to be conveyed
and, within the naturalistic framework, only a limited means of
conveying it. We must be told we are in Bath, who Captain
Absolute is, with whom he is in love, and the expedient he means
to use. Accordingly, two servants are brought onto the stage to
give a detailed resumé of the doings of their masters, implausibly
disguised as conversation. Sheridan knew his own weaknesses,
and was later to parody them delightfully in *The Critic*; but Fag
and Thomas have their counterparts in the innumerable gossiping
servants of French and English domestic comedy, whose sole
function is to serve as an extended programme note.

Presentational theatre skips over these difficulties. It can make
announcements directly to the audience, instead of obliquely. If
we can, for the moment, conceive of an impossible situation in
which *The Rivals* could be given as a *noh* play, it might open something like this: As the introductory music plays, Absolute John
advances down the *hashigakari*. He wears the costume of a
*daimyo*, with a scarf knotted round his head to show that he is
disguised as one of the lower orders. Reaching the *sh'te* pillar, he
addresses the audience: 'I am the son of a rich lord in the
provinces. Today I have arrived at the end of a long journey to this
remote shrine where many come to be healed. To win the lady
whom I seek to be my wife, and to avoid my father's anger, I
have disguised myself as a humble retainer, and must seek a way
to cheat her guardians and see her.'

Here imagination falters, for the complex domestic trivialities
of *The Rivals* would wither in the austere framework of *noh*
(though the older drama might have found Lydia's confusion be-

tween illusion and reality productive). The point is that the presentational actor presents himself. He announces who he is (or is announced by another character or the Chorus). And to establish his character with verbal economy he displays a costume, as a shop hangs out a sign, to indicate what is going on within. The use of formal stage costume to reveal character is one of the distinctive features of presentational theatre.

Presentational costumes are not meant to resemble real clothes, though they may derive from them. Instead, they employ agreed conventions – often intricate – to give information about the wearer. We know, from seeing him, his station and his temperament; and with a set of costuming conventions as complex as those of *noh* and *kabuki*, we may have a detailed conception of him before he speaks a word. This is not usually true of representational theatre. When George enters in *Who's Afraid of Virginia Woolf?*, he might be a businessman, a politician or a plain-clothes policeman, for all we know by looking at him. It is only through his conversation that we can place him more exactly. The conventional use of costuming is economical in exposition, but baffling to the uninitiated. If you do not know the rules, you cannot play. Faubion Bowers, in his study of *kabuki*, admits that at his first performance he could not even distinguish men from women. All the performers were male; the distinction was made by costume, the rules of which had to be learned. Each society evolves its own theatrical code, based on its own assumptions and traditions. The foreigner may be totally at a loss, or, worse, misled by superficial similarities (as when an Englishman sees his first game of American football). The same possibilities for error occur in everyday life. If we see a man carrying a spear or a gun, we infer from his accoutrements that he is a soldier. But we identify a general from his insignia, though there is nothing about his appearance that automatically connects him with war and battle. We know what he is because we know the code. A visitor from Mars would not distinguish between a general and a postman. If we see a man in a red robe and white wig, we know him for a judge, though these things in themselves do not express his function. A child's more limited frame of reference might take him for a deficient Santa Claus. We have already made one parallel between drama and language; another might be made here. The costume conventions of Japanese plays have their literary counterpart in *kanji*. The Chinese characters present an enormous barrier to initial understanding, but once they are mastered, rapid reading becomes immediately possible, because each ideograph conveys a whole word to the eyes. In the same way the conventional costumes convey a wealth of information, bypassing the need for verbal exposition.

The presentational actor, then, reveals himself by externals, and it is these that dictate his performance. The representational actor starts from the inside and works outwards. His first concern is a study of the psychology of the character, and identification with it; from this, he evolves the gestures and business that seem appropriate. The outward acts are conditioned by the inner frame of mind. But the presentational actor, conscious always that he is an actor, starts from the outside. He assumes a character, not by working himself into a state of mind, but by literally assuming a mask and a costume, and adopting those movements and attitudes which tradition and convention deem appropriate, and which can be relied on to trigger the right responses in the audience. A Method actor prepares for his performance introspectively. He may improvise dialogue which is an extension of his on-stage personality; he may run several times round the theatre if he is required to enter in a state of physical exhaustion. *Noh* and *kabuki* actors prepare by contemplating themselves in full costume. Both theatres have a mirror-room at the end of the 'bridge' where the actor may study himself before going on stage. The Greek actor, it seems, used the same approach. A number of well-known and much-reproduced paintings show the tragic performer, in full costume, contemplating his mask. These have often been identified as the actor after performance or sometimes as a symbolic representation of the author contemplating the masks of his characters. It seems much more likely, by *kabuki* analogy, that they represent the actor *before* performance, conceiving his role in terms of its outward presentation. Mary Renault has adapted such a picture on the cover of *The Mask of Apollo*, and makes the actor's contemplation of his mask a *leitmotif* of her novel. As usual, her artist's imagination has led her to perceive intuitively something to which scholarship dares not wholly commit itself.

This has its effect on theatrical vocabulary. A character in a play is in Greek *prosopon* and in Latin *persona*, both words referring literally to the mask. Japanese has no precise equivalent. It is significant, however, that *monomane* used by Zeami to denote the purely theatrical element in *noh*, means literally 'imitation of things' (*mono*); and that *mono* is regularly used in Japanese compounds to objectify a quality or emotion. *Monokanashi* means 'sad', but *mono* intensifies the quality of sadness by according it its own personality (as a Navajo Indian will say 'Hunger is killing me' for 'I am hungry'). *Monogatsku*, 'insanity' or 'possession', literally signifies 'a thing attaching itself to one'. For Zeami, then, acting was the art of imitating externals; though, as we have seen, this process of imitation was modified by conventional usage.

What we are saying here may seem to conflict with our earlier remarks on *noh*'s distrust of the sensory world. There is, in fact, no discrepancy. A drama has to assume material form if it is to appear on the stage at all. We are talking now specifically of this material form, and of the way in which an actor manifests his character to the audience. The actor is preoccupied with externals in his presentation. The drama seeks, by manipulation of these externals, to conduct our minds to the higher reality.

When such emphasis is placed upon the costume, the costume is, to all intents and purposes, the character. The actor is the machinery that gives the character movement. Their personalities are distinct and that of the actor is of no more importance than that of the stage assistants or property men, who, like him, put objects into motion. In his case, too, the artifice is always apparent. We see the machinery working, just as we see the assistants carrying a property across the stage, but we make a clear distinction between what is relevant and what is not. In *noh*, for the most part, the only complete costume – a wig, mask and robe – belongs to the *sh'te*, who, as we have seen, is strictly speaking the only actor. The *waki* signifies by his name, his position and his partial costume (no mask) his peripheral role. Nor is the mask in any sense a disguise. This is not its purpose. *Noh* masks are small, leaving the wearer's neck and part of his face clearly exposed. There is a distinction between the mask and the man behind it, and it is the former that demands our attention. The same is true of the exaggerated *kabuki* make-up, which is really a mask painted directly on the face, and may often leave areas of skin untouched. The painter Earl Hubbard, watching Baiko making up, said that he 'painted a picture of another person on himself'.

These uses seem to derive from the origins of the mask in ritual. It is reasonable to assume that the first mask was worn for two reasons: to overawe the spectators by assuming the image of a higher power, and to divert possible divine jealousy by making a clear distinction between the mask and the wearer. We see this in well-attested non-dramatic usages. The Roman general, entering the city on his triumphal procession, had his face rouged in imitation of the statue of Jupiter standing on the Capitoline Hill; but his soldiers, following him in the procession, poured scurrilous abuse on their leader to make clear the distinction between the divine simulacrum and the mortal behind it. The masks of noble dead (*imagines*) were kept in Roman houses. In processions they were worn through the streets. There was no intention of impersonating the dead. The wearers simply gave temporary mobility to simulacra which had their own permanent and independent existence.

In Japanese theatre practice this distinction between the character and the individual personality of the wearer can be seen in a number of examples. In *Okina*, the patriarch-god mask has its own identity. It does not represent the god; it is the god. Offered on the dressing-room altar before the performance it establishes its kinship with the divinity. The actor removes the mask from its box on stage, signifying that the god has come. He replaces it, and the god has departed. This is also apparent in the *kabuki* version of the *shishi* dance, described at length on pp. 44 f. Here the mask, apparently an inanimate object of brown carved wood, has a life and spirit of its own, and begins to demonstrate its independence as soon as it is worn. Unknown to the dancer, it snaps at the butterflies; its strength is greater than hers and dominates her performance. Finally, in the second part of the dance, it engrosses her completely, so that the feminine personality of the dancer is submerged in the masculinity of the lion. The transformation is represented by the change of costume; which is no more than to say that the mask has grown until it covers the whole body. A modern Western analogue may be found in Archibald MacLeish's *J.B.*, a version of the Job story done as Greek tragedy. The two commentators, Zuss and Nickles, appear first as ringside vendors at a circus; they then put on masks representative of Heaven and Hell, which transform their vision and dominate their will. The mask asserts itself upon the wearer.

In the Western world a similar idea inspired a well-known story by Max Beerbohm, though here the mask is a benevolent one which moulds the dissolute features of the wearer to its own likeness. In Japan a recent film, Shindo Kaneto's *Onibaba* (1964), works a variation on the same theme. A woman wears a devil-mask that she is unable to remove from her face; when she finally wrenches it off by brute force, it takes the face with it.

This is no less true of costume. In both the *noh* and *kabuki* versions of *Matsukaze*, a girl puts on robes left by a departed lover. She immediately goes mad and assumes his personality. In the *noh* play *Tomoe* the spirit of the warrior woman who gives the play its name tells of her lover Yoshinaka's death in battle, and how he left his outer robe for her to wear. When she puts this on, she assumes his personality and dances his story, not her own. In the *bunraku* version of *Honcho Nijushi Ko* the girl who carries the fox helmet herself becomes a fox; its spirit attaches himself to her, and dominates her. And, by the same token, an important character may be represented on stage by an untenanted costume. In *Aoi no Ue* the sick lady Aoi has no dialogue and is not required to move; we see only her unconscious body, over which the possessing spirit hovers. She is represented, therefore, only by a costume. At the beginning of the play two assistants carry in an orange robe and spread it carefully along the forestage. Significantly, the *hashigakari* curtain is ceremonially lifted for its appearance, as for the entrance of a character. If the robe were considered merely as a property, stage etiquette would require the curtain to be opened only at one corner.

Once we grasp this fundamental convention, many apparent anomalies resolve themselves. It does not matter who plays the parts, providing they are wearing the right costumes; or, at least, it matters only so much as the skill of the individual driver affects the performance of his car. It is not incongruous, for example, that men should play women, as in *noh* and *kabuki* and in Greek and Elizabethan drama. Mask, costume and make-up proclaim 'woman': the actor gives them speech and motion. Similarly, an adult actor can play a child. In *Kokaji* (the *noh* play in which the swordsmith seeks divine assistance to forge a weapon for the Emperor) a miraculous child recites the history of famous swords of Japan. He is played by a mature performer, as he must be; this is the *sh'te* role, with exacting technical demands; but the mask and costume announce him as a boy. In *Funa Benkei* we have what seems a double contradiction. The great warrior Yoshitsune is played by a *ko-kata*, child actor, according to the regular convention for roles of such exalted station, and his mistress, Shizuka, by a man. But for an audience concentrating on the costumes, there is no contradiction at all.

In the same way one actor may play several irreconcilable roles in the same play. In *Sakura Gimin Den* the same actor, Matsumoto Koshiro, takes three parts in succession: Sogo, the farmer-martyr; Kozen, a priest turned demon; and Hotta, Sogo's arch-enemy and executioner. Such feats, of course, are not unknown in the West: Paul Scofield played twin brothers in *Ring Round the Moon*, Louis Jouvet took double roles in several of his films, and Alec Guinness and Peter Sellers have played half a dozen parts singlehanded. But these were intended as displays of expertise in make-up, facial and vocal impersonation: one actor tried to convince the audience that he was several. Matsumoto's performance was still a technical *tour de force*, but of a different order.

When the costume is the character, any change in the one signifies a change in the other. The examples cited above show how, when one character assumes another's garment, he also takes his personality. For this reason, disguises in presentational theatre are usually rudimentary: a scarf tied round the head, a veil across the face, a hat pulled over the eyes. A complete or even partial change of costume would imply something more fundamental. In the *noh* play *Kamo Monogurui* a madwoman dancing at a shrine is sought and recognized by her husband. She signifies that she has come to her senses by putting on a green robe, patterned with autumn leaves, over the drab grey and white she wore before; it means that she has become virtually a different person. In *Kokaji* the swordsmith shows by the increasing grandeur of his costume (one layer being added over another) his growing affinity with the divine spirit that will aid him in his work. We may compare the 'double costume' worn by the spirit in *Aoi no Ue* (see p. 117). These examples give point to Zeami's remark that the actor, when portraying a character possessed by a spirit, must try to distinguish between the nature of the possessor and that of the possessed; his acting, like his costume, must reveal different layers.

To return to the problem of disguise: when a character does assume a complete change of costume to deceive his enemies, plot complications ensue which are, by Western standards, extraordinary and illogical, because he is immediately assumed to be, and acts in every respect as though he were, the person he is dressed as. In *Kamakura Sandai Ki* Takatsuna Sasaki impersonates a farmer and enlists as the Shogun's man. As soon as he puts on the armour which marks him as his enemy's retainer, he becomes the Shogun's man both in dress and in spirit. He carries out his instructions to the letter, though they run contrary to his own interests; not until he has changed back into his own clothes does he reveal his own personality. A more elaborate development of this convention appears in *Kanadehon Chushingura*, the *kabuki* vendetta play. Act IX surveys the consequences of Lord Enya's humiliating death and the cautious testing of individual loyalties among his retainers before the revenge-conspiracy is finally formulated. Kakogawa Honzo is suspected by Enya's other followers as a coward and an appeaser. He himself is suspicious of Oboshi Yuranosuke, with whose son his daughter had a marriage contract, because he seems to be spending his time in frivolity, rather than plotting vengeance. In this atmosphere of mutual mistrust he presents himself at Yuranosuke's house disguised as a wandering, flute-playing acolyte, in the appropriate robe, trappings and face-concealing straw hat. Forced by circumstances to reveal his identity, he lays aside the hat and flute, but still retains the robe. This is significant; it means that, under the superficial disguise, there lies a deeper level of deception. Honzo is still not speaking as his true self. In a long taunting speech to Yuranosuke's wife, he accuses her husband of idleness and debauchery. In fact Yuranosuke is affecting frivolity to fool the enemy and put them off their guard. Honzo suspects this, but is not sure. His sneers and taunts do not come from the heart, but are his way of sounding out the situation. The continued wearing of the 'disguise' robe signifies as much. It is not until Honzo has confronted Yuranosuke in person and obtained a frank admission from him (though at the cost of a quarrel in which Honzo suffers a fatal blow) that he fully abandons his pretence and strips off the last of his disguise. His pretence, like his costume, is removed in layers. Significantly, when Yuranosuke leaves to further the plot, and himself assumes the convenient disguise of the wandering acolyte, he wears only the bare elements of the costume, the belt and hat. His deception has only one layer.

For this reason, as we have noted, disguises are usually kept to a minimum, because of the complications they induce. There is an interesting example in the *kabuki Kanjincho* (see p. 152), where Prince Yoshitsune and his retainer Benkei disguise themselves as mendicant monks to escape the enemy police. They are stopped at a bridge check-point, suspected and examined. The officer asks Benkei to prove himself by explaining the significance of the leggings and sandals he is wearing – the footwear actually worn by monks of the sort they are pretending to be. But on the stage Benkei and his companions are wearing none of these things, though everyone talks as if they were. The disguise is purely imaginary, for, by the conventions of this theatre, if they were fully dressed as monks they would *be* monks, and not Benkei and Yoshitsune in disguise.

Just as, in *Kokaji*, the added layers of costume suggest the spiritual ascent of the character, any impairment or deprivation of the costume suggests the impairment, or even destruction, of the character. Obvious examples are *Hagoromo*, where the angel is incomplete without her robe, and the elaborate *kabuki* sword-fights where the failing warrior is successively disrobed by the property man. The device may also be used to indicate psychological damage or spiritual weakening. In *Yoritomo no Shi* (*Yoritomo's Death*) a retainer kills the woman he loves rather than have her submit to dishonour. In falling, she pulls one sleeve off his robe, indicating his own loss at her passing. In *Sakura Gimin Den*, the priest Kozen, distraught by the despot's oppression of the people, breaks his rosary, burns the *sutras* and announces that he will become a demon to persecute the house of Hotta. (His behaviour is very similar to that of Cassandra before she meets her death in Aeschylus's *Agamemnon*.) As he rushes down the *hanamichi* a servant tries to hold him back; the sleeve tears from his robe, both showing his spiritual impairment and foretelling his coming death.

In the same play a dissolute relative planning to inform against the farmer-hero, Sogo, is himself pursued by the police. They chase him to the *hanamichi* and seize him by the coat. Ducking out of it, he runs away naked but for a loincloth. While this action is comprehensible in realistic terms, it has a deeper conventional significance: he has become an outcast, a 'nothing', and is no further danger to Sogo. Later still in the same play, a retainer who has been caught plotting against his master is deprived of his robe, and thus, by implication, of his status. It would be going too far, of course, to say that every costume change has deep significance. Some have spectacular value only, as in the *kabuki* 'Wistaria Maiden' dance, where the performer, passing behind a tree, assumes a succession of increasingly beautiful costumes. The split-second changes demonstrate his technical virtuosity. But in most cases the deeper significance exists, and every action, even the smallest, that involves the costume must be considered with this in mind. When, for example, the sympathetic minister of *Sakura Gimin Den* thrusts the petition into the fold of his *kimono*, the action has more than its surface value. It signifies that he is literally taking the appeal to heart. By the same token, the untying of the *obi* string has profound erotic connotations. It is interesting to see how these ideas are still embedded in the Japanese concept of play production. They may be damaging (as the review of Pirandello's *Henry IV* in Chapter 6 shows) or helpful. Kurosawa's *Red Beard*, filmed in 1965, shows a doctor's acceptance of his duty to serve the community by his ultimate donning of the uniform he had at first contemptuously rejected, and a prostitute's rejection of her way of life by her tearing up of the *kimono* put on her to attract customers. Kurosawa's manipulation of these symbols, and his deliberate counterbalancing of one with the other, rests on centuries-old assumptions.

While this examination is confined to theatrical usage, it will be obvious that similar conventions operate in other spheres. In societies like that of feudal Japan itself, where clothes and hair-styles were a mark of class, their mutilation denoted social degradation, just as shaving of the head implied a withdrawal from society. A well-known German play, *The Captain from Köpenick*, founded on fact and enjoyed as a joke against the Junker mentality, shows the importance of costume conventions to military life: a humble civilian takes a captain's uniform, and while he wears it is not only respected by everybody as a captain, but behaves like one physically and mentally. Such conventions do not originate from the theatre. They derive partly from animistic beliefs, according to which material objects possess a spirit of their own (we see this in the Shinto worship of the Imperial accoutrements) and partly from the practices of sympathetic magic, in which clothes and personal possessions acquire, by association, something of the wearer's spirit, and may in certain cases represent him. Such beliefs exist to a greater or lesser extent in most primitive religions, are embodied in their ritual and pass into the vocabulary of the presentational theatre. In Greece, notably, they inspired a set of theatrical conventions remarkably similar to the Japanese. The example of Cassandra in *Agamemnon*, already noted, is only one of many in which a change of costume prefaces the impairment, by death or some other disaster, of the character. China provides numerous stories, many of which found their way into Japanese literature, of violence done to an enemy's clothes when his person was inaccessible. Such beliefs are also fundamental to *voodoo*, where damage done to the image of a person will result in his harm; it is essential, however, that the image be dressed in something belonging to the person it represents. In Japan the transference of vital forces from the person to his simulacrum underlies certain customs preserved to this day as picturesque ceremonies. The well-known Doll Festival of 3 March (the third day of the third month), in which girls set out their dolls in formal array and pay them honour, derives from the belief that any sickness in the person could be transferred to the image and absorbed. Each year, on the river at Asakusa as in other parts of Japan, worshippers perpetuate this belief by floating paper cut-outs of themselves and their families down the water, to carry away any ills that might be present in the flesh. The primitive belief that to surrender your image was to place yourself in another's power provoked sharp resistance to the introduction of photography in the Meiji Era; it was one of the few Western innovations that encountered popular disfavour. The full-face photograph of the Emperor Meiji used to be worshipped as if it were the Emperor himself; and David and Evelyn Riesman, in *Conversations in Japan*, report the story of a high school principal who committed suicide when his portrait was destroyed in a school fire.

The affinity between the puppet theatre and its live counterpart should now be obvious. They live in the same world and operate according to the same conventions. Psychologically orientated Western actors, perceiving that the puppet has no psyche, regard it as deficient and contemptible; for them it can only ape the surface of the role, without access to the inner logic that gives the outer manifestations coherence. The Japanese actor, who shapes his role primarily by the assumption of external characteristics, sees in the puppet an actor who is a logical extension of his own techniques: all externals, and therefore admirable; an actor who, moreover, can in skilled hands acquire

absolute precision of balance and movement. The operator holds
the puppet in front of his body as the actor conceals himself behind a costume, or holds a mask before his face.

This affinity extends to detail. The 'black men' of *kabuki* may
not manipulate the actor, but they frequently control his costume.
During the progressive disrobement of the *kabuki* duel, it is not
uncommon to see three assistants clustered round the actor at
once, pulling the intricate coloured threads which loosen panels
of his dress, holding up his sleeves, and adjusting his wig. In one
play the actor wears frames in the sleeves of his *kimono* to extend
their full magnificence. When the fight begins they are removed
to free his arms for action; when, the duel over, he falls into a
triumphant *mie*, the assistants rapidly replace the frames and hold
out the sleeves in a tableau. At such moments the similarity between the presentational actor and the *bunraku* puppet is striking.
In the *kabuki* version of *Okina* the actor goes one stage further by
impersonating a marionette. Sambaso, the comic character,
emerges from a box. His 'manipulator', dressed in black, goes
through the motions of checking strings and making final adjustments, then puts him through a lively dance. But something goes
wrong: the invisible strings tangle, the actor-puppet pirouettes;
one snaps and he flops to the floor. When the dance is over, he
is put back into the box. The conceit recalls the removing and
replacing of the Okina mask in the *noh* original. In presentational
theatre, mask, puppet and actor are simply three similar and
interchangeable ways of securing the same effect.

If this affinity is clear in *bunraku*, it is even more so in a less
publicized local variant, *koruma ningyo*, 'puppets on wheels' –
though in fact it is the operators, not their charges, who roll
themselves along. Adapted from *bunraku* a century ago by
Nishikawa Koryu, this form has been transmitted through the
farmers of the Tama district of Tokyo, where it survives today.
It employs one operator for each puppet instead of three. He sits
on a small box with wooden wheels, by which he can propel
himself across the stage with considerable agility. Hands and feet
control the four-foot-high puppet. The left hand, inserted in the
trunk, controls head and body movements; the right works the

arms and articulated hands, one directly and the other by a spring mechanism; the feet are attached to pegs in the feet of the puppet, so that the figure walks as the operator trundles himself along. As in *bunraku*, the operators are dressed and hooded in black, and are practically invisible against a dark background. Words and music are provided by a chanter and *samisen*.

I saw a two-part performance of this nature in Tokyo. It began with a solo Sambaso dance in cap and bells; this was followed by a full-length play, the story of Kiyohime, a deserted wife. Searching for her husband, she meets first a villager, then a wood-cutter, and grows increasingly irate at their unhelpfulness. Finally a priest tells her the truth: her husband has gone off to live with another woman. At this point the black curtain falls to reveal a gaudy painted scene, a river with a boat. Kiyohime is increasingly distraught. She shows this, significantly, by her dishevelment, tearing the pins and combs from her hair; disinte-gration of costume, as usual, implies disintegration of character. Tearing off her outer robe, to the consternation of the boatman, she throws herself into the river (at this point the operator throws her bodily over the strip of painted water, rolls himself behind at great speed, and picks her up again) and appears above the surface several times, as though drowning. Then, climbing into the boat, she turns into a serpent. Her wig flips over to re-veal a devil-mask (a popular device in *bunraku* also) and her body sinuously extends; a smoke-bomb is let off, and the play ends magnificently with the demonic woman writhing in a shower of fireworks. It is wry comment on Japanese marriage that the play is described as showing 'the dreadful lengths to which a woman's egotism may lead her'.

Here again the relationship of operator to puppet is the same as of actor to mask, or actor to costume. The puppet is a mask that has grown arms, legs and body. Though the actor controls his mask and costume directly, he still recognizes a dissociation from them which is no less real than the physical separation between the puppet and his operator, or the puppet and the chanter. In puppetry we see more of the machinery, but the machinery is essentially the same; and disassociation is hardly greater than in

H

*kabuki*, where the role is twice-removed from the actor's own personality – first by his assumption of a stage name and traditional title (implying his identification with other actors, not with roles), and second, by the use of traditional techniques which he assumes together with his costume. Jean-Louis Barrault has written of the excitement of his first performance at the *Comédie française*, where he was issued with the breastplate worn by the seventeenth-century creator of his role; by substituting for the mystique of this breastplate the whole of the actor's art, we can begin to appreciate the state of mind of the *noh* and *kabuki* performer.

The future of *bunraku*, like that of *noh*, is hard to predict. It owed its emergence to a fad, but its success to a strict discipline, the product of an age at once more leisurely and more circumscribed, when there were fewer distractions, fewer opportunities and every inducement for a young trainee to accept an arduous apprenticeship which promised fame and honour at the end. Like the live-theatre forms, it was not so much a profession as a way of life, demanding total involvement. Only recently has this tradition vanished. The director of a Tokyo marionette theatre looks back nostalgically to the golden time, only five years ago, when his company would work uncomplainingly seven days a week, fifty-two weeks a year, even through the New Year holiday during which the most austere Japanese relaxes. Now, he says, they demand Sundays off and regular vacations. Changing times have done even more harm to *bunraku*. Financially it has fallen on evil days. Enthusiasts tend to be the older people. The art is no longer self-supporting. For fifty-five years it was run at a loss by Shochiku Enterprises; then for three years by NHK Television; now by the government, which has constructed the smaller hall of the National Theatre with *bunraku* in mind. Critics claim that subsidies have made the theatre lazy and that *bunraku* is now at the bottom of the trough, waiting for a genius to revivify it. For the present it must be admitted that *bunraku* is rapidly becoming a cult-art, like the *kabuki* with which it has been inseparably associated, and is cherished more for its historic past than for its artistic present.

# 6

## The Age of Translations

The Meiji Restoration, as we have seen, disrupted the traditional structure of the Japanese theatre, forcing the old families to make difficult adjustments and introducing new theatrical concepts. The recognition that drama could be valuable propaganda for the new regime produced, about 1890, a new form known as *shimpa*. Like much of the later theatre, it had political affiliations and was basically antagonistic to *kabuki*, considering it decorative but mindless. *Shimpa* argued that the theatre was not merely a medium for displaying art. Rather, it should present a realistic picture of the world and illuminate its problems. *Shimpa* took national themes and presented them in a realistic manner. *Kabuki*, groping for favour, often borrowed its subject-matter; in 1904 both old and new companies were dramatizing events from the Russo-Japanese war. *Shimpa*'s appeal in recent years has somewhat diminished, though plays along these lines continue to be written, and a distinguished film actor has formed his own *shimpa* company, the Morishige Gekidan, which plays to packed houses.

Contact with the West produced a hunger for American and European plays. These could not be handled by existing companies, whose traditional art was not equipped to deal with so radically different an approach. The first *shingeki* ('new plays') were given by amateurs, members of the newly formed Literary Society, who opened on 17 February 1906. November of the same year saw a mixed programme of classical excerpts, including the trial scene from *The Merchant of Venice*, which remained a firm favourite for several seasons. This period saw the first serious translations of Shakespeare, the manuscripts of which are now part of the Waseda University collection. Other groups were formed. The Free Theatre (Jiyu Gekijo) gave its first performance in November 1909. This company had a hard core of mature *kabuki* actors, who foresaw the difficult transitional period through which the Japanese theatre would have to pass. They thought in terms of an 'age of translations', out of which would emerge new forms both modern and distinctively Japanese. Their first production was Ibsen's *John Gabriel Borkman*, followed the next year by a season including *Hamlet* and *A Doll's House* and in 1912 by Shaw's *You Never Can Tell*.

The gulf between the Japanese theatre and its Western counterpart embraces more than different social standards and unfamiliar subject-matter. They are two forms built on different aesthetic foundations, and divided by the actor's concept of his relation to his role. The extrovert and presentational style cultivated for centuries in Japan cannot be easily reconciled with plays written for actors trained in a different mode and expected to identify themselves psychologically with their roles. This is the most serious difficulty that the Japanese actor has to face. He is forced, in effect, to relearn the fundamentals of his trade. The varying success with which this has been accomplished will be apparent in the following reviews. Japanese actors, on the whole, are more secure in Western plays to which the traditional presentational methods can be applied. They are conspicuously successful in the 'epic' style, cultivated by Brecht and others, which comes close to, and indeed borrowed from, their own traditions. The 'alienation effect' demanded by Brecht from his characters is founded on the premises of presentational acting. But the wholly naturalistic style continues to elude them, with results sometimes disastrous to the play. In Brecht the actor is moving in a world he knows.

The extent of this affinity may be seen in the National Theatre's production of *Mother Courage*, a modern play which fits perfectly into the Japanese pattern. The setting employs isolated naturalistic fragments against a formal background of burlap curtains; the costumes are appropriately timeless, deriving equally from feudal Japan, the Thirty Years War and the Great Chinese Cultural Revolution: the hand-drawn *kabuki* curtain serves as a screen on which Brecht's slogans and descriptions are projected; and the actors continually assert their identity as actors, and their divorcement from their roles, by stepping forward, acknowledging the audience and breaking into song. (This production showed, incidentally, one danger to which the subtitled foreign film in Japan is also prone: Brecht's descriptive titles, translated into Japanese, took far longer to read, and the production was slowed, up thereby.) What works so well in Brecht, however, is fatal to the psychological nuances of a work like Robert Bolt's *Flowering Cherry*, and ruins a poignant scene in Anouilh's *Antigone* by turning the guards into posturing buffoons.

Theatrical politics of this period are almost as complicated as feudal history. Administrative and artistic dissent disrupted the Free Theatre and brought about the formation of a new group, the Arts Theatre. This was to expire in turn, but not before producing Wilde's *Salome* and Ibsen's *The Woman from the Sea*. Companies multiplied, and Western drama grew in favour. Ibsen was particularly popular, as he is in India today for the same reasons: when feudalism turns into democracy, the public instinctively looks to a dramatist whose plays expose the rottenness of the traditional social structure. Matsui Sumako, one of Japan's first 'emancipated women', made her name by playing Ibsen heroines. *Shingeki* posed considerable problems for Japanese actors – in approach, in technique, and, not least, in make-up. The Japanese often refer to the importations as 'red hair' drama, a joke which conceals a serious difficulty. Japanese hair is universally black, and the only shade to which it can be dyed is a rich auburn. For any other colour the actor must use a wig. Make-up for these plays is often as complicated as anything required for *kabuki*. Many a production sags under the weight of nose-putty. A play like Arthur Miller's *Incident at Vichy*, which has French and German characters, a gipsy and a Jew, calls on every method of facial disguise the actor knows. This exemplifies the larger problem. The contemporary Japanese actor is struggling, with more or less success, to adjust to techniques which are not his own, and to break habits which are no less strong for being unconscious.

The theatre as a whole suffered from the nationalistic fervour of the police state before and during the Second World War. Even *noh* did not escape; the censors were alarmed by its fundamental democracy (all things are equal before the Buddha) and restricted performances to audiences unlikely to be politically active. Contemporary criticism, particularly of the film, still suffers from an overdeveloped political consciousness. Donald Richie, in his study of the Japanese cinema, has amusingly illustrated the Japanese critic's habit of finding political allusions in the most unlikely places. *Shingeki* companies were shaken materially by the war itself – all 'high-class' art, including live theatre, was banned in 1944 – and by the occupation that followed. Only a handful of theatres escaped the bombing. Space was at a premium and the entertainment-tax exorbitant. Added to this was the vigilance of the occupying forces, suspicious of anything that might remotely be interpreted as national propaganda, and bombarding the cultural leaders with suggestions. One of these, put forward in all seriousness and perhaps in memory of the Japanese objections to the original production, was that performances of Gilbert and Sullivan's *The Mikado* would help to bring the ruler-cult into disrepute. Another was the banning of *Kanadehon Chushingura*, which only served to inflate the play in popular esteem. Fortunately the Army of Occupation had good advisors, many of them Americans who had spent much of their lives in Japan, and avoided the worst abuses of a censorship, which would, in any case, have been difficult to enforce. As one Japanese said, 'When most of our own people don't understand what *kabuki* is talking about, how can the Americans?'

Out of this confusion the Mingei (People's Arts) Theatre was born, and continues to contribute to the Tokyo theatrical scene. Opening in 1950 with *The Seagull*, it went on to a highly successful play about the life of Vincent Van Gogh. In 1954 Miller's *Death of a Salesman* had a record run of 142 performances, although its style of production was then something completely new in the Japanese theatre. In 1956 the Mingei produced *The Diary of Anne Frank*; then came *Shima*, the first stage treatment in Japan of the results of atomic bombing. Throughout its career the company has been interested primarily in the realistic drama and plays of contemporary social significance. It receives no subsidy, but continues to be self-supporting through its wide popular appeal. Cultivating a working-class public, its most popular dramatists are Arthur Miller and Arnold Wesker, whose aims and language the audiences find comprehensible. Like other companies, it has its own school. Actors train as they go; the usual policy is to mix older and younger members in any given production.

Theatrical Tokyo is now geographically divided. The larger theatres and first-run cinemas lie east of the Imperial Palace, around the Ginza and in the neighbouring Marunouchi and Hibiya districts. The Kabuki-za marks one limit of this strip, the Imperial Theatre the other: two poles of dramatic art, two symbols of modern Japanese society, the one preserving the national past, the other imitating the Western present. Appropriately aloof from commerce, secure in its subsidy, the National Theatre stands in isolation on the far side of the Palace. To the north, near the Korakuen fun-fair, are the two *noh* theatres in most frequent use, the Kanze Kaikan and the Suidobashi Nogaku, the latter housing the Hosho family and the Nomura *kyogen* players. 'Off-Ginza' can be anywhere. Some of the smaller groups have their own premises, like the Actors' Theatre in the embassy district of Roppongi. But in the frantic search for *Lebensraum*, most companies must fit in when and where they can. Several operate in the suburbs of Shibuya and Shinjuku. They inhabit attics and basements, or cinemas when the film is over, a vacant lot under a full moon, or a tent erected in the precincts of a shrine: places unmarked on maps, unknown to taxidrivers. Even major productions are forced to seek shelter in a community hall or hotel. The more prestigious theatres publicize their activities widely, if sometimes erroneously, in a monthly news-sheet. *Noh* has its own bulletin. The smaller groups often give the impression of avoiding advertising altogether and communicating with the faithful by word of mouth, or by telepathy.

The Ginza enterprises and the National Theatre operate on a monthly basis, with a few days' respite between productions and a sensible system of ticket distribution. Most seats are reserved, but a large block is held for sale one hour before the performance. Prices vary. Orchestra stalls at the Imperial, Nissei or National Theatre may cost up to 2500 yen, an *avant-garde* work in the suburbs 300. The larger theatres now have English information desks and special clerks to handle foreign reservations; they also offer programmes printed in English, or at least a translated synopsis of the play. Around this bustle of activity has grown up a formidable array of critics. In the Japanese manner, they specialize: some devote themselves to *kabuki*, others to *noh*, *bunraku* or the new theatre. They guard their own provinces jealously, and are equally hesitant to intrude on others'. This means that the Japanese theatre is spared one menace that afflicts its American, and to a lesser extent its English, counterpart. The critics do not form a judicial tribunal with power of life and death. Reviews, in fact, seem to have little effect on attendance; theatres are usually full. The only place where I have regularly seen half-empty houses is the National Theatre, which seems to have much work yet to do before it acquires a following of its own. It is doing its best, however, to educate the younger generation by holding illustrated lectures on *kabuki* given by accomplished actors and followed by a complete performance. The large school-parties that attend begin by giggling and end by being enthralled. There is high hope here.

It is possible to see, within a short space of time, an astonishing diversity of productions. The following reviews give some idea of this in a survey of the chief events of one season. If they seem to deal predominantly with Japanese productions of foreign plays, they give an accurate picture of the theatre as it now is. Tokyo is still living in the 'age of translations'. There are, of course, Japanese plays, ranging from naturalistic drama to the *avant-garde*, but these are largely off-Ginza productions. One of last season's most successful experiments was Kara Juro's *Long*

*John Silver*, which resurrects Stevenson's hero and transplants him to a Japanese bath-house, and a milieu not unlike that of the Brecht-Weill *Dreigroschenoper*. It is a play, in fact, very Brechtian in mood, with a touch of Beckett. Long John, like Godot, never appears; the characters who wait for him indulge in desperate make-believe, clinging to the tinselled memories of the twenties, underneath which lies the yawning reality, the total meaning-lessness of life. And there is 'pop-art' in Terayama Shuji's *The Hunchback of Aomori*, set against a backdrop of the rising sun; it is the story of a deformed child born in the wilds of northern Hokkaido, a dark, brooding tale set in a framework of contrived puerility, with a schoolgirl narrator who consistently misinter-prets the sinister happenings in the light of her own innocence. The same author's *The Crime of Miss Debuko Oyama* uses a similar detective-story framework, pop-art background, and deliber-ately flat dialogue: the first production was irreverently mounted in one of Tokyo's traditional *yose* music-halls. Devotees of these theatres sneer at the 'froth' of Giraudoux and Anouilh with which the larger companies occupy themselves.

Yet the fact remains that Japan's leading actors and directors are still primarily concerned with Western works. They are anxious to learn more about the Stanislavsky system, first intro-duced to Japan in 1913 by Osanai Keoru, who had also worked with Max Reinhardt, and was an important figure in the early Japanese cinema. They are fascinated by the Actor's Studio, where one of the present Kabuki-za company, oddly enough, has studied; they examine the Theatre of Cruelty and the Theatre of the Absurd, and want to adapt them to their own uses. Their choice of plays is dictated, inevitably, by what Japanese audiences can reconcile with their own social background. There is much interest in Edward Albee, though the Japanese could not under-stand *Who's Afraid of Virginia Woolf?* either as play or film. It presented a view of married life that they could hardly begin to comprehend, and the translator admitted to enormous language problems. *The Zoo Story*, on the other hand, was highly popular. Playing at a Shinjuku cinema after the film was over, it had queues winding three deep round the building. It is a meaningful

H 2

play for the Japanese, in portraying an archetypal fear: middle-
aged complacency confronted with inexplicable irrational
violence, and forced in the end to perpetrate violence of its own.
The audience that watches it is conscious of a similar upheaval in
its own society; there are many Japanese experiencing the same
fears now. Another reason for the play's popularity, perhaps, is
its stylistic kinship with *noh*; *The Zoo Story* has a cast of two – an
inquirer and his informant – dialogue which verges on the ritualistic and an almost total lack of action.

As the following reviews are concerned solely with professional
productions, it would be as well to say something here about the
amateurs. A number of such groups flourish extra-curricularly in
schools and universities. The educational system, for better or
worse, takes little cognizance of the theatre; in this it comes
closer to the British than the American attitude. There is little
attempt, even, to bring students into contact with the literature
of the classical theatre. A British schoolchild begins reading
extracts from Shakespeare at an early age, and by the time he
goes to university will have studied a number of the major plays.
The status of *noh* literature in Japan is more like that of Chaucer
in the Western curriculum, a specialist interest because of its
language problems. High school students learn something of *noh*
and *kabuki* in historical surveys, but do not read the texts.
*Kabuki*, academically speaking, still bears the stigma of a popular
art. The universities offer few practical theatre courses. There is
no equivalent of American departments of speech and drama; the
courses cover history and theory only. At Waseda University,
well known for its dramatic studies, about half of the teaching is
concerned with the Western theatre. Students may perform in
plays at junior (third-year) level, but anyone with a serious interest in acting and production is advised to join a company and
attend its school.

The students organize for themselves many things that they do
not find in the curriculum. This serious club-life is one of the
most valuable features of modern Japanese universities. Several
have *noh*-clubs, devoted to the study and performance of classical
drama, and they learn, from a professional instructor of the Five

Families, the techniques of chanting, and perform choral passages from the more familiar plays. One such group at Hosei University is taught by a member of the Kanze family. They make up parties for performances, and give the theatres loyalty, if little in the way of financial support. But most of the audience learn about the theatre not from books, but by going to plays, and many are surprisingly ignorant of the history of what they see while still enjoying and applauding its present manifestations. I have been given enough enthusiastic misinformation, by students and others, to fill a sizeable book of its own.

Another less admirable feature of the contemporary theatre is a new chauvinism determined to guard Japanese culture against foreign interference. Although the theatres are full of Western plays, there seems to be a plot to keep out Western audiences. Many foreigners spend months in Japan without being aware of the vast amount of theatrical activity, and this is not entirely their own fault. There is a bland official assumption that tourists will be interested only in the Kabuki-za, the strip-shows of Asakusa and the Nichigeki Music-hall. Anyone wishing to penetrate further finds difficulties. Visiting professionals are welcomed with open arms, but for the middle group, those who are not professionally orientated and yet have more than a passing interest in the theatre, there is little aid. Even the National Theatre, which aims to become a living museum of Japanese drama, pays scant attention to attracting the visitor. For this reason it draws precisely the wrong type of foreign audience: culture-hungry ladies for whom all is quaint and wonderful, and American sophomores who sneer at what they cannot begin to comprehend, sit grudgingly through two Acts and rush for the nearest *discothèque*. In Paris, once one has established that one is interested in something other than the *Folies Bergère*, information is plentiful and access easy. In Tokyo the new isolationism persists in regarding as eccentric any foreigner determined to see all aspects of the theatre. This is a pity. In most cases, language is a minor obstacle. A production like the Nissei's *Anna Karenina* would be meaningful to those who spoke no Japanese, and even, I dare surmise, to those who knew only the bare outline of the story; and it would give a far more accurate impression of the contemporary theatre than the obligatory few hours at the Kabuki-za.

## The naturalizing of the musical

Japan's first public introduction to the musical theatre of the West came in 1903 with the production of Gluck's *Orfeo*. But Western opera is ill-suited to the Japanese style: modern composers have found more satisfaction in creating their own, with musical settings of *kabuki* stories. In 1965 Japan saw its first American musical, *Hello, Dolly*, in Osaka. This had considerably more appeal, and Tokyo now has a theatre, the Imperial, devoted to this genre. It is aptly named. The original Imperial Theatre, built in 1911, was modelled after the typical European opera house and was influential in introducing Western theatre techniques to the country. Its glittering ultra-modern successor confronts the Imperial Palace, next to the square, grey, unprepossessing building that served as General MacArthur's Occupation headquarters. The lobby is magnificent, overhung with lights shaped like bronze stalactites; it leads into an avenue, almost a small township, of restaurants to suit every Japanese and American taste. Almost every theatre in Japan does what England permits only at Glyndebourne, and allows a long intermission for dining. Performances at major theatres rarely last less than four hours, a length hallowed by tradition and now almost mandatory, even for Western plays. Six or six-thirty is the normal curtain time, in deference to an audience largely limited to public transport; the subways close at midnight. An evening at the theatre thus becomes a major undertaking, requiring physical stamina and the ability to go for long periods without food or drink. Fortunately the auditorium of the Imperial Theatre is as luxurious as the stage is well-equipped. Apart from the National and the Nissei, it is the only comfortable theatre in Tokyo.

Japan has traditionally excelled in imitation. If any proof were needed, *Half a Sixpence* gives it. This is the British musical based on H. G. Wells's *Kipps*; not a slavish duplication of the London or New York production, but the next worst thing. There are several moments where *kabuki* influence reveals itself – in the frantic choreography of the draper's shop with its mobile curtain screens, and in the split-second costume changes, particularly when Kipps transforms himself from shop assistant to gentleman behind a moving chorus, bobbing up at intervals in various stages of metamorphosis. The Japanese have infused the play with their own love of spectacle.

But this is as far as national independence goes. If you shut your ears to the language and overlook the pagoda-like cast given to the view of London from the bridge, you could swear you were on Broadway or at Drury Lane watching this, or for that matter any other, musical. The tyranny of the present musical form, like the anonymity of the international hotel, overrides national traditions and native genius. The sight of something so familiar in surroundings so exotic fanned my smouldering resentment against the standardization which this form imposes on its practitioners.

When *Oklahoma* broke upon the world, it was hailed as a decisive break with the clichés of musical theatre. This was no longer Vienna three times removed, but something new and vital. It embodied a distinctively American spirit; it had a partly tragic theme; it revolutionized choreography by taking it seriously. Its successors continued to rise above triviality. They handled such hitherto unheard-of subjects as race relations (*South Pacific* and *West Side Story*), union disputes (*The Pajama Game*) and municipal politics (*Fiorello!*). It could be objected that these were superficial and romanticized, but at least the new musicals had a hard core of argument that Strauss, Lehar, Romberg and even Porter and Kern lacked. They created a new theatrical language, a new fusion of action, speech and song; in their own way and from their own standpoint they were moving towards the same concept of 'total theatre' that attracted writers in the so-called legitimate fields. Brecht and Weill, on the one hand, and Rogers and Hammerstein, on the other, were not so far apart.

Those happy days are gone. The musical still bases itself on serious works, but only to dignify itself by association. The libraries are ransacked for material: Dickens, Austen, Thackeray, *Ah, Wilderness!* and *Goodbye, Mr Chips*. Theatrical experiment has fossilized into another set of clichés. All of these are in the Imperial Theatre performance, and all the more obvious for being done in Japanese. The sets perform a perpetual and monotonous square dance, up both sides and down the middle. A follow-spot flirts coyly with the leading man. Stage movement is dictated by acoustics, which is no longer a matter of the performers' voices, but of the placing of the microphones. The stage has grown so large that actors cannot cope unaided. Any dialogue scene must be played downstage centre. Even the chorus is trapped. As they mass and sing, a thicket of microphones descends to dangle over their heads. There could be no more convincing demonstration of their incompetence to do what they have been trained and paid for. *Half a Sixpence* is one form of imitation that the Japanese theatre could afford to do without.

For those who thought that the two-part costume extravaganza went out with Dryden, the Imperial Theatre offers, for the first time on any stage, and with the benediction of the late Margaret Mitchell's husband, *Gone with the Wind*. Part One, which I was unable to see, opened the theatre in November 1966 and took the story up to the burning of Atlanta. Part Two, after a brief recapitulation, discovers Scarlett gnawing roots on the blasted soil of Tara, and making her famous vow that she will live through this and never be hungry again.

*Gone with the Wind*, in Japan, is not so much a book as a national obsession. A fan club in Kyushu studies it in English and holds lectures on it. The film originally grossed $1,110,000 in Japan, and when recently revived here in the 70-mm version drew packed houses for months; school parties attended as a history assignment. The reasons for this popularity are not hard to find. For an audience brought up on *kabuki* and the noble melancholy of the Japanese novel, *Gone with the Wind* has all the approved virtues. It is genteel and lachrymose. It has a civil war and the flower of the aristocracy sacrificing themselves to the call of duty. The Code of the Old South (which no-one here would dare to call a myth) substitutes effectively for the decorum of feudal – and modern – Japan. Add to this, in Part Two, the death of a father in the first Act, a husband in the second and a beloved daughter in the third, together with True Love discovered and immediately blighted, and there is nothing more to ask.

Part One set a number of Japanese records, playing for 197 performances and attracting audiences from as far afield as the southern states of America. Part Two, determined to surpass them, has spent 30,000,000 yen on décor alone (three times the cost of Part One) and as much again on the costumes: in total, about one-third of the $3,900,000 spent on the film, no small budget for any play, and by Japanese standards fantastic. The play leans heavily on the film, of which it is frequently and deliberately reminiscent. Its prologue includes several shots from the film version. We see, first, back-projected on a screen that fills the stage, a huge map of the Confederate States, seared by the explosion at Fort Sumter, while the massed Southern aristocracy cheer on the forestage. The picture changes to the subsequent carnage, and the patriots are jostled from the stage by fleeing refugees. Clark Gable drives Vivien Leigh out of the conflagration of Atlanta, and the play proper begins with Scarlett, ragged and famished, grovelling on the turnip patch. It is theatrical ancestor-worship in a new form. The stage production reveres the film as *kabuki* actors do their predecessors. The definitive statement has already been made; the stage can only hope to imitate, and not surpass. And so the film is constantly before our eyes, if not in excerpt, then by suggestion. Back projections reinforce the exterior scenes throughout; the method of the prologue is continued through the play. The settings duplicate as far as possible those of the film. The Japanese Rhett Butler and Ashley Wilkes are living images of Clark Gable and Leslie Howard. When Scarlett stands poised against the sunset in the final tableau, we miss only the whirr of the projector. This interweaving of film and play also recalls the Japanese theatre's fascination with the new medium in the early years of this century, when actors were used for interior and film for exterior scenes. *Gone with the Wind* is an interesting throwback, in more senses than one.

The play is staged with the solemnity proper to a national epic, albeit an adopted one. Strictly speaking it is not a musical at all, though it is so billed. There is no singing, apart from occasional snatches of 'Marching through Georgia', and the music (by Stephen Foster out of *Madam Butterfly*) is incidental. *Gone with the Wind*, in this version, is spectacle pure and unashamed. It unfolds in a series of elaborate pictures, separated by long dark patches during which the scenery trundles across the stage, directed by its own system of traffic lights. In fact the whole colossal enterprise is like a film with an intermission every few frames: Part Two alone runs nearly five hours. The producers, aware that most of the obvious spectacle is over with Part One, have done their best to compensate. The hall of Tara is appropriately vast and continually revolving to show side rooms and galleries. Ashley and Scarlett play one of their scenes of thwarted passion before the menace of a gathering thunderstorm while the mansion glows sullenly on the hill. To match the burning of Atlanta in Part One, Shanty Town is fired by the Klan in Part Two: silhouetted against a filmed conflagration, the buildings on the forestage flare and topple, belching alarmingly realistic flames and smoke.

For all the preposterous nature of the story, it is a far happier adaptation than *Half a Sixpence*, for the reasons cited above. It fits perfectly into the national pattern; it is mint-julep *kabuki*. Everything is several times larger than life. The villains – Wilkerson, the discharged overseer turned Yankee, and the Union army *en masse* – rant, swagger, twirl their moustaches and laugh diabolically. Big Sam, an underprivileged Sukeroku, fells ten (count them, ten) would-be rapists in a fist fight; the film was content with three. Even the cavalry snorting at the door sound more like Union Pacific than the Union army. The acrobatics are here too. Scarlett tumbles down a flight of stairs which flatten out obligingly, like the trick staircase at a fun-fair, to make her fall easier. And, of course, there is the constant weepiness. In one short scene Scarlett suffers her miscarriage and learns that she can never have another child; the adorable Bonnie is killed while ponyjumping; Rhett takes to drink, and Melanie to her deathbed. The negro servant, the only one left standing, promptly goes into raving hysterics. In the circumstances, it seems the only thing left to do. Like *kabuki*, the play is largely static, punctuated by moments of intense violence. Like *kabuki*, it is enormous fun.

*Two plays at the Nissei*

The Nissei is one of Tokyo's newer theatres, antedating the Imperial, its near neighbour, by two years. It was created to fill a theatrical and political void; in Japan the two things usually go hand in hand. Conservatives allied themselves with *kabuki*, left-wingers with the *avant-garde*, and political allegiances determined where one would work. One Japanese film took its subject from this ideological battle in the theatre, showing a *kabuki* troupe forced to share quarters with a left-wing company, and being taught social responsibility in the process. It was virtually impossible for a conservative director to produce a left-wing play if he was interested in it solely on its merits. To some extent the cleavage still exists, but the Nissei, as the following will show, provides at least one meeting-ground for old and new.

The auditorium is two stories up; ground-space in central Tokyo is too valuable to waste. Magnificent red-carpeted stairs lead up to it, and are nearly always empty. The Japanese prefer the narrow escalators which wind covertly up the sides. We need not wait till curtain-rise for spectacle: the auditorium is good for fifteen minutes. Its walls are encrusted with mosaic, shimmering in aquamarine and gold. They curve and bulge, bursting from time to time into a glass-domed excrescence through which one peers hopefully, expecting to see, at the least, Captain Nemo conducting an underwater funeral. It is disappointing to find only ventilators. You blink at the curtain; the curtain, woven of metallic thread, blinks back. It is Neptune's palace, Aladdin's cave from a Palladium pantomime, enormous, opulent and exquisitely vulgar.

What happens on the stage, fortunately, is not. It is *Anna Karenina*, written by many educated Japanese as *Kalenina*, as if to compensate for *Herro*, *Dorry*; the production is by the dean of contemporary directors, Senda Koreya. It is a treatment, from a distinctly unusual point of view, of one of the most famous Western love-stories.

A gong sounds, the curtain rises, and we are peering into a black void. Out of the darkness shuffle the peasants. There seem to be hundreds of them. They are worn, wrinkled, silent. Their movements are tentative and groping; they blink their eyes and shake their heads in a puzzled way, as if they have been behind that curtain, in the dark, for centuries. They look out at us, un-comprehending, as if they are scared of what they might see. Their mute presence dominates the action; and it is not always mute. Sometimes they sing. Sometimes a few girls fall laconically into the rhythm of a folk-dance. Once, to bridge a scene-change, a line of fat old women snakes along the forestage, holding out their wares for us to buy – cakes, fruit, sausages. At these moments they move in a curious puppet-like way, their eyes silently mock-ing themselves, and us, 'We are the folk,' they are saying, 'and this is a folk-dance. Isn't this what you expected?' Then they are still again, watching us and the main characters with the same disturbing intentness. They are the sub-text of the production, but a sub-text written in red letters, and one which grows more obtrusive as the play proceeds, until at last it jostles the love-story for chief place. The peasants are always there, somewhere. Even in the boudoir scenes there are one or two of them squatting on the steps, or half visible in a dark corner; the myriad skeletons at the feast, a perpetual reminder of how the other ninety per cent lives.

The stage now flickers with light. Railroad tracks are projected over the peasants' faces, on the drab brown wings, on a translu-cent screen lowered over the forestage. A train roars; the lighted windows hurtle past us on the screen. It is suffused with red. There has been an accident, one of the peasants has been killed. The others crowd round his body like sleepwalkers, not crying, not angry; simply noting. Then they turn to look at us. We shud-der. They move back into the darkness, to take up their positions as silent sentinels over the main action.

In the middle of the stage is a multi-tiered revolve. It is turned by hand – the peasants' hands – and it turns continually. On this structure the aristocrats cavort and go through the motions of love, hate and despair. It is light on the platform, in contrast to the dark below. The sets are built and rebuilt, a changing succes-sion of beautiful, fragmentary, flimsy pictures. A wisp of curtain,

four pictures and a door-shape: a room. A spire and a truncated
arch poised against the night sky: the perspective of a street. Two
screens, a few tables and some gorgeous costumes: a restaurant.
These scenes merge into one another as the revolve turns. The
restaurant passes into a street, the street into a ballroom. We
can see one scene being erected in the background as another is
being played. The action is similarly fluid. Movement may cry-
stallize into brief moments of ballet. In the ball scene the other
dancers freeze into immobility when Vronsky sees Anna, and
they perform a rapt *pas de deux* among the living waxworks.
Vronsky's fellow officers at the race-course turn into a musical-
comedy chorus, mocking him. A line of peasants makes a frieze
with their scythes against the sky, while the landowner sprawls
reading on a grassy bank, Vronsky walks straight out of his own
scene into Anna's dream, and we see, simultaneously, spread out
across the stage, the military world that Vronsky has just left,
the sleeping Anna, and the dream-Anna and her lover. Time can
be telescoped as easily as it can be frozen. A proposal merges
instantly into a wedding; the girl accepts at the top of the stairs,
changes into her wedding dress half-way down, and finds her
family assembled with the priest on the ground floor.

Between the peasants and the nobility – literally – stand the
servants. They provide a spoken, the peasants an unspoken, commentary on the frivolity of their masters. They walk to the front
of the stage and address us, as in Brecht, directly, in speech or
sardonic song. At the end of Act II our attention is divided three
ways. At stage right, Vronsky seduces Anna in a boudoir. In
Vronsky's bed on the revolve, two of his servants make furtive,
fumbling, ugly love. Across the stage, an emaciated pair of serf-
musicians with drawn faces and gaunt staring eyes play romantic
music on harp and violin. It is a commentary upon a commentary
upon a commentary.

But the main characters also mock their own pretensions.
Vronsky and Karenin, meeting by chance in the street, freeze
into attitudes of melodramatic horror: the modern equivalent
of a *mie*. When Karenin surprises Vronsky with Anna in her room,
he hides behind her skirts and sneaks out by the back stairs. The

actions constantly belie the sentiment of the words, and the lovers continually parody themselves, standing revealed as feeble, posturing and anti-heroic.

The stage is used like a cinema screen. It is divided, fragmented, a montage of vivid vignettes that relate to and remark upon one another, so that we see the same action through several sets of eyes at once. There is a wonderful scene at the opera, when Anna has left husband for lover and is snubbed by her social circle. Isolated objects loom out of the half-light: a swirl of crimson curtain, a scattering of plush chairs, an enlarged fragment of a programme. We look across the footlights of the opera house into the audience. On our side a tenor and soprano protest undying love. Between bars they hiss abuse at each other under their breath. Anna enters. We hear the comments of the audience as their faces turn into the light and they whisper and gossip among themselves. The singers join in the gossip, forgetting their own quarrel. Again the message is obvious. The 'true love' of Vronsky for Anna has no more reality, no greater value, than the pretty charade of feigned love on the stage.

During the first two Acts the peasants have grown more menacing. We have seen their shadows groping behind the walls of Anna's bedroom, turning into the hallucinations that haunt her. Huge pictures of them have been flashed on the wings. In Act III they become still more insistent. They are no longer content to sit quietly at the side. They worm their way through the scaffolding of the revolve, like malevolent vermin. They stroll across and lean on it insolently while a dignitary is making an official speech. He peers at them nervously, wipes his pince-nez, loses his place. The Act opens with a grand tableau. On the platform stands the massed aristocracy, singing a solemn chant. At their feet reel the carousing peasantry, drunk, angry, noisy, offensive. Their choruses interrupt the chant, drown it, and bring it to a halt. War is announced. We see Vronsky drunk and maudlin in the now empty restaurant, torn between Anna and his career. He makes his choice – it is significant, in this production, that he makes it when he is almost too drunk to stand – and leaves to join his regiment. Anna is alone on a bare stage.

Once more the projectors whirr, and the railroad tracks are superimposed on the screen. The lights flicker, the train roars, she jumps. Peasants gather round her body; but over it is projected another image, a heap of skulls. What is one death among so many? What is her personal tragedy when set against the tragedy of a whole people?

We are back, briefly, on the farm. Again the peasants are scything, but this time the landowner works with them, sweating in his shirtsleeves, following their rhythm. And, as the cast assembles for the curtain-call, it is the peasants who are triumphant on the revolve, and the aristocracy who push it round.

This is a production which puzzled many and annoyed some. Sentimentalists who had wept over the film adaptations of the novel – the first with Garbo, and the other with Vivien Leigh – were upset by this disparaging treatment. And yet it was no parody for parody's sake. It brought out the social issues implicit in Tolstoy's work, and which dominated his whole life. Whatever one may think of the treatment of the love-story, the production is a masterly comment on an era and on a changing set of social values.

When the *kabuki* theatre visited Leningrad and Moscow in 1928, with a company led by Ichikawa Sedenji and honoured by the attendance of Stalin, it found an audience wholly sympathetic to its techniques and intentions: perhaps the only country, at that time, where such an audience could be found. Russia had, in Meyerhold, a director who had developed his own presentational theatre, which applied cinematic technique to the stage, fragmented the stage picture, translated action into a sequence of vignettes and externalized emotion in terms of acrobatics. The Nissei *Anna Karenina* recalls the spirit of Meyerhold; it recalls, too, the sardonic social commentaries of Brecht and his disciple Roger Planchon's ridicule of the pretensions of history. In fact Senda's production and Planchon's *Les Trois Mousquetaires* (a *succès de scandale* in Paris, seen also in London in 1960) have much in common. Both take romantic figures hallowed by literary associations and reduce them to creatures of straw. Both show up philosophy as pomposity, grandeur as play-acting, heroics as self-interest. Planchon's Richelieu conducts diplomatic negotiations while making an omelette. The posturings of Senda's Vronsky belie his heartfelt protestations of love. In both there is a levelling process. The grand of the earth are shown in their all too human absurdity: high sentiment is equated with lust.

And yet, in its techniques, *Anna Karenina* is entirely homespun. The visual magnificence; the episodic structure; the rapid changes of set and costume, revealing their own mechanics; the mixture of song, speech and dance; even the hand-operated re-volve, which goes back to the early days of the popular theatre – all these are born out of *kabuki*, as is the presentational method of the actors and their alienation (in the Brechtian sense) from their roles. An ancient technique is adapted to a theatrical philosophy which is, once more, modern. Where *kabuki* recognized the distinction between the costume, which was the character, and the actor who wore it, this production distinguishes the social mask from the underlying reality; and the point of the play is in this division. What we have here is *kabuki* plus thought. Brecht himself was deeply influenced by the theatre of the Orient. His characters are designed at once to attract and repel; we are half moved by them, half revolted by their pretensions. It is precisely this effect that *Anna Karenina* so brilliantly achieves. Senda's use of the revolving stage exemplifies his attitude to the whole work. A piece of stage machinery acquires social significance, just as the episodic structure, in *kabuki* an end in itself, is used to show per-sonal relationships as fragmentary, unco-ordinated and, ulti-mately, meaningless.

*Anna Karenina* was followed at the Nissei by *Eurydice*, Anouilh's fair-to-middling treatment of the Orpheus legend, directed by Asari Keita. It was another *tour de force*. By all the rules a pro-duction in which one is immediately, and at times wholly, con-scious of the lighting should be classified as bad. This was not. Asari has taken that hoary device, the follow-spot, and given it point and meaning. A tilted black platform fills the depth of the stage. On it people and furniture are ranged in isolation. Each character exists in his own pool of light. The spots are so deftly handled that they follow the actor to a hair's-breadth. They state the loneliness, the failure to communicate, that is part of the play's theme. Sometimes they assume a life of their own. Orfée first meets Eurydice in the dingy station café. The railway intrudes upon the set. Signals hang overhead, steam rises through the bridge, lights flicker as the trains come and go; it is a transient world, where contact is fleeting and accidental, where we pursue our own voyages and only momentarily impinge on those of others. We see, as islands of light in a sea of darkness, the cashier's desk, a couch, and a few scattered chairs and tables. Travellers settle for a moment and then pass on into the night, to the next train, the next caravanserai. When the lovers come together, the black floor blooms with spotlights, sharp bright circles, quivering, beautiful and evanescent, like lilies on the surface of a pond. When Eurydice is drawn back into the orbit of her odious family. Orfée is separated from her by a gauze curtain. As he claws at it to get back to her, the spotlights play upon it, transforming an intangible barrier into a solid one, like finger-smudges on a window pane. It is a production where the actors form only one element of the theatre's technical resources, and accept this subordination cheerfully.

Once again *kabuki*'s apparent weaknesses are transformed into assets. It is no accident that these modern productions rely so heavily on film techniques, for the cinema, which constructs drama from a succession of momentary images, is the logical successor to the ideas implicit in *kabuki*. It is also in the film world that traditional and modern actors may most easily meet. *Kabuki* actors are assumed within the traditional hierarchy, while *shingeki* operates its own schools, but both are driven to the film, while deploring it, from financial necessity. And even modern actors have fallen heir to a frame of mind that three centuries of *kabuki* have produced. They tend to see the play as a series of individual performances, rather than an ensemble; they see each scene as self-contained, rather than as part of a larger whole. Asari has capitalized on this fragmentation of the dramatic impulse as neatly as Senda did in *Anna Karenina*, though to a different end. The concept of the isolated actor whose performance should not infringe on those of others subserves the play's theme of non-communication; the loneliness of the actor becomes that of the character. One notices how the minor figures in the café scene – the waiter and the cashier – and, afterwards, the waiter in the hotel bedroom, freeze when nothing is required of them. This too is venerable *kabuki* practice. The focus is on one figure at a time, and the rest become so much stage furniture.

*Kabuki*, too, though actor-dominated, recognizes the independent existence of the setting, and its right to its own moments of glory. This influences Asari's use of lighting. The moving spotlights have their own dramatic statement to make, and the actors recognize throughout that they are not necessarily the most important things on stage. The Nissei productions are the true heirs of the *kabuki* tradition; by a process of evolution and the acquisition of a director, the Japanese theatre has arrived at the form which the West reached by a different path and called 'epic'.

### *New* kabuki

It is doubly disappointing to walk next door to the Takarazuka Theatre and see the travesty which the Japanese themselves have chosen to regard as *kabuki*'s successor. Female emancipation, theatrically speaking, went to the heads of the post-Meiji Japanese much as it did in England after the Restoration. Women had for centuries been prohibited from the stage. Once the break with tradition had been made, companies rushed to the other extreme. Not only were actresses seen again, but whole troupes of actresses. The conventions were reversed; if men had played women why should not women now play men? This exploitation of the feminine, of which Okuni would wholly have approved, produced such transvestite manifestations as the Girls' Opera, which regularly attracts huge audiences, themselves mostly women, as well as all-woman *kabuki*. It has also begotten the hybrid form known as new, or mixed, *kabuki*, mounted here by Toho Enterprises.

The pundits dismiss new *kabuki* as contemptible, and for once the pundits are right. Not that the actresses are to blame; they are elegant, decorative, even talented. But their material is sadly inferior. Its creators have borrowed the genres of *kabuki* – historical, domestic, low-life – its scenic expansiveness and some of its mannerisms. They cannot approach its art. The first sight of the stage is ominous. There is a full Western orchestra, including the ultimate horror, an electric organ. A runway, cabaret-style, separates this from the stalls, and a truncated *hanamichi* bridges the orchestra-pit to the stage. Curtained alcoves on either side of the proscenium arch open from time to time to reveal musicians or scenery.

The first play is a historical piece dealing, predictably enough, with one of the many amours of Prince Genji. The set is a huge picture-book, from which *kimono*-clad figures peep coyly forth to turn the pages. Choruses emerge; there is much dancing with fans and occasional bursts of song that might have been written by Sigmund Romberg cultivating Japanalia in his dotage. The performance, in fact, combines the worst features of *kabuki* and Western musical comedy. From its honourable ancestor it has taken the least worthy characteristics, the sentimentality and the deliberate cultivation of the superficial; but where these in the original were redeemed and disciplined by high art, in the adulterated version they exclude all else, and are emphasized by the music, which intrudes at any pretext for pathos. Its emotions are as synthetic as its costumes, which glitter but have no weight; it is as banal as a picture postcard of Mount Fuji. As the revolve turns and the scenes become gaudier and drearier, one has an increasing sense of *déjà vu*. And of course one has seen it all before, with better music and an infinitely better script, in *The Mikado*.

Some things work well. There is more sense of direction, the tempo is faster and the *longueurs* of *kabuki* are absent. The sword fights are well choreographed. One hero dispatches seventeen of his enemies, by my count, singlehanded. Their bodies drape the stage in picturesque distortions; one falls head first down a well. By cabaret standards the dancing is well done, particularly by a chorus who parade along the runway with lanterns on their heads. For half an hour, in a night club, it might pass. But when it uses the traditional *kabuki* devices it defeats its own ends. One of the side stages opens on *joruri* chanters – an amplified *joruri*, but still drowned by the orchestra. There are even fans in the audience who shout their favourites' names, in approved style. But their cries ring false, as if they were not so much applauding the actors as trying to convince themselves. These delusions of grandeur show up the shoddiness of the whole proceedings. *Kabuki*, which has already established categories – 'cotton' and 'silk' – to distinguish peasant plays from those about the aristocracy, should now admit a third, nylon *kabuki*, to describe an offshoot which is cheap, glossy and all too obviously factory made.

### The examination of conscience

From one of the largest theatres to what, surely, must be the smallest; located near Roppongi, under a plate-glass store, and inhabited by the Free Theatre, Jiyu Gekijo. The company has borrowed a name of honour in its own country and in others. It was Antoine's *Théâtre libre* that offered the first decisive challenge to French romanticism in the late nineteenth century, and in Japan the original Jiyu Gekijo, in the Meiji Era, broke new ground by offering its audiences controversial Western plays.

We descend a flight of break-neck stairs and squeeze into a fifty-seat auditorium. The audience is late in coming, but makes up in numbers what it lacks in punctuality. More chairs are brought in and crammed between the front row and the stage and into the side, and only, aisle. It is now impossible to get in or out. If fire breaks out – which is more than likely; part of the freedom is that everyone smokes as heavily as possible – we shall die like rats. There is no stage. The actors' end of the room is divided from ours by a cheap muslin curtain, badly dyed. We sit back in uncomfortable resignation and reflect that Antoine's opening night must have been like this. At least the play's title is tantalizing. It is *Oedipus in Hiroshima*.

Once the lights dim, things improve. It appears that the muslin curtain has a purpose other than economy. It becomes a screen through which illuminated objects are revealed to us. The play's prologue, in fact, uses no actors: it is *son et lumière*, a recorded voice supported by sudden, dramatic illuminations. Tilted in a red spotlight, a tape-recorder announces the end of the world. Clouds of butterflies, held on rods by *kabuki*-like property men, rise into the light, flutter for a moment, fall and die. The recorder grows slower and fainter, grinding to a halt. In another corner of the stage a large picture of a human foetus comes into view. It pulses in the light to the beating of a drum, the rhythm of the human heart. Like the voice it fades and dies. We are looking into nothingness.

The play, unfortunately, never quite lives up to this beginning. It is based on the strange, tortured personality of Claude Eatherly, the airman who gave the all-clear signal for the dropping of the first bomb on Hiroshima, and thereby sealed its fate. It leans heavily – perhaps too heavily – on the book written by Gunther Anders about Eatherly, and the letters that passed between them. Its format – a trial in the afterlife – has already become something of a cliché, both on the stage and in such films as *A Matter of Life and Death* and *The Story of Mankind*. Eatherly is the defendant. One advocate, a sabre-rattling, whisky-gulping Napoleonic general, argues military necessity. The other, robed and banded, represents the Church and the sanctity of human life. What the judge represents is difficult to say. A whiskered Chinese, he spends most of the trial not merely inscrutable but asleep. His waking moments are occupied in building towers of children's blocks and knocking them down again. He is meant, perhaps, to symbolize the ultimate indifference of history. A sign hangs over him, *Dura Lex Sed Lex*; but here law itself seems to have abdicated.

But, as Kenneth Tynan once said about a similar play by Pearl Buck, no treatment of this subject can ever be dull. Here the evidence redeems the trial. Pictures flash upon a screen, sometimes erotic, sometimes horrifying, culminating in a montage of the Hiroshima devastation. A twittering, *kimono*-clad couple dance onto the stage: Old Japan, picturesque and quaint. A flash, an explosion, and they return in seared and tortured masks. Again and again Eatherly re-enacts his mission, the events that have come to haunt him. Abandoned by the court without a verdict, he becomes his own judge and executioner. It is at this point that the title becomes relevant. Like Oedipus, he feels himself guilty, though of a crime forced on him by higher powers, and one that he could scarcely have avoided. Like Oedipus, he responds to the pressures upon him by blinding himself. Masked and sightless he gropes his way across the stage, exemplifying our horror, our pressures, our insistent sense of responsibility for things which, none the less, seem to be beyond our power to control. At the end, when the play regains contact with actuality, it finds its most powerful moment: the reading of Eatherly's own letter to Anders, shorn of dramatic embellishment. It is simple, poignant and moving.

It is not, perhaps, a good play. If its middle had reached the quality of its beginning and its end, it would have been a magnificient one. Like so many plays of this type, it falls into the trap of overstatement; it preaches too much, and relies on shock tactics which fail to shock because they are too obvious and too predictable. The advocates bellow their challenges directly at us; we are separated from them only by a flimsy balustrade. A doll is guillotined on the stage. There is a great deal of ritual marching about by figures in green aprons and rubber gloves, representing the contributions of science. For all this it should be made compulsory viewing for those who think that the contemporary Japanese theatre begins and ends at the Nichigeki Music-hall.

It is interesting to compare this with a European importation that employs the same form, many of the same techniques and substantially the same theme, with considerable greater success: Peter Weiss's *Die Ermittlung* (subtitled *Oratorium in* zwei *Gesängen*), directed by Senda Koreya at the Toshi Centre Hall. By careful planning or sublime accident, it takes place, literally, over the heads of the International Conference for the Advancement of Science. In *Anna Karenina* Senda had a script that demanded the utmost mobility. Here he has one that is largely static. We are once again in a courtroom. A tribunal sits in judgement on the administrators of the Nazi extermination camps. The defendants, eighteen of them, sit in numbered ranks on our right. They wear identical black suits, identical dark glasses; they are the machine.

Except when individuals are picked out for questioning, they move and react as one. They fix their unified, ironic gaze upon the witnesses; from time to time they turn to look, appealingly, at us. A small railed platform in the centre, lit by an overhead light, is the witness stand. On it the former prisoners re-enact their suffering. Linked with the pictures that flash on the screen behind it, it serves to indicate a railway truck or a cell. The black curtains which enclose the trial are diagrammed with plans of the death-camp. These too are used as screens for Senda's beloved projections.

It is by this device that Senda illuminates the austerity of the script, and the elements are held in perfect balance. In *Oedipus in Hiroshima* the histrionics often drowned the message. Here the emotions are deliberately held in check. There is no ranting. The tone is one of factual reporting, and the brutality of those facts made apparent by the visual images. They begin (in much the same dispassionate way as the Nazi mind must have worked, treating human slaughter as a problem in logistics) with a map of Europe charting the areas chosen for deportation of the Jews. This is followed by a diagram of the camp itself, with the railway lines leading to it. The pictures come closer and grow more personal. We see the camp gate with its derisive slogan: *Arbeit macht frei*. We see the huts and the walls; the roll of prisoners, with significant deletions; the rations, the uniforms, the identification cards. At one point the double fence of barbed wire spills over from the centre screen to the whole stage, as if defendants, witnesses and court were all prisoners, caught up in a common crisis from which they could not escape. Then come the poison gas, the graves, the ovens; the piles of spectacles, the canisters of extracted teeth. And round the court, in a sinister *obbligato*, glow the names and marks of the giant companies – not merely Krupps and Siemens, but ICI and others nearer home, all symbols of the subjection of the individual to the corporate interest. Against these the repeated picture of chimneys belching smoke takes on a double meaning.

At the end the defendants retaliate. Leaping from his seat, one of them, blonde, bespectacled, challenges the prosecutors on their humanity. The death-camp images vanish from the screen and are replaced by others, equally horrible, equally familiar: the mushroom-shaped cloud, the tormented victims of Hiroshima. The play which opened with a starved and wizened corpse closes with an H-bomb explosion. *Die Ermittlung* ends with a challenge. It answers no questions, but provokes more. It was one of the few plays I have seen in Tokyo where the customary Japanese restraint in applause was entirely appropriate. The only possible applause is thought.

## *Shogun* Oedipus

Tokyo is cosmopolitan in its eating habits. It has Viennese, Russian, Chinese, Persian and Hungarian restaurants, Italian pizza parlours, German bierkellers, Korean barbecues and a Hamburger Inn. The Café Giraud in Shibuya, one of the brighter suburbs, offers, as its name suggests, French chansons and Paris prices, together with a backroom production of *Oedipus the King*.

Certain resemblances between the classical dramas of Greece and Japan have already been discussed in these pages. In many ways the two are temptingly similar. Japanese students are regularly taught that Greek drama is 'like *noh*', and some scholars have attempted to show a historical connection between them. It is impossible to prove. We can trace the Greek theatre to India, and part, at least, of the Japanese back to China, but scholarship cannot, and probably never will, bridge the yawning gulf between. Others have argued that the resemblances are purely superficial, and that one cannot be properly discussed in terms of the other. This view, I believe, goes too far to the other extreme. The number of possible theatre techniques is, after all, finite; and it is not unreasonable that two forms of dramatic art, founded on similar aesthetic premises, should evolve independently into similar forms of expression. Both were created from a fusion of the epic tradition with the dance; both took their material from historical and mythic sources; and both universalized this material by adopting a noncommittal stage, spatially and temporally undefined. It seems also, as I have suggested earlier, that the Greek and Japanese actors shared a common attitude towards the playing of their roles, particularly in the portrayal of character by external symbols. The later histories of the two forms also have much in common. Both were tradition-bound and reluctant to countenance innovation; and Greek tragedy, preserved largely by academic favour, has resisted theatrical experimentation hardly less effectively than *noh* since its adoption by the Shogunate. Most productions seen today adhere to some vague notion of the 'classical' approach, though few would be prepared to commit themselves as to what this was. Greek tragedy and *noh*, in their later days, have both been smothered by the odour of sanctity.

It is doubly interesting therefore to see a Greek play interpreted by techniques which, though themselves ancient, come much closer to a living theatre tradition. The greatest stumbling-block for Western – even Greek – directors is the Chorus, which has virtually disappeared from our theatre except in its truncated Elizabethan form. Most productions try to rationalize its existence in terms of stage action, a self-defeating compromise: the Chorus is essentially a formal device, and any attempt to treat it as a stage crowd merely makes the formality more apparent. There is no such problem in Japan, where *noh* has perpetuated the choral tradition. In this production, beautifully directed by Hayano Toshiro, the Citizens of Thebes were treated frankly as a *noh* chorus. The stage was a small platform at one end of the hall, which itself held little more than seventy people. The chorus took its position on the balcony above, appropriately framing the action, and never moved except to rise and chant. The actors, too, were spared the endless perambulations inflicted on them by Western directors to compensate for a largely actionless script. Movements, again as in *noh* were limited, and gained intensity from the restriction. The most powerful passage of the play, in fact, was a moment of complete stillness, when Oedipus, silent on the stage, waited impassively for the arrival of the shepherd and the sealing of his fate. Hardly less powerful and all the more effective in contrast to its largely static context was Oedipus's pouncing on the shepherd to wring the information out of him. The transition from the all-wise king and father of his people to the desperate and lonely man could hardly have been more clearly marked. Hayano had informed the Greek text with his knowledge of the Japanese temperament: the long silence broken by the sudden berserk rage. Most of the cast, except for Oedipus and Jocasta, wore masks (again a convention of the original foreign to us, but familiar here) and the protagonist himself donned a mask after the blinding. The Chorus wore open-work masks, through which their own faces could be seen; Hayano concerned like most modern Japanese directors with bridging the gap between the play and the audience, sought by this device to establish the Chorus as an intermediary, belonging to both worlds.

This production revealed differences as well as similarities. It was a convincing demonstration that Greek tragedy and *noh* exist in the same aesthetic world, and that the imperfectly known techniques of the one can safely be expanded from a knowledge of the other. At the same time it showed the great difference in their philosophies. Up to a point *Oedipus the King* fits perfectly into the Japanese pattern. The theme of an individual struggling against forces beyond his control, placed in a predicament where he is innocently guilty and submitting to a self-inflicted punishment, conforms with the Japanese concept of the hero and his relation to society. By Japanese standards, however, the play should have ended with the submission and the blinding. Sophocles' tragedy conspicuously does not. The hero suffers but endures; more than this, he gains understanding and a new nobility that will be consummated by his saintly death in *Oedipus at Colonus*. Jocasta, not Oedipus, is the perfect tragic character in Japanese eyes: she dies, and her submission is complete. It is here that Sophocles and *noh* diverge. For him, Jocasta is the weakling, the apparently invincible spirit who snaps under strain. Sophocles' humanism, his championship of the fortitude of the human spirit, has no counterpart in the Japanese philosophy.

Three days after I saw this production, the theatre was closed by police order because of the fire hazard. The old enemy of the Tokyo theatre had struck again.

*Two plays by Pirandello*

Pirandello is popular in Japan for reasons which are not hard to find. His speculations on the problem of identity intrigue audiences who have already heard such questions asked in *noh*; his concern with the mask and the face, the gulf between truth and illusion, is readily adaptable to Japanese conventions. *Six Characters in Search of an Author* was offered by the Aoyama Arts Theatre, typically well hidden in a back street, above a kindergarten: shoes to be removed at the door and replaced by slippers far too small. There is no sympathy with the size of Western feet. A minuscule lobby, hung with posters of Joan Baez, Marcel Marceau and a Picasso ceramics exhibition; a huge photograph of Alan Ginsberg in an Uncle Sam hat: and a production in the half round, with the audience along two sides of a large room and the actors in what was left. No stage and only the fragments of a set; the acting area marked out by a coloured floorcloth, with a few chairs and a stepladder scattered around. It was not a bad arrangement for a work which deals, after all, with a play in rehearsal. The actors came and went among the audience, dropping into vacant chairs when out of the action. There is a fierce concern among contemporary Japanese directors with breaking down stage formality and restoring contact between the stage and the spectators – an immediacy which *kabuki* once had, before time and increasing unfamiliarity erected their barriers. The production used its spatial limitations to establish a rapport, made easier because the actors, most of the time, form their own audience to watch the play within a play.

*Six Characters* embodies the same issue as the *noh Yamamba*: art confronting reality and recognizing its own limitations. A company in rehearsal is interrupted by an anonymous and sinister family, who introduce and play their own story. The actors, attempting to reproduce it, find themselves at first inadequate, and then overwhelmed by its horror. Western productions, in differentiating between the two groups, often fall into the trap of making the actors too theatrical, too frivolous, too inadequate. This detracts from Pirandello's purpose; he wants to show the

I

gap between reality and art, not reality and bad art. In this production the problem was neatly solved by adapting a venerable
Japanese convention: the *noh* tradition in which the *sh'te*, the
masked actor, is the only 'complete' character. The visitors were
made up in an approximation to *noh* masks, with the central
portion of their faces (the area which the mask covers) painted
dead white; and the rest was normal flesh colour. The Japanese
convention, of course, reverses that of the West. For us the mask
is a disguise and the face beneath real; in *noh* the mask is real and
the face beneath unimportant: the unmasked *waki* lacks full
definition. The visitors were thus established as prototypes, compared to which the actors were inadequate approximations, and
Pirandello's intention was perfectly fulfilled. Their costumes
were distinguished by the same abstraction. They were dressed
in unrelieved black, like tailor's dummies, with the seams and
basting drawn in white chalk: everyday clothes refined, like the
costumes of *noh*, to their essentials.

The conventions so ably adapted in this production proved
ruinous to *Henry IV*, which cruelly revealed the difficulties the
Japanese actor still has in conforming to a style which is not his
own. The play deals with a man who, thrown from his horse in a
costume pageant, is shocked into the hallucination that he is
Henry IV, the eleventh-century German monarch he was representing at the time. Protected by his friends and relatives, he
lives in medieval surroundings, with all the panoply of the era
in which he imagines himself to be. His servants dress as courtiers
and soldiers; his friends, when they visit, don appropriate
costume. In the course of the action he regains his senses, but is
so horrified by the world around him that he returns, by choice,
to the pretence. The conflict of illusion and reality is constantly
before us, in the contrast between modern language and attitudes
and the medieval costumes into which the characters scramble
when their 'king' appears; it is Pirandello's commentary on the
elaborate pretences we all use to cloak our lives and make them
bearable.

This production was by the Mingei company, a group more
mature and far more technically accomplished than the Aoyama

players; and yet it failed, through no fault of the actors' own. I had seen and admired this group before, in *Incident at Vichy* – the director's nightmare, an almost completely static play. The characters do nothing most of the time but sit on a bench and talk; and I remarked earlier in this chapter on the weight of make-up a Japanese cast has to assume. In spite of these disadvantages they presented a version that was taut, moving and far more successful than the original production at the Lincoln Centre in New York. From *Henry IV* it became obvious that the apparent disadvantages of Miller's work were, for the Japanese actor, assets, and that elaborate make-up is still a psychological as well as a physical necessity. Old habits die hard. Although few modern actors have any close connection with *kabuki*, they preserve, instinctively, the traditions by which the Japanese theatre was for so long bound. Added to this there is, perhaps, something of the Oriental dislike of appearing barefaced: they prefer the concealment afforded by the mask or the inscrutable expression. In practical terms this means that the modern actor is happiest when subjected to a strong external discipline, as in the Nissei productions, where he is used virtually as an instrument; or where he can put some strong barrier of make-up or mannerisms between his own personality and the public. Character parts, therefore, are extremely well played, while straight parts are not. The actor has not yet fully adjusted to the other sort of discipline, the kind which comes from within; he has not learned how the psychology of the character must motivate his outward behaviour. He does the right things and makes the right moves, but only because the director tells him to; he carries no conviction and tends to stop acting when he is not in motion – a failing that became even more obvious when, some weeks later, I saw the production repeated on television. In *Henry IV* this attitude is particularly damaging because it reverses the play's values. By and large the actors when in modern dress are unconvincing. As soon as they climb into historical costume, they become real. But Pirandello demands that the robes be illusory, and the characters beneath them real. Thus the actors go to great lengths to feign an uneasiness in costume that they obviously do not feel.

They smoke cigarettes, hold their halberds upside down, and wear their armour crooked. These heavy-handed attempts to redress a deficiency which is in truth no fault of theirs makes for a confusing evening, so far as the play is concerned, but one which illuminates the crisis of the modern Japanese theatre: the actor still prefers to operate at one remove, and has not learned, yet, to come out from behind the mask.

*Pop Puppetry*

Out to Waseda by three changes of subway; through the narrow, student-packed streets lined with cheap restaurants, and, after several misdirections, up a fire-escape to the Waseda University Little Theatre. It has seventy-five seats. We swelter in the early heatwave. A spokesman apologizes for the failure of the air-conditioning. This is evidently an old, familiar joke. The audience laughs and sweats in good-humoured resignation.

It is difficult to give a name to what happens on the tiny stage. I call it 'Pop Puppetry' because it bears the same relation to the traditional art as pop art does to its own predecessors, using for the most part enlarged advertisements or cartoon characters, mounted on poles and used as rod-puppets. Sometimes balloons appear from their mouths, giving the dialogue. But human actors are used also, sometimes to provide a forest of waving hands, sometimes full length to converse with the puppets and with us. It is directed by Aoki Shin, a young man whose chief interest is in painting, not in the stage, with twelve assistants. His programme gives his own note on the work, and a title. He tells how, from his work in television, he has become increasingly aware of the remoteness of the transmitted image from the person it is intended to reach. The marvel of living pictures has become little more than a background for our daily activities. Therefore he seeks to restore a vital relationship between the image and the spectator, and has called the first part of the programme 'One Hundred Inch Colour Television'.

It consists of a series of sketches, bitterly satirical, in which inanimate objects come to life and change their natures, and intermingle with live actors. The first shows an actor as Hitler, making a speech in mock-German on a swastika-draped dais. The speech is periodically interrupted by banal music as enlarged soft-drink advertisements and rows of bottles are floated across the stage. Gradually the bottles line up and assume a martial posture. As the speech reaches a crescendo, soldiers appear, use the bottles as revolvers or grenades, and aim them at us. Tableau and curtain.

A radio commentator conducts interviews with a series of monsters. Each is larger and more ferocious than the one before. Her questions are always the same: 'What about you? What is your name? What do you do? Are you happy in your present occupation?' They are all quite clear about what they do; they eat things and are perfectly happy. The larger they are, the more voracious they become, and the less interested in anything except eating. The larger visitors cannot even remember their own names, so great has their obsession grown. The last almost fills the stage, and tries to devour the microphone and the inter-viewer with it. Rising from the tussle limp, wounded and covered with bandages, she reaches out towards us, the audience, and asks, '*Anata-wa?*' And you?'

*Eternal Love.* An unseen choir sings a chorus from Handel's *Messiah*. On the stage a diminutive priest waits beside an enor-mous bride. Her face is turned away from us. Where is the groom? Missing, apparently. The puppeteers rise from hiding and search for him. At last he is found and dragged onto the stage. He is even smaller than the priest. The marriage service is read over the incongruous couple. 'Will you take this woman for your lawful wedded wife?' No answer. The priest seizes the groom and tries to force an answer out of him, beating him savagely to the floor. Picking up his limp body and propping it up against the enormous woman, he pronounces them man and wife. The man turns and runs desperately to the front of the stage, searching for escape. As the lights dim his bride turns, and we see her face for the first time. It is red, blotched, distorted, the face of a monster. Her eyes light up. One huge meaty hand poises for a moment above her husband, then descends to pinion him fast as the puppeteers shower the stage with confetti.

There are other incidental delights, such as a number called 'Party a go-go', showing Mao Tse-tung and the Red Guards cavorting to a jazz rhythm. Mao turns round to reveal a hollow body and a heart hung upside down, swinging like the pendulum of a clock. Militarism is the main target throughout. Huge shapes, vaguely like soldiers, loom out of the semi-darkness; harmless objects turn into guided missiles and point at us. The director has certainly established the contact for which he sought.

The second part of the evening is wordless, and called *Dialogue '67*. It is an abstract political fable, using simple, meaningful cut-out shapes, moving to the sound of a tambourine. Against the black curtain hover a crowd of white figures. Each has a triangle for a body and a circle for a head, like pawns in a chess game, or stylized representations of the human shape. A different, more sinister shape appears – a blue pillar, crowned. The Queen? The Whites freeze as it approaches and begin to quiver again as it retreats. This manoeuvre is repeated several times. Finally they lose their fear and crowd round the visitor. It exerts its influence upon them, and one by one they turn blue. There is one abstainer, who keeps his distance from the crowd and resolutely remains white. The Blues go out after their new leader; the remaining White is now the odd man out. The same pattern is repeated with another group and a Red visitor. The Whites become Reds – again, except for one, who joins his fellow exile.

Now Reds and Blues begin to fight each other. First each party peers and runs in turn. Then they take a more menacing stand, surround the Whites and try to carry them away. After a mêlée they retire for reinforcements and bring up their armament, the Knights, grey spiky figures whose mouths snap angrily. As Reds and Blues lock in mortal combat, the two Whites, over whom the battles had begun, go up in flames. The others surround them, flickering nervously from one colour to another, no longer knowing who or what they are, or what the fighting has been about.

This programme is worthy of attention if only for its marked departure from Japanese tradition. There is no real history of satire in Japan; there has been no equivalent of Juvenal, Rabelais, Swift or Pope. Deference for authority is still, perhaps, too strong. Japan, as I write, has just produced *MacBird*; it will be some time before it writes one of its own. Tokyo as yet has no Establishment or Second City. The Waseda performances suggest that, in the next ten years, it may have.

## Noh *in modern dress*

Eda Kazuo has been mentioned earlier in these pages as one who follows in the footsteps of Zeami: a Buddhist priest and *avant-garde* director who gives theatrical expression to his Zen philosophy. The Actors' Theatre includes two one-Act plays under his direction in its programme for this season. They are interesting examples of the application of Zen principles to contemporary life, and of the direction which Japanese playwriting is tending to take; they also illuminate, like the Pirandello plays discussed above, the difficulties of the actor when he ventures outside familiar territory.

*Butter-Inferno*, by Iwata Horoshi, invokes the negative aspect of Zen to show the meaninglessness of existence. The protagonist is a prosperous businessman, president of a medium-sized company. His life bores him; the routine of the business world affords no satisfaction and the play follows his aimless quest for 'something interesting'. He sets off on a taxi ride to seek distraction. The driver, affable and loquacious, conducts him to a middleman, a Virgil to his Dante, who guides him to the first ring of Inferno. It is a smart bar, with a homosexual waiter. After a while the owner appears and tries to entertain him with a story: 'A man was digging a hole in the ground, just wide enough for one. When he had dug down very deep, he heard a noise; it was someone else digging through from the other side. The man thought for a while, then climbed out and began to fill the hole.'

The man finds the story pointless. His restlessness has not been eased, and he is anxious to go on somewhere else. He is passed on to a woman who, the owner says, has been waiting avidly for him. But she has nothing new to offer: like the owner, she is interested

only in telling stories. As the man leaves her in disgust, a supernatural voice summons him to Hell. Death, it promises, is the
only thing that is really interesting. But even Hell, as shown here,
is aimless. We see it populated by bull- and horse-headed monsters, formed into a choir by the Infernal Judge and rehearsing
a dreary song about the fleeting nature of time. The Judge
examines the man about his past life, his hopes, fears and ideals.
After a rambling and incoherent monologue the man falls asleep;
he is put into a centrifugal separator, which reduces him to his
component atoms and assimilates him with the rays of the sun.
As the play ends the actors reveal themselves as actors, take off
their animal heads and begin to clear the stage. One of them is
struck by a sudden inexplicable pain. As he lies writhing on the
floor the others scatter and the curtain falls.

The play is a reverse *Everyman*, in which the protagonist passes
into a limbo which is neither life nor death, and where every
step in his quest takes him closer to a Hell which itself is no more
than a mockery of the pointlessness of life above. Each new contact abuses or denies the existence of the last. The middleman
warns him not to trust the taxidriver, the waiter quarrels with
the middleman, the owner tells him to avoid the waiter, the
woman denies the owner's existence; each lives in his own aimless world, denying the others and shunning contact with them,
like the man digging the hole who withdraws at the first sign of
human company. Time is meaningless. The man's watch stops as
soon as he enters the taxi. The waiter tells him that time is not
only delusory but fatal; the great observatories which watch the
planets, and so ultimately regulate our clocks, have deadly
poison on their telescopes which seeps into our lives. As he
plunges deeper, the man remembers less of his own past.
Examined by the Judge of Hell, he can recall his life only in brief,
incoherent snatches. He remembers his wife's cry when she died;
he remembers, with difficulty, the name of his chief competitor,
and rambles on for a while about his plans to expand his company.
The Judge finds this as meaningless as the man had found the
stories told to him. But Hell too is pointless, preoccupied with
trivia and routine. Every day a man must be placed in the machine

and assimilated with the sun. This is the Judge's drudgery; he asks why, but finds no answer.

*Butter-Inferno* moves in the *noh* world, where time is suspended and past and present, illusion and reality may mingle; where our preoccupation with the passing moment is shown to be absurd, where individual concerns are limited and trivial, and where the individual himself, at the end, is absorbed into the universal continuum. It employs the *noh* motif of the quest to explore the modern malaise, spiritual hunger amid material prosperity, exemplified here both by the protagonist's dissatisfaction and the actor's whimpering at the end: we are sick and do not know why. Eda Kazuo has dressed the play in appropriately modernized *noh* trappings, a compromise between the old stage and the new. The taxicab is shown in outline only, as a frame of neon light. The furniture is sparse, the properties imaginary. The setting reveals itself in layers, successively removed like the protagonist's illusions. Behind each door there lies another; the gate of Hell itself is not the end, but reduplicates itself in a long vista of identical gates extending to infinity. Each new reality reveals itself to be a new illusion; the actors' doffing of their costumes at the end is simply part of the same process.

It is the acting that jars. The play's concept presents a technical challenge that most Japanese actors – and particularly this fledgeling company – are not yet adequately equipped to face. *Noh*'s premise, that the phenomenal world is illusory, is this play's conclusion. *Butter-Inferno* shows a man probing the world around him and being successively disillusioned by what he finds; but the shock of that disillusionment depends upon the completeness of the illusion. *Noh* can dispense with the literal reproduction of actuality, but this play, by its own terms, cannot. It must show actuality to denounce it. The characters must assume a temporary substance: their own world must seem real to them, and they themselves seem real within it. The play demands, in fact, convincing naturalistic acting; it asks from the actor an inner conviction and a psychological awareness that this company could not give. The production consequently suffered from the same embarrassment of styles that beset the Mingei's *Henry IV*, and weakened the argument in much the same way. The Japanese actor out of a mask is, very plainly, an actor; but a play whose point is the distinction between illusion and reality demands that he seem real.

*A Study of the Possessed*, by Terayama Shuji, avoids this problem by putting the actor back behind a mask, and in a formal setting where the company obviously feels more at home. It is a parable about intolerance, a study of the loneliness of the odd man out in society, told in the form of a folk-tale. A girl has been raped by a dog. The neighbours mutter ominously among themselves, fearing that she will produce a puppy, not a human child, and the air is thick with superstition and ill omen. As the dogs howl in the forest, the baby is born, human in shape, but possessed by a dog spirit. His mother dies when he is five years old; two years later his father runs away, leaving him in the care of his old grandmother. He grows up amid animosity, shunned by villagers and animals alike. Yearning desperately for the sympathy that is withheld from him, he grows morose. There are incidents in the village, random acts of destruction committed by some man – or animal. The boy is suspected and beaten. His ways grow stranger. The teacher finds him sniffing like a dog. In class he draws a flower covered with hair. Driven further in upon himself, he takes to living in trees. Then he finds a companion: a stray dog, a pariah like himself. He adopts it. The incidents in the village continue. Rumour-mongers ask who is to blame: the boy or his dog. They try to have the dog killed, but he saves it; the two grow closer together until in their solitude they become one. The boy grows up and is to be married. He is frightened by the thought and runs from it; the years of insidious persecution have done their work, he is estranged from human beings. At last he goes unwillingly to the altar. The following morning the bride is discovered alone in their bed, dead from a neat round wound in her throat.

The actors wear black and perform against black curtains. A narrator reads the story, while the principals move in white masks in the spotlights and use *noh* gestures. Behind them sits the Chorus, chanting from time to time, voicing the rumours of the village and imitating the cries of dogs and owls. Its members are black-hooded, like the assistants who move silently across the stage with properties. The stray dog is a cut-out figure, white, and worked on strings: when master and dog become one, the boy enfolds the animal in his own costume. It is drama which has, once again, become ritual; a perfect modern *noh* in using the traditional appurtenances of the drama to make a folk-tale timeless, and to elevate a simple story into a protest against discrimination and hate. The Japanese theatre, at its most modern, looks back to its earliest beginnings.

# Appendix I: *From Epic to Melodrama: Three Plays of Shunkan*

As an additional comparison of the major dramatic forms it may be interesting to examine the same subject treated successively by *noh*, *bunraku* and *kabuki*. *Shunkan* lends itself admirably to such examination. It has produced one of the most tragic *noh* plays and one of the most emotional of *kabuki*.

The common sources are the old battle annals, *Heike Monogatari* and *Gempei Seisui Ki*; the plot and characters are based firmly on history. *Shunkan* also exists as a *kowaka* text (see pp. 66 f.), which may itself have influenced the *noh* form. Shunkan (b. 1142) was a Buddhist priest of noble family. Rising to high office under imperial patronage, he became dissatisfied with the despotic rule of the Prime Minister, Taira no Kiyomori, whose abrogation of power had brought the Imperial House into disrepute. Shunkan accordingly conspired with Fujiwara no Naritsune, general of the imperial bodyguard, Taira no Yasuyori, a lay priest and high police official, and others to overthrow Kiyomori. The abortive *coup* took place in 1177, and its leaders were killed or exiled. Naritsune's death sentence was commuted, through family influence, to banishment on Kikaigashima (Devil's Island), a barren rock remote from civilization. Shunkan and Yasuyori accompanied him. The two younger men found consolation in religion and set up improvised shrines on the island, while Shunkan, a sceptic, held himself bitterly aloof. Some time later a general amnesty was declared to celebrate the imminent motherhood of Kiyomori's daughter, now Empress. Shunkan was excluded from the

list because of Kiyomori's particular grudge against him: it was
in his house that the *coup* had been planned. The others returned
to the mainland, leaving Shunkan to end his days in solitary exile.

The *noh* version of this story, by Zeami, is classified as a 'fourth
group' play, that is, among those which have a more immediate
and violent dramatic content. It is unusual in having no clamactic
dance.

The play opens with the entrance of the imperial envoy (*waki*)
followed by a sailor (*kyogen*) carrying his sword. Standing by the
*sh'te* pillar, the envoy announces his identity and purpose. The
amnesty has been proclaimed; he is on his way to the island with
a pardon for Naritsune and Yasuyori. He instructs the sailor to
prepare a boat, and both leave the stage.

This much serves for prologue. The play proper now begins,
with the beating of the drums and the entrance of Naritsune and
Yasuyori (*sh'te-tsure*). It is assumed that the scene has shifted to
Devil's Island. Naritsune is dressed in blue, Yasuyori in green,
with a priest's mitre and beads. Both carry fans and wear straw
aprons partially dyed in harmony with their costumes. The
colours are, for *noh*, unusually muted, a concession to the im-
agined privations of the setting; this is the closest *noh* can come
to realistic costuming.

Advancing downstage and facing each other and the audience
alternately, the characters identify the place by its dismal name.
Echoed by the Chorus, they chant of the three shrines they have
built. While still on the mainland they have vowed to make
thirty-three pilgrimages to the shrines of Kumano, which their
punishment had interrupted. They have therefore built replicas
of the shrines on the island and do the best they can. Makeshifts
must serve: homespun garments for pilgrim's robes, white sand
for the offerings of rice, the flowers of a local plant for the prayer-
staff.

This is more than keeping up appearances. Their attitude is
founded on simple piety. Zen teaches that the divine does not
concern itself with externals, and that faith can dispense with the
trappings of worship. The gods are not rooted in Kumano, but
omnipresent; devout hearts can appeal to them, even from a

barren island. 'Now we have asked the gods of Kumano', they sing, 'to take up their abode on this island . . . though far from the Kumano hills, our shrines are sacred to their gods . . . thus we go upon our holy way.' Both cross to the *waki* side, in front of the Chorus, and remain standing through a long musical prelude to the entrance of Shunkan.

He too wears a priest's mitre, a dark robe over pale gold and a black straw apron. His distinctive mask is pale brown, with the mouth open, eyelids closed and the bones prominent in the wizened face. He carries a small wooden bucket, and a fan tucked in his waistband. His opening words are spoken beside the first pine on the *hashigakari*. They are full of bitterness; he compares himself to a dweller in Hell, and to the cicada at autumn's end, perched on a barren tree and singing of its coming death. Entering the stage proper, he is greeted by the others. Showing them his bucket, he announces that he has brought wine, and answers their surprise by explaining that 'wine was originally another name for water with medicinal virtues. So this water may well be excellent wine.' It is the ninth day of the ninth month, the Feast of the Chrysanthemum. They hold a mimic feast, with their fans, by the usual *noh* convention, serving for cups. The Chorus, speaking for them, repeats their longing for the mainland.

We now see, as it were, two places at once: the ship on its journey and the exiles on the island. A stage assistant sets the framework of the boat on the *hashigakari* and coils a rope round the prow. Standing within the boat are the envoy and the sailor, the latter with a slim bamboo pole. Miming the action of steering, he comments on their speed before the wind and announces their arrival at the island. All this while the exiles have sat motionless. Entering the main stage, the envoy unfolds the scroll containing the pardon; the sailor props the boat against the rear wall of the *hashigakari*. Gratefully the exiles take the scroll, and Yasuyori reads it aloud. Shunkan's name is not there. He takes the scroll and reads it for himself. It must be a scribe's error; their crime was identical, and so should their punishment be. He makes the 'weeping' gesture, while the Chorus reiterates the letter's gloomy contents. (Yasuyori and Naritsune, with true *noh* impassivity, have shown no flicker of emotion on their faces, either at their good fortune or their companion's distress.)

Replacing the boat on the *hashigakari*, the sailor ties one end of the rope to the prow and brings the other to the centre of the stage. The envoy enters the boat, summoning the pardoned exiles to follow him. As they turn to leave, Shunkan rises and puts his hand on Yasuyori's shoulder. All are grouped around the *sh'te* pillar at this point. The envoy makes a single gesture of fending Shunkan off with the pole. The priest narrates his own actions: 'Shunkan turns and grasps the mooring rope, trying to hold the departing ship.' But the rope is cut by the sailor. Shunkan clasps his hands and weeps. From the boat the others cry that they will intercede for him; 'Wait patiently!' Shunkan again acts as his own Chorus. 'Shunkan stops his bitter tears . . . he listens with a rapt intent, under the pine-trees on the shore. 'Wait with hope', they shout.' 'Wait with hope and confidence,' chants the Chorus; and they speak of the boat growing smaller in the distance. The voyagers walk slowly out; the sailor carries the boat out after them. 'The waves hide ship and men.' Shunkan is alone on the stage, weeping. The music stops; the play is over; he too turns and exits down the *hashigakari*.

Comparison with Greek tragedy is inevitable and illuminating. Sophocles' *Philoctetes* involves an exile on a desert island, but in issues which are largely social. Sophocles uses his protagonist's plight to explore the relationship between the individual and the community, and to insist that man's ultimate duty is to his fellows, even when they have shown themselves conspicuously unjust. No man is an island, even though he may be forced to live on one. Philoctetes, who at first rejects the proffered reparations, is led to rise above his animosity and return to his proper station.

In its emphasis on the transcendence of self, the Greek play has something in common with *Shunkan*. In the one, the individual must submit to the group will; in the other, the sufferer must restore his faith in the compassion pervading the universe, before which pain is transitory and misfortune an illusion. But here the resemblance ends. Reunion with society is seen as a legitimate goal for Philoctetes. For Shunkan, it is part of his error. Seen with his companions, he seems as resolute as they. But he has merely adjusted; his bitterness has made him self-sufficient. They have accepted. Their reconstruction of the shrines of Kumano on the island is an act of faith. Shunkan's pretence that the water is wine is an act of self-defence. Yasuyori and Naritsune, in being deprived of the physical pleasures of life, have discovered faith (by a process analogous to that of *noh* itself, which refines the temporal to disclose the immanent). The gods are clearer in this barren place. Shunkan has merely found philosophy, which is not proof against the new disaster. His grief at the end of the play stems from 'ignorant attachment'.

The play closes with a cry of consolation: 'Wait with hope; wait with hope and confidence.' Wait for what? Not, surely, for the faint possibility of reprieve, though this may be the superficial meaning of the words. Shunkan's fellows are telling him to have confidence in the ultimate rightness of things: to find the patience they have found, which can dismiss the temporal as unimportant and see good and evil as one. Some modern critics have found their farewells callous. I cannot agree. It is, perhaps, significant that Shunkan, at the end, talks of himself as another person; he becomes his own Chorus. Though this objectivity is a familiar *noh* device, it has particular relevance here. Shunkan begins to see his suffering as something apart. What seems to be a dismal end is really the beginning of the beginning.

The puppet *Shunkan* is one scene of a five-part play, *Heike Nyogo no Shima* (*The Heike on Lost Island*), written by Chikamatsu Monzaemon in 1719 for performance at Osaka. The setting is a lonely rock. A tree springs from its summit, and reeds grow round its base. Behind lies the sea and the unbroken horizon, desolate, forbidding. We are presented with Man against Nature, which in this genre is as familiar a theme as Man against the State. The chanter's voice recites the background as the operators bring in Shunkan. Both in the setting and in his person it is obvious how the stark quality of *noh* has been romanticized. His face is lined and haggard, the cheekbones almost starting through the skin; his hair is sparse and straggling, his beard long and unkempt; his clothes fall in rags around him. Supported on a rough stick, he

hobbles across the rocks to join his companions. *Bunraku* emphasizes the painfulness of his progress. Yasuyori and Naritsune, like
him, grasp at creepers to drag themselves along. Bowing to Shunkan, they sit with him; linking hands, they lament their misery.

At this point *bunraku* introduces a new character and a significant shift of values. Naritsune has fallen in love with an island
girl. He introduces her and announces his intention of marriage.
This exploitation of love interest, foreign to *noh*, is familiar in
the popular forms. The girl is shy; she enters through the side
curtain, hesitates and runs back out of sight. Finally, overcoming
her timidity, she brings things for the wedding ceremony: water,
not wine, in a hollow bamboo, and an abalone shell to make a cup.
(Note how the hint of this in *noh* is worked up for its own sake,
and elaborated into a more picturesque incident.) Shunkan performs the wedding, but their celebration is interrupted by an
unbelievable sight. A boat is coming. They look out across the
audience, tracing its progress along the horizon. It comes nearer,
is visible to us, and enters at stage left. Seno-o, the envoy, disembarks, carrying fan and scroll, and escorted by two servants.
Seated majestically on a stool, he reveals the exiles' destiny. He is
a forbidding figure, white-bearded and ornately dressed, con-
trasting sharply with the suppliants before him. Naritsune and
Yasuyori are elated at the news of their recall. Shunkan is desolate.
He takes the scroll in quivering fingers and reads. His name does
not appear. Desperate, he seizes the wrapper of the scroll and
scans that; it is barren. He falls into a frenzy of grief, writhing
and shaking, his hands clasped in prayer, his eyebrows working
rapidly; a *mie*.

As he lies on the ground, a second envoy disembarks – a
younger, kinder man. There is still hope. Another scroll is read.
Although Shunkan may not return to the capital, he is to be
allowed as far as the mainland. The worst of his exile is over. He
makes a grateful obeisance, and his friends congratulate him. But
there are complications. As they joyfully embark, the girl
attempts to follow her new husband. Seno-o and the escort drive
her back. They are authorized to take three and no more.
Naritsune, beside himself with grief, tries to come to her assist-

ance, but is dragged into the boat. The messengers argue among themselves, but Seno-o is adamant. (It is here that the rigidity of the puppet countenance assumes its greatest value; there is nothing more forbidding than a puppet saying 'No'.) The girl is left prostrate on the rock, gazing at the vessel, trembling. It is typical of this genre that her passionate solo is the longest single episode of the play. With great strides, she wades out to the boat, but it is too far for her, and she returns in grief.

Shunkan returns from the boat to comfort her and offers an exchange – his person for hers. She may return to civilization with her husband, and he will voluntarily continue his exile. But he is interrupted by Seno-o, who refuses point-blank to take the girl. Shunkan pleads in vain. Seeing that protest is useless, he draws near to Seno-o and snatches his sword, striking and wounding him. Seno-o staggers back; the operators remove his outer robe and disarrange his long white hair. They fight. It is a typically grotesque *bunraku* scene, for both are weak, Shunkan from his privations and Seno-o from his wound. They stagger towards each other, striking, missing; the girl seizes a wooden rake and waits for a chance to intervene. Shunkan sees an opening. Lunging forward, he slashes his opponent's belly. Seno-o falls, his sword dropping over the edge of the stage. Shunkan, himself barely able to stand upright, brandishes his sword above the prostrate body. There is a tableau, a moment of crisis, a warning. If Shunkan kills Seno-o, he will forfeit all hope of restoration. He hesitates, but only briefly. Down comes the sword. On the boat, Naritsune weeps. Shunkan drags the frightened girl into the water and forces her on board. As his friends shout farewell and encouragement, the envoy gives the word to sail. Shunkan is left on the shore. With mounting anguish he scrambles to the peak to catch his last glimpse of the outside world. His climb is agonizingly protracted; he stretches out his arm in a last gesture of farewell as the diminutive boat bobs along the horizon and night falls.

This version was adapted for *kabuki* the following year, again for performance in Osaka. It was not successful, and has never again been given in its entirety. The Shunkan scene, however, has often been revived as a self-contained episode in recognition of its superior merit. It has also been performed abroad, at the West Berlin Arts Festival in 1965, and in Paris, where the audience particularly approved: the exile on the island reminded them of their own history.

The production described here is that of the National Theatre in 1967; thus it was a directed production, which leans towards the Western concept of theatre. It opens with an additional episode set in Kiyomori's capital and involving Shunkan's wife, Azumaya, who has been captured and brought back to the tyrant. He offers to spare her life if she will become his mistress. His cruel wooing becomes an excuse for spectacle. A procession of dancers tries to entice her into an amenable frame of mind. She remains adamant, and commits suicide with a dagger left by a sympathetic intermediary.

In the room below, Kiyomori is boasting with his generals Seno-o and Shigehira of their impious conquests. They have ravaged the great temple of Nara, which was sympathetic to the enemy cause. Shigehira relates how he decapitated the Great Buddha. A messenger enters with Azumaya's severed head. Kiyomori tries to conceal his discomfiture by ordering the court ladies to continue the entertainment, and they perform, at his command, a popular dance which, unknown to him, is a satirical attack on his regime. This underscores the action that follows. Kiyomori sees Azumaya's ghost and throws the severed head at it: it is replaced by another and more terrifying apparition, the head of the decapitated Buddha. Azumaya's head has come to mean more than the persecution of one innocent victim. It symbolizes the tyranny and blasphemy of the whole regime.

The scene now moves to Devil's Island. A white floorcloth suggests sulphuric rock. It is studded with small boulders, solid constructions but with shadows artificially heightened: a painter's composition. One large rock rears against the sky; there are blasted trees hung with seaweed and a tiny hut, a cave hung with matting. Behind, the floorcloth is painted with a wave pattern, and this is continued on the background. Chanter and *samisen* are in evidence.

The play follows the *bunraku* story, but enlarges its visual scope and embellishes it pictorially. The exiles are dressed in stylized rags and have additional pathetic business; when we first see Shunkan he is gathering dry seaweed to make a fire. The girl's tentative entrance is more prolonged; she runs all the way up the *hanamichi* and then back again. The ship is huge, resplendent and full of retainers. Once again we have the episode of the two scrolls. There seems at first sight to be illogic here, in both the *bunraku* and *kabuki* versions. The two envoys carry different orders; why have they never, apparently, discussed these on the boat? The reason is partly dramatic – *kabuki* cultivates the double reversal of fortune, from joy to despair and back to joy again; but the answer lies chiefly in the bureaucratic mentality and the Japanese concern with protocol. Each envoy has his own instructions and will fulfil them: no more, no less. This attitude also explains Seno-o's refusal to take the girl on board. He has only three entrance permits, and the letter of the law must be respected. Of course, he relishes the situation. In what the English synopsis endearingly calls 'another bit of nastiness', he tells Shunkan of his wife's suicide. It is this that makes him offer to exchange himself for the girl; life on the mainland would now be no less bleak than on the island.

One incident symbolically present in the *noh*, but passed over in *bunraku*, is exploited here to the full. After the duel, when Shunkan has sealed his fate by killing Seno-o, the others go on board, and the mooring rope is trailing on the stage. As the ship puts out, the rope is drawn along the sand. Shunkan grasps it. In *noh* the rope is cut, representing the severing of Shunkan's ties with the outside world. Here it is used for a desperate tug-of-war, with the castaway clinging to his last link with civilized life. Shunkan is drawn the width of the stage until he surrenders his hold and sees the end fall limply into the water and disappear from sight.

Now occurs one of those scenic transformations that *kabuki* so enjoys. The revolve turns and Shunkan follows it, as if keeping pace with the ship along the shore. The white floorcloth on the forestage is drawn aside to show waves underneath. Another strip of painted waves is drawn by rope and pulley up the *hanamichi*. We are on the far side of the island now, seeing it across the water through the sailors' eyes. The great rock is towards us. Shunkan climbs it, looking out beyond the audience to where the ship is vanishing over the horizon. He gazes for what seems eternity, while the curtain mercifully closes on his isolation.

The same story, cast in two different modes, exist in opposed worlds and demands different responses. The *noh* play asks us, like Shunkan, to transcend emotion. Human ties are represented as fallible and, in the true test, irrelevant. Man must be led, or forced, to come to terms with the absolute. In the *bunraku* and *kabuki* versions, the emotions despised in *noh* become central. *Noh* gives us metaphysics, its successors high melodrama. The one pares a situation to the essence, the others embellish it. The one abstracts the protagonist from life, the others surround him with life's urgent and conflicting claims. *Noh* appeals to the mind, the popular theatre to the heart.

Most obviously, the later versions duplicate, and even triplicate, the crisis. In *noh* the possibility of dramatic surprise is eliminated at the beginning; the envoy announces on his first entrance that his scroll contains only the two names. In the later versions we are offered a succession of surprises, so that Shunkan's fortunes and his emotional state follow an irregular course throughout the play. The boat brings hope, the first scroll despair. The second scroll heartens, and Seno-o's refusal to take the girl throw all into gloom once more. Shunkan's self-sacrifice is countered by Seno-o's refusal. Seno-o falls, and Shunkan must finally choose between the girl's reprieve and his own.

The *kabuki* Shunkan's motives are honourable, but earthbound: love of his friends, the memory of his wife, the desire to suppress a wrong, and, by killing a merciless enemy, to bring mercy about. His self-sacrifice is not wholly altruistic, but dictated by his own sense of loss. By killing Seno-o he makes this decision final. It is the act of a brave man, and at the same time an act of submission: the ideal *kabuki* combination.

And in all this, it must be noted, the foundations of the society which has produced these disasters are not questioned. Rule is rule, though it may be imposed by a tyrant; crime is crime, and must be paid for. Shunkan's position after the death of Seno-o is substantially that of the forty-seven *ronin*: an act has been committed which loyalty and humanity declare to be the right one, but which is still an offence against established authority. Shunkan's case is also Azumaya's. Loyalty and nobility demand self-sacrifice. It is this that invests Shunkan with heroic stature. He performs high deeds and accepts the consequences. *Noh*, too, advocates acceptance, but in a different frame of reference. In *kabuki* we are caught within the limits of our own society, whose pressures are closer to us. We feel them and their consequences more. In *noh* we see a Shunkan who exemplifies Man, in *kabuki* one who is a man; and though we may follow the former with our reason we applaud the latter with our tears.

# Appendix II: *Theatre and Film*

Western audiences have had few chances to see the classical Japanese theatre in the flesh. It does not travel well. *Kabuki* has toured in the United States, with the dubious benefit of simultaneous translation; *bunraku*, more from financial necessity than a desire to proselytize among foreign audiences, has performed in California, New York and London; *noh* has recently visited England, Norway, Poland, Germany and Portugal; and Utaemon's *kabuki* company and a folk-dance team have represented their country at Expo' 67 in Montreal. Most Westerners, however, have their sole contact with the Japanese performing arts through the film. Since the international success of *Rashomon* in 1950, Japanese productions have become increasingly popular. San Francisco has had its Japanese cinema for some time; New York now has another, the Toho on 45th Street; Germany recently saw a Kurosawa retrospective; and the films have been seen regularly on television and in art cinemas in Great Britain. It is appropriate therefore to consider how far the concepts of the classical drama have made their mark on the film, and to what extent the modern Japanese cinema is influenced by traditional theatrical practices.

The emergent art, in Japan as everywhere else, leaned heavily on the theatre. Tokyo's first cinema, the Kanda Kinki-kan, was a converted playhouse of the old style with the screen hung at the back of the open, pilastered stage and the audience seated on the floor. Other borrowed theatrical devices were the clapper-boards, used to recall the audience's attention after each change of reel, and the *benshi* (narrator) who functioned in much the same way as the *gidayu* chanter of the *kabuki* and puppet stages. It was his job to interpret the silent action to the audience in a more or less relevant monologue. The *benshi* became so firmly entrenched that many acquired large personal followings, irrespective of the merits of the picture. When the film developed as an independent art and began to divest itself of its literary associations, the *benshi* were indignant, and resigned their positions only after noisy protest.

Early subjects, also, were taken from stage plays. *Kabuki* performances were filmed without change, 1904 brought *Momiji-
gari* (*The Maple Viewing*), a *kabuki* version of a *noh* original, and
starring two prominent actors from the traditional theatre. This
was followed by selections from the famous *Dojo-ji*. The actors,
however, were far from convinced of the merits of the new
medium. While admitting its documentary value, they viewed
the cinema with the same disdain that their own art had suffered
at its beginnings. The earlier film versions of *jidaimono*, historical
pieces, therefore employed mostly *obeya* actors of the inferior
grades. It was not until acquaintance with American films, with
their more accomplished technique and faster pace, brought
about a change in audience-demands that the *obeya* influence declined and the Japanese cinema cultivated a new type of actor.

1913 saw the first film version of *Kanadehon Chushingura*, shot
as a stage play from the viewpoint of the front row centre. It has
remained a favourite subject, with at least one new version
appearing annually until the present day. The early films continued the tradition of using female impersonators, even for
works derived from *shimpa* and *shingeki*. A Japanese version of
Tolstoy's *Resurrection* (1914) still used men in women's roles.
These *onnagata* actors, like the *benshi*, were removed only after
considerable argument. Other well-worn *kabuki* devices were
adapted to the new medium. The traditional white-face make-up
found new purpose in the ill-lit studios, and the first colour films
(with each frame separately hand-tinted) cultivated the same
flamboyantly artificial colours as the live stage. *Souls on the Road*
(1921) used cross-cutting to imitate the pattern of Chikamatsu's
parallel-action stories. Even today one may find traces of *kabuki*
influence in the glorification of the natural setting for its own
sake, with the action punctuated by shots of trees and water.

Direct derivations from *kabuki*, however, have become increasingly rare. The early film-makers made their own condensa-
tions of the traditional subjects, and found *shimpa* players more
amenable to their requirements. When *shimpa* in turn hardened
into costume melodrama, they turned increasingly to *shingeki*, or
created their own plots. *Kabuki* has not been entirely forgotten.

Ichikawa Kon made a puppet version of *Dojo-ji*, banned by the American Occupation for the sole reason that its script had not been submitted for preliminary censorship. Kurosawa Akira's *The Men who Trod on the Tiger's Tail* (1953) took its plot from *Kanjincho* (see p. 152), with the addition of a new character, a servant played by the leading comedian Enomoto Kenichi. One critic has compared the result to *Hamlet* with an interpolated valet's part played by Stan Laurel. There can be no doubt that the servant stole the show, and there is still discussion as to how far the film was intended as a parody of feudal values, and how far as a defence of them. 1954 saw Mizoguchi Kenji's *A Story from Chikamatsu* – a tale of runaway lovers – and 1955 Yoshimura Kimiseburo's *Bijo to Kairyu* (*The Beauty and the Dragon*), which applied to the *kabuki Nakurami* the same methods as Olivier's *Henry V*, opening with a reconstruction of a classical performance of the play and moving into the wider expanse of film. As late as 1958 Kinoshite Keisuke could adapt *kabuki* stage techniques for *The Song of the Naroyama*, based on a short story by Fukazawa Shichiro which has become well known in the West. It tells of an old woman, near death, who forces her loving son to abandon her on a mountain-top, in accordance with the age-old customs of her people, so that she will no longer be a burden to him. Kinoshite's film opened with the drawing of a *kabuki* curtain, and the scenery throughout, instead of using cinematic wipes and dissolves, slid away in imitation of stage mechanics.

*Noh* influence, understandably enough, has been more limited. A drama whose action lies wholly in the mind does not adapt easily to a visual medium. The slow tempo and quietism of *noh*, which themselves reflect the traditional pace of Japanese life, have influenced the film in various subtle ways. Kurosawa, in one of his early films, had adapted *noh* conventions to portray an insane man, and had used *noh* as well as *kabuki* music for *The Men who Trod on the Tiger's Tail*. His first explicit attempt to convey *noh* style on the screen was *Kumonosu-jo* (*Cobweb Castle* or *Castle of the Spider's Web*), released in the West as *Throne of Blood*. This Japanese version of *Macbeth* began and ended with a Chorus. The make-up and movement of the leading actress were clearly reminiscent of *noh* performance (she used the *noh* walk), and inspired by Kurosawa's recollections of his own theatre-going. So was the treatment of the single witch who replaced Shakespeare's three. The *noh* conventions made this character appropriately sexless, an effect prescribed by Shakespeare, but rarely realized in performance, even when, as most directors prefer, one or more of the witches are played by men. At the end she – or he – did not so much vanish as disintegrate, by an interesting extension of the costume techniques described earlier; the costume, and thus the character, literally fell apart. In the despot's castle the banqueters were entertained by *kyogen*. *Throne of Blood* also showed its *noh* affinities in other, less obvious ways. In one scene two horsemen, lost on a moor, endlessly crossed and recrossed the screen to find the track. Like the angel's protracted exit in *Hagoromo*, the repetition, at first merely tiresome, ended by being engrossing. The scenic economy was no less striking. Kurosawa refined his pictures like a Zen garden, using the minimum of natural components and concentrating on textural contrast; the witch's hut was a *noh* property. Another *noh*-influenced film, unseen in the West and relatively unsuccessful in Japan itself, was *Yokoku*, written, directed and acted by Mishima Yokio, author of the well-known *Golden Pavilion*. The subject of this short film, the military revolution of the 1930s, was strange to *noh*, but the setting used an actual *noh* stage, with *sh'te* and *waki* working in a serene and contemplative atmosphere. Where Kurosawa had used modern reconstructions of *noh* music, Mishima sought for a contemporary abstract accompaniment that would give the same effect. Kurosawa himself returned to *noh* themes in *The Hidden Fortress* (1958): the plot turned on a princess who disguised herself in the first half of the film and appeared in her true shape in the second, and was accompanied by *noh* music.

In various indirect ways, however, the traditional theatre has perpetuated itself. It would be wrong, perhaps, to seek for influences here; one can find them anywhere by looking hard enough. One leading Japanese critic pointed out to me that Westerners, looking at the film from outside, are more prone to find influences than the Japanese themselves, many of whom would deny any connection of the contemporary cinema with the traditional theatre. It would be safer, on the whole, to say that the modern film industry shares certain basic assumptions with *kabuki*, which in turn derive from deeply rooted habits and a native temperament which has not changed as much as the superficial modernization would lead one to suppose.

The film companies, for a long time, were organized on the old hierarchical basis. Directors worked their way up through the ranks, accepting a master-disciple relationship hardly less rigid than that of the Kabuki-za. This pattern now shows signs of disappearing; the great names of the past are in decline, and in an atmosphere where work is judged on a purely commercial basis it is easier for a young man to make an immediate success. The film world also accepted distinct genres, in the *kabuki* manner, and a system of classification far stricter than that operating in the West.

These too are beginning to blur, though companies still tend to be identified with a particular type of picture, and audiences base their choices on the company image rather than on the advance publicity for any particular film. Toho specializes in horror, Nikkatsu in sex and crime, Shochiku in reverential treatment of Japanese history. Daiei broke the rules and baffled its public by following a sequence of potboilers with several prestigious art films, including *Rashomon*.

*Jidaimono* have always been popular, and most obviously reveal the continuity of the theatrical tradition. They now account for about one-third of the cinematic output. Earlier examples, while discarding *kabuki* staging, perpetuated its values. The *samurai* hero was always honourable and invulnerable, bound by his loyalty and expert with the sword. (Cuba is currently negotiating for the purchase of *samurai* films to boost national morale.) In the wave of social criticism that accompanied the Taisho Era (the Japanese twenties) the mood changed; directors began to use historical situations for critical purposes, paralleling the *kabuki* movements of the Meiji years and after. Kurosawa's *Seven Samurai* belongs to this class, as does *Peerless Patriot* (1932), which ridiculed social pretensions by replacing the *daimyo* with an impostor.

With the outbreak of the Sino-Japanese war and the subsequent commitment to the Axis, these manifestations came under increasing displeasure. The historical film **was** compelled to be patriotic, and to glorify war and self-sacrifice. Censored in turn by the American Occupation, which prohibited what the police state encouraged, it has tended in recent years to become increasingly escapist. Kurosawa's more recent films, *Yojimbo* (1961) and *Sanjuro* (1962), both starring Mifune Toshiro, take a less sentimental view of the values of feudal society. The all-conquering hero is much in evidence – in both, Mifune scatters countless opponents like chaff – but the brutal reality of the code of the sword is emphasized throughout. In *Sanjuro* Mifune acts as champion and mentor of a group of young men, who learn, by his example, the ruthlessness cloaked by *samurai* ideals. After the carnage he strides out of the picture and out of their lives like a Japanese Shane, leaving them triumphant but sadder in their hastily acquired maturity.

*Chambara*, historical melodramas with much sword play (the name comes from *cham cham*, the children's vocalization of the clash of *samurai* swords), are still highly popular, and offer audiences a cheap substitute for what their fathers enjoyed at the Kabuki-za. They have found a new market in television, which offers at least one such drama a night. Kyoto, which once provided locations for historical films, has now largely been taken over by the television companies. Technically, the home screen has brought about many improvements. In the economic panic of recent years film companies sold their old *jidaimono* to the new medium and created a new public, which began to press for higher standards. Televised *jidaimono* are usually pictorially brilliant. One popular series, *Sword* (tracing the history of a famous weapon through a succession of owners), is written by Hashimoto Shinobu, who worked on the script of *Rashomon* and models his style on that of Reginald Rose and Paddy Chayevsky. *Jidaimono* has also discovered, with considerable delight, its affinities with the Western, which holds an equal place in the affections of the television public. The Way of the Warrior, at least in its more melodramatic forms, is seen as equivalent to the

Code of the West. Kurosawa's favourite director is John Ford. The influence has been mutual. *Seven Samurai*, exploiting the familiar plight of the *ronin*, showed dispossessed warriors banding together to save a persecuted village. Widely popular in the West, it inspired an American imitation, *The Magnificent Seven*, with Mexico substituted for rural Japan. This in turn produced a sequel, *Return of the Seven*, which drew huge audiences in Tokyo cinemas. Conversely, Noguchi Horoshi's *Duel in the Setting Sun* (1955) was a Japanese remake of *High Noon*.

Of all the films that have achieved foreign distribution, *Yojimbo* perhaps most deserves attention for the way in which it summarizes, in two hours, the primary influences on the contemporary Japanese cinema. Its story of feuding gangs whose rivalry obliterates a village carries a strong flavour of the Western: one of the bravos carries a pistol which almost – but not quite – defeats the traditional sword, and there is even the American cliché of the coffin-maker who profits gleefully from the mutual slaughter. In its parody of the *samurai* superman it shows a cynicism typical of the modern artist's view of his own history. But it also uses, sometimes very subtly, *kabuki* devices, retaining their old force under a naturalistic coloration. A nervous watchman patrols the streets. The clack of his wooden clappers signals climactic moments of the action, reminding us equally of the traditional theatre and of the film clapper-board that precedes a take – in either case a virtually presentational device that both commands our attention and enforces emotional distance from the horrors we are about to witness. The beating of a prayer-drum accompanies the grimaces of a dying man to give the cinematic equivalent of a *mie*. Mifune's face, brutalized by his opponents and covered with blood and bruises, is reminiscent of *aragoto* make-up. *Yojimbo* is an object-lesson in how the old may blend effectively with the new.

The Japanese film notably cultivates *aragoto* and low-life pieces in which individuals, often criminals, pit themselves against society. Once again disbanded *samurai* are natural subjects; the film returns endlessly to the new *ronin* of the Meiji Era, as well as to their modern gangster equivalents. Western importations in this genre are well liked; one of the most successful films in the current season has been Jean-Pierre Melville's *Le Deuxième Souffle*.

Another recognized genre is *gendaimono* (films of contemporary life), corresponding roughly to the *sewamono* of *kabuki*, though at the present time the boundaries are beginning to blur. The early cinema produced a spate of 'mother pictures', glorifying the self-sacrifice of the domestic heroine. Younger modern directors have been greatly influenced by *cinéma vérité*, using non-professional actors and unscripted dialogue. Hani Susumi's *She and He*, shown at the Berlin Film Festival in 1965 and afterwards in London, used mainly amateurs; Hani, significantly, began his career in documentary films. This tendency has recently been taken to its extreme by Imamura Shohei's *The Evaporating Man*, a cinematic examination of an actual disappearance, which proceeded on the lines of a police investigation, interrogating witnesses, many of whom never realized they were being filmed. It has been pointed out that only in Japan, where law-suits are time-consuming and costly, could such a film be made without libel actions. In their technique, such films are trying hard to break away from the old dramatic framework. In their fascination with the more scandalous aspects of everyday life, they adhere to a tradition at least as old as Chikamatsu.

The film has also inherited the Japanese fondness for ghost stories. *Kabuki* traditionally staged these in high summer, to chill the blood in lieu of air-conditioning. July is also the time of the Buddhist O Bon festival, when the spirits of the departed are believed to return to earth. Hani suggests another reason for this seasonal popularity. In summer most Japanese sleep under mosquito nets and with the house doors wide open; this gives an eerie atmosphere to nature, conducive to the telling of horror tales. *Yotsuya Kwaidan* (*The Horror at Yotsuya*), a spectral *kabuki* masterpiece based on a scandal some three hundred and thirty years old, has been remade over ten times as a film. Japanese ghosts are traditionally vengeful, thus perpetuating another *kabuki* theme. In this case the spectre is that of a murdered wife, Oiwa, returning to haunt the husband who killed her. In fact Oiwa seems to have committed suicide, but the Japanese prefer the more colourful version, and have elevated her to the status of a national monster. Oiwa's direct descendant, a tranquil school-teacher apparently unembarrassed by the family notoriety, still lives at the same site in Yotsuya. *Three Strange Tales*, directed by Kobayashi Masaki, a more delicate exercise in this mode, has been recently seen in the West; the same director has also produced *Kwaidan*, based on a collection of supernatural stories by Lafcadio Hearn.

And finally the erotic, present at *kabuki*'s beginnings and always popular in Japan. On the average, the major companies produce seven hundred films a year (though for 1965 and 1966 the total dropped to 250). On top of this there are a number of small companies specializing in 'pink movies'. This implies no political orientation: merely *cinéma bleu* through rose-coloured glasses. They have a vast public and film-makers appreciate their cheapness. A pink movie costs about 3,000,000 yen, a serious film from ten to twenty times as much. Meiji censors attempted to eliminate the erotic from the performing arts, but recent years have seen an increasing numbers of sex films. Although relished by servicemen on leave, they are not widely exhibited outside Japan. Nakahira Yasushi's *Crazed Fruit*, released abroad as *Juvenile Passion*, and dealing with a teenage girl's sexual relationship with two brothers, is an honourable exception. Considerable scandal was caused a few years ago when a German producer bought a pink movie and presented it as at the Berlin Film Festival as representative of Japanese work. Television produced its own equivalent in the notorious *Pink Mood Show*, a highly popular programme devoted to late-night erotica.

Is the influence of the theatre, then, confined to the classification of films? Not entirely: though here again one must be wary of seeing influences that the Japanese themselves deny, and acknowledge the considerable effect of foreign works. Just as the Japanese theatre influenced Eisenstein's *Ivan the Terrible*, its cinema has shown itself susceptible to the European novel. Kurosawa's *Rashomon*, which won first prize at the Venice Film Festival in 1950 and was the first Japanese film to make a strong impression on the West, is a case in point. Based on two stories

by Akugatawa Ryanosuke, it seems at first to espouse the *noh*
doctrine of the deceptiveness of the senses. A *samurai* and his wife
meet a bandit in the forest. The *samurai* is killed and his wife raped.
We see this story in three versions, through three different sets
of eyes, as told by the wife herself, a woodcutter who witnessed
the incident, and the husband's ghost speaking through a medium.
Each version apportions the blame differently. Truth is seen as
relative, and it is impossible to distinguish the illusory and the
real. Akutagawa, however, was immediately influenced not by
*noh*, but by the contemporary European novel, and in particular
by Pirandello, whose methods he pursues. Nonetheless, Kurosawa's constant fascination with the conflict between illusion and
reality betrays, surely, some residual *noh* influence. His *I Live in
Fear* (1955) took as its protagonist a Tokyo industrialist haunted
by terror of the atomic bomb, ending his days in a lunatic asylum
gibbering through the bars at the sun, which he took for nuclear
conflagration. Kurosawa's current film, *Tora, Tora, Tora*, studies
the Japanese attack on Pearl Harbour. More than half is devoted
to the battle games and tactical planning preceding the battle;
these are then contrasted with the reality.

   The Japanese film is still, like *kabuki*, largely actor-centred.
Stylistic unity is difficult to obtain because the actors themselves
come from such diverse backgrounds, and many of them combine
film work with performances in the traditional or modern theatre.
Financial necessity drives most actors to work in several media.
Matsumoto Koshiro, a leading *kabuki* player, appears regularly
with his wife and son (the latter also famous in *kabuki*), reading
prayers on television in *How Joyful Our Family*. Of the modern
film stars, Hasegawa Haza began filming while still a *kabuki*
apprentice. Awashima Chihage is a graduate of the Girls' Opera.
Mizutani Yaeko came from *shimpa*. Many actors have enormous
personal followings, and the public comes to see them rather
than the film. *Grand Prix*, when it opened in Tokyo, was billed as
'starring' Mifune Toshiro, though the part he played (a Japanese
millionaire industrialist and racing-car owner) was comparatively small. In such conditions it is hardly surprising that films
are conceived, like *kabuki* productions, as a collection of indi-

vidual performances, rather than as an artistic unity. Directors with a firm sense of their own style may overcome this: Kurosawa's *Yojimbo* (*Bodyguard*), for example, happily wedded the talents of Mifune and Tono Eijiro, though the former has a *kabuki* background and the latter comes from *shingeki*; but elsewhere the disparity is often obvious.

Japanese directors are often surprised when Western critics interpret their work in *kabuki* terms. This is partly due to the fact that most reviewers know as little about *kabuki* as they do about the Japanese film, but it does not mean that the influence is entirely absent. Kurosawa, when told that the characters of *Rashomon* were modelled on *kabuki*, denied any such intention. Hani was equally surprised when reviewers claimed that the male lead in *She and He* was giving a *kabuki* performance, for the man in question was an artist by profession, and only an amateur actor; he had never appeared on the *kabuki* stage. I suspect that part of the difficulty here lies in the Japanese actor himself, and the problems already discussed in Chapter 6. While some actors (particularly Mifune) carry their *kabuki* training with them, and cannot eradicate it from their movement and delivery, others inherit, unconsciously, what was for centuries the only acting style. The Japanese are not given in ordinary life to expressing their feelings by facial expression. Such frank displays of emotion as even the supposedly inhibited English indulge in are foreign to them. This is the reason why the Western naturalistic style continues to elude them: they see no middle way between no expression at all and the exaggeration developed by *kabuki*, and in performance fall instinctively into the latter. An actor like Akutagawa Hiroshi, who makes his effects by understatement, is rare. As a natural consequence of this emphasis on the individual actor, one may see the directorial pattern in many instances reverting to *kabuki* habits: scenes are frequently prolonged after the Western director would have shouted 'Cut!' simply so as not to deprive the performer of the attention due to him.

Nor must we minimize actor's physical skill. The Japanese film uses few stunt-men. *Jidaimono* actors are accomplished athletes and swordsmen, and the duels combine the actors'

K

expertise with astute mechanical effects in a way that recalls *kabuki*'s fascination with violent combat and protracted death. In *Throne of Blood* the despot dies stuck like a porcupine with arrows. In the climactic duel of *Sanjuro*, the combatants face each other, motionless, for what seems like eternity; then the screen erupts with violence, the villain is slashed, and his blood spurts like a fountain into the air. This delight in mechanical ingenuity, though it may not derive directly from *kabuki*, responds to a similar interest on the part of the audience. The first Japanese science-fiction film, *Godzilla* (1954), begot scores of others, inspired by the American *King Kong* and given a typically Japanese political coloration by linking the emergence of these monsters of the deep to nuclear experiments: the monster symbolizes the brute forces of nature unleashed. It is noticeable, too, that in these films the trickery is usually apparent. We are allowed to see how the monsters work, for the film-makers are not so much creating an illusion as demonstrating their own technical prowess. In less alarming ways, television continues the tradition. One of the most popular weekly serials, *Kamen no Ninja Akahage*, transposes science fiction to a feudal setting, with magicians masquerading as Shinto priests, the Shogun threatened by a walking monolith, and a magic kite that wafts the heroes to safety. *Captain Ultra* indulges in similar cavortings, with the setting changed to outer space. But in these examples, and others of the type, it is significant that the ultimate weapon is always the *samurai* sword, which succeeds when all electronic devices have failed; and one may perhaps note, without being accused of hunting too fancifully for analogies, that the favourite cliché of the contemporary Japanese animated cartoon is the character who divides himself into several simulacra, so that his opponents cannot distinguish the illusion from the reality.

# Appendix III: *Some English Imitations*

Chapter 6 has shown how heavily Japan, in the twentieth century, has been indebted to the West. The reverse influence, for obvious reasons, has been weaker and more sporadic. In a sense it is only just beginning, as European and American dramatists rediscover the value of the mask and of the blank, undetermined stage. The most conspicuous attempt to translate Japanese theatrical values into Western terms remains one of the earliest: the work of William Butler Yeats, whose *Four Plays for Dancers* applied *noh* methods to themes drawn from his own culture, and who even in his last plays continues to reveal the great influence that the Japanese religious drama had on him.

Yeats was led to the *noh* drama for several reasons, some of them, perhaps, the wrong ones. The attraction sprang in no small part from the mysticism that was so strong in his own nature, and his researches into other religions and philosophies. As a Platonist he espoused the concept of an ideal world of which our own is but an imperfect representation; as a student of the classical Indian philosophies, he was drawn to the use of ritual and symbol. F. A. C. Wilson has demonstrated, in *W. B. Yeats and Tradition*, how complex and pervasive this use of symbol is. Some of his influences were closer to home. The French symbolist writers, particularly Maeterlinck, struck a sympathetic chord. A spiritual affinity existed, and the groundwork was laid, before Yeats ever came into contact with *noh*. He saw tragic art as having the power to allure us into an almost trance-like state, in which we could achieve rapport with otherwise inexpressible ideas; he believed that the symbolist drama, in particular, carried out a Platonic function in rejecting the empty images of the actual world to suggest the elemental forces operating behind it.

Yeats never visited Japan, though he much wished to. He planned the journey several times, but was always prevented by other arrangements or lack of money. He lacked the personal contact with the language that he enjoyed when Purohit Swami helped him to translate the *Upanishads*, and his sketchy Japanese correspondence is not particularly illuminating (although, heavily annotated, it has served as the excuse for several books). His most important contacts were made at second hand: through Ezra Pound's free versions of Fennolosa's *noh* translations, which he read between 1913 and 1915; through Lady Gregory and her own imitations of *noh* drama; from a fragmentary amateur performance of *Hagoromo* in London and a professional recording of the same play. Pound himself gave considerable advice and encouragement, and actually participated in one rehearsal of *At the Hawk's Well*, an incident which one wishes had been more graphically recorded. Yeats also worked closely with a Japanese dancer, Ito Michio, though the latter had himself no professional connection with *noh*.

These contacts crystallized Yeats's striving towards a dramatic verse form that would stimulate by imposing new disciplines, and at the same time avoid the mere pursuit of novelty; for Yeats of all writers was the most conscious of the value and dignity of tradition. His cultivation of *noh* also satisfied his ambivalent attitude towards the theatre. He was fascinated by the stage and by the power and immediacy of the dramatic as opposed to the purely lyric statement. At the same time the practical necessities of the commercial theatre bored him. As a good patriot he saw the need for a living Irish theatre, and spent some years in its management, though grumbling at the time wasted. Yeats saw his national culture as a growth distorted by the prevailing wind from England, and it was probably this as much as anything else that led him to seek more distant models. Duty impelled him to an interest in practical stagecraft, though from his own accounts of some of the performances he was forced to witness in the sacred name of Ireland this must at times have been irksome indeed. Something of this distaste spills over into writings on *noh*. He repeatedly refers to Zeami as a 'critic', as though this had been his only function, and chooses to ignore his involvement in the highly practical business of play production. Yeats wanted to have the best of both worlds, but was constantly frustrated in his stage work by the problems of giving concrete form to the imaginings of the lone poetic voice. The things he evoked were often impossible to realize in scenic terms. A case in point is *The Player Queen*, which in its first scene calls for 'a place where three roads meet'. How does one show this on a stage? It cannot really be done, except in an arena production. Yeats never seems to have visualized the play in these terms, though it has been so staged in at least one recent performance. Of the many stories of his theatrical embarrassment, one of the best concerns the original production of *The Shadowy Waters*, which requires, at the end, a harp to burst into flames. Yeats sat gloomily in the auditorium trying one lighting effect after another. and finding none satisfactory. When he had given up and called for the lights to be extinguished, he found the stage bathed in a red glow. Leaping to his feet, he cried 'That's it. That's exactly what I want!' From the wings came an outraged shout: 'Well, you can't have it. The bloody switchboard's on fire!' Privately he yearned for a theatre in which the lyric voice could speak without trappings or encumbrances. He was thus naturally led to the contemporary experimenters who were breaking away from the naturalistic stage: to William Poel and his Elizabethan revivals on a bare platform; to Gordon Craig's settings created out of neutral screens; to Adolphe Appia and his substitution of light and shadow for painted canvas.

For all these reasons the *noh* theatre exercised an immediate appeal. Yeats ignored its popular origins. It was its later, artificial, semi-private nature that attracted him. The commercial theatre, the theatre that seeks a wide audience, he found distasteful. One of the reasons for his rewriting of *A Full Moon in March* seems to have been that at its first production at the Abbey Theatre it was a popular success. When he revised it as *The King of the Great Clock Tower*, he omitted most of what the general

public had found pleasing. He asked rather for 'an unpopular
theatre, and an audience like a secret society'. He embraced the
economy, both artistic and financial, which *noh* offered. The plays
required a minimal cast. Yeats economized even more by removing the standard *noh* Chorus of eight and asking his musicians,
three in number, to perform in both functions, besides acting as
stagehands. The plays could be inexpensively staged. (In Japan
this has never been true, but Yeats's adaptations require comparatively simple costumes and masks and the most rudimentary
indications of setting and properties; no special stage is needed.)
An audience of fifty would make the play self-supporting. There
is a charming and quite characteristic story of Yeats turning
away a baffled newspaper reporter prepared to offer him a full-
page coverage, because he needed no publicity. Above all, *noh*
utilized an apparently simple but in reality highly allusive verse
style dear to Yeats's heart, and particularly suitable for stage use.
This can perhaps be seen most easily in his translations of Sophocles. His version of *King Oedipus* is still consistently preferred
for stage performance above more elaborate versions, because
the lines are written so that actors can speak them. His language
is simple and unadorned. The profundity lies beneath the surface.

His plays, then, most immediately show the *noh* influence in
their staging. *At the Hawk's Well* (1917) and *The Only Jealousy of
Emer* (1919) call for a screen against the wall of the room, and a
black cloth bearing the design of a hawk to be unfolded and hung
by the musicians. A chandelier lights the acting area. For *The
Dreaming of the Bones* Yeats suggests a screen symbolically indicating sky and mountain, thus reverting to strictures on the
naturalistic stage voiced some years earlier: 'One often needs
nothing more than a single colour, with perhaps a few shadowy
forms to suggest wood or mountain.' The latter plays are more
expansive, using larger casts and more complex settings, but
some of the old simplicity remains. *The Herne's Egg* (1938) uses
a toy donkey to stand for a real animal, and *Purgatory* (1938),
though in some ways more realistically conceived, reduces the
setting to a ruined wall and a barren tree, perhaps reminiscent of
the gnarled pine of *noh*.

Yeats's musicians used simple instruments – drum, gong, zither, flute – and his actors were masked. Some of the earlier masks were created by Edmund Dulac (later to distinguish himself rather less signally by designing the coronation stamps of George VI), who also wrote the music. This, and that written later by other composers, was not always successful. Yeats was tone-deaf (a fact which colours his directions on the actors' vocal delivery) and the music he thought appropriate was not always so. *Noh* normally permits a mask only to the *sh'te*. Yeats allowed more, and suggested as an addition or alternative that faces should be made up to resemble masks. In *A Full Moon in March* (1935) and its simplified revision, *The King of the Great Clock Tower*, the head of the decapitated swineherd is indicated, appropriately, by the empty mask. Yeats wished to eliminate facial expression and refine movement to the bare essentials. For him, the voice was the actors' prime tool: 'Greek acting was great because it did all but everything with the voice.' In another context he relates an idea he had for moving his actors about the stage in wheeled barrels, to allow them to forget everything except the diction. He asked his masked actors to comport themselves like marionettes – again a not entirely accurate rendering of the Japanese prototype, but still permissible within the conventions he was establishing. Ninette de Valois had established a ballet school in Dublin and several of her pupils filled his roles. She danced for him herself, and he apologizes in a dedication for having to conceal the expressiveness of her face.

Yeats thus approximated the essential performance conditions of *noh* before a similarly select and informed audience. Drama had again become ritual, and 'ritual', said Yeats, 'the most powerful form of drama, differs from the ordinary forms because everyone who hears it is also a player'. As on the *noh* stage, the act of communal participation and conventions apparently restrictive, but in fact liberating, allowed the author freedom from the normal limitations of space and time. On Yeats's stage, as in its Japanese exemplar, past and present may merge. In *The Dreaming of the Bones* a young man fleeing from the Dublin rising of 1916 meets the ghosts of two lovers, revenants from a vanished heroic age. In *Purgatory* the Old Man's past comes to life before his eyes. As he gazes at the ruined wall of his family mansion, burnt down by his drunken father, the window lights up to show his parents in their youth. His own son, a boy of sixteen, is blind to these visions: for him, there is nothing but a hole in an old wall. The same ambiguity operates in regard to the characters. In *The Only Jealousy of Emer* the personality of the hero is divided so that the Ghost of Cuchulain confronts his enchanted mortal image in a scene reminiscent of *Aoi no Ue*. One character may speak for another: in *A Full Moon in March* one Attendant speaks as the Queen, another as the Swineherd's severed head. Characters merge into each other; and, by the same token, the same character may appear in different manifestations. In *At the Hawk's Well* the Old Woman casts off her robe to appear as the Hawk. In *The Only Jealousy of Emer* a similar effect is achieved by the change of mask.

Yeats's faithfulness to his sources varies from play to play. *At the Hawk's Well* shows the purest *noh* style, though the Woman-Hawk, the well's guardian, does not dominate the play as the *sh'te* properly should: the conflict is rather between the Old Man and the Young Man, who compete to drink from the well's grudging waters. In *The Cat and the Moon*, a tale of two beggars before a saintly shrine, Yeats reconstructs a virtually perfect Irish *kyogen*. (He seems to be reverting, incidentally, to the explanatory *kyogen* of the *noh* play proper in *The Death of Cuchulain*, where an Old Man, 'looking like something out of mythology,' speaks the exposition.) But detailed resemblances are less important than themes and attitudes, and in this respect, even in the later plays, the similarity is striking. Yeats's own favourite among the *noh* plays seems to have been Zeami's *Nishikigi* (*The Decorated Tree*), in which a travelling priest meets the ghosts of a man who died of a broken heart and the woman who rejected him. By his prayers he unites them and brings respite to their souls. It is basically this story that Yeats adapts for *The Dreaming of the Bones*, and the same principles govern his composition of the other plays. For the legends of feudal Japan he substitutes his own country's heroic past, and the nostalgia for long-departed glories

common to both cultures, at their worst when they attempted to graft foreign forms onto a vision that was essentially modern, and essentially Irish. The most successful are the later plays, which retain *noh*'s simplicity while compromising with its outward forms; the earlier imitations seem to have been embarrassing to audience and performers alike, for the simple reason that one culture cannot so easily adopt another's ritual. It is interesting that the more recent productions (usually by university companies, such as the Trinity College, Dublin, players at the Edinburgh Festival) have departed from Yeats's directions and distributed, for example, the choral passages among several speakers, using the same techniques that many modern directors are applying to the choruses of Greek tragedy. Nevertheless the Yeats adaptations remain one of the happiest instances of the transposition of styles: perhaps because of the striking similarities between the Japanese and Celtic temperaments; perhaps because, in Yeats, they found the rare combination of the mystic and the practising dramatic poet.

For our last example we may turn to an adaptation both more recent and, so far as one may predict, destined to have considerably more popular success: Benjamin Britten's *Curlew River*, a 'parable for church performance', composed and performed in 1964. For both Yeats and Britten the discovery of *noh* caused an immediate excitement and gave a new turn and a new form to ideas they had already been pursuing. Britten had for some time been interested in giving Christian meaning to material drawn rom other than sacred sources: his *Rape of Lucretia* is a prime example of this. He was also interested in exploring the musical and dramatic vocabulary of the Middle Ages. *Noye's Fludde* (1958) is a musical realization of a medieval cycle play designed to be staged with the simple formality of the age that first produced it. *The Burning Fiery Furnace* applies the same treatment to the story of Shadrach, Meshach and Abednego; *The Prodigal Son* is now being written.

Britten visited Japan in the early part of 1956, in the company. of Peter Pears and Prince Ludwig of Hesse and the Rhine. His exposure to traditional oriental forms in the intervals of conducting his own works was productive both of the ballet *Prince of the Pagodas*, and, in a completely different vein, *Curlew River*. While touring he was able to see two performances of the *noh Sumidagawa* (*The Sumida River*). This play, a 'fourth group' composition by Motomasa, has had considerable appeal for newcomers to *noh* and has been frequently translated. The story is a characteristically simple one, and involves two standard *noh* themes, the Madwoman and the Journey. A Ferryman (*waki*) about to cross the Sumida River is told by a Traveller (*waki-tsure*) that a Madwoman is approaching. She has been demented by the loss of her son. The Madwoman (*sh'te*) appears and enters the boat. During the crossing the Traveller asks why so many people are assembling on the far bank. The Ferryman tells him that they are performing a rite for a young boy who had been taken from his home and left to die there the previous year. Weeping, the Madwoman identifies him as her son. They disembark and recite prayers over the grave; the voice of the boy (*ko-kata*) is heard, and he eventually reappears to her, only to vanish with the coming of the dawn.

Both Britten himself and Prince Ludwig have written of the great impression this performance made on him. *Curlew River* is a translation of *Sumidagawa* into Western terms. It succeeds where Yeats's adaptations partially failed because Britten recognized from the outset the artistic invalidity of merely imitating the Japanese conventions. He sought instead for a workable equivalent, and a ritual form more immediately meaningful to a Western audience. This he found in the same material that had served him for *Noye's Fludde*, the religious drama of the medieval Church. In the latter work he had given musical form to a cycle play, and by various musical and dramatic devices restored the sense of communion between spectator and performer from which the play derived its initial impact. Spectators once again became participants, to the extent of playing simple instruments handed out by the child performers. For *Curlew River* Britten goes further back in time. It is an imaginative reconstruction of that point in history, only hinted at by our surviving documents, when a new and vital drama was beginning to evolve out of religious ritual;

when the wordless tropes were being adapted to present the Christian story; and when liturgical reforms were still concerned with creating works of art and not, as now, with destroying them.

*Curlew River* is designed to be played in a church, and the simplicity of its setting derives equally from *noh* and the bare ecclesiastical furnishings among which the earliest Christian plays were performed. A long ramp, at once *hashigakari* and church aisle, leads to the acting area. This is a raked platform bare of scenery; there is only a tall wooden structure, which serves both for the mast of the ferry-boat and the bell-tower of the shrine. All is made from natural wood; it shows the hard work and devoted care of human hands. The play begins with a formal procession, after which the players, musicians and Chorus take their appropriate places on the stage; it ends with a similar procession, so that the performance is framed within a church ritual recalling the formal opening and closing of *noh*.

Britten is faithful to both his sources in that all performers are male. They enter first as monks, acolytes and lay brethren: the last are the musicians. The Abbot, as prologue, addresses the audience directly and informs them of the content of the play. With some of the monks, he remains on stage to provide a Chorus: they represent both the travellers in the boat and the crowd on the far shore. The leading players are ceremonially attired while the music plays. A tenor takes the Madwoman's part. They wear ornate robes and half-masks which, as in *noh*, make no attempt at disguise; they present the personages, rather than imitate them. Acting is correspondingly simple and ritualistic. Apart from the entrances of the characters, movement is rigidly restricted: the *noh* dance is here reduced to a few steps.

Britten follows the story-line of his original almost exactly and reproduces its main structural features. The Ferryman's extended central solo is the equivalent of the *kyogen* narrative setting out the story in simple language. The climactic unison prayer, with its spiritual exaltation culminating in communion with the divine, reproduces the force, if not the form, of the *sh'te*'s dance.

Characters announce themselves with *noh* formality. To achieve the timeless quality that the Japanese theatre secures by its use of myth set in the remote past, Britten deliberately refrains from identifying his characters with any specific time or locality. For the Sumida River he substitutes an imaginary landscape obviously inspired by his beloved East Anglia, but not geographically precise. We are in the fen country; we are told of two kingdoms, the Eastland and the Westland, divided by the river; the Madwoman comes from the Black Mountains. These are abstract characters, moving in a world as sparse and as suggestive as the landscape of a Zen garden. And although this is a professedly Christian work, even the Christian references are initially minimal. Although a Latin hymn opens and closes the play, the action for the most part is as timeless as the setting is anonymous. It is not until the final prayer that we have any substantial mention of Christianity or use of its terminology. William Plomer's libretto universalizes even beyond the scope of its original.

The symbolism, as in Yeats, is strong, but more effective because less constantly obtrusive; more effective too, because Yeats is confined within a literary-historical frame of reference, while Britten, by his association with still meaningful ritual, touches normal experience more closely. He takes the Japanese idea of the holy places separated from the actual world by water, and gives it a Christian coloration. The woman distraught is all women, all mankind and, at the same time, Mary; the child kidnapped by a heathen, left to die and miraculously resurrected, is equally a saint, Christ Himself and the whole of the Christian Church. Like *noh*, Britten's work admits of a multiplicity of interpretations by insisting on none.

Yeats came to *noh* by way of language, Britten by way of music. His composition in no way attempts to reproduce the structure of Japanese music, though he uses certain of its devices; the flute occasionally speaks for the character (as when the Madwoman is first heard offstage) or conveys an image (the flight of the curlew, itself symbolic of the women's distraught wanderings). Some of the Madwoman's falling cadences are reminiscent of *noh* chant. Yet the music does recapture the spirit of the original, by using traditions equally venerable and with equally strong associations. The parable, to use Britten's word, or mystery, to use the Abbot's, succeeds because it has once more made ritual an effective, corporate, dramatic experience.

# Bibliography

It will be obvious that the following list makes no attempt to be comprehensive. It contains a selection of standard works on the major dramatic forms (including some of the earliest, whose usefulness has by no means diminished); general studies in related subjects; some of the better handbooks designed for those attending the performances in Japan; and a few translations. Not included is the increasing amount of periodical literature devoted to the Japanese theatre and film. The reader who has access to the publications of the Kokusai Bunka Shinkokai will find many articles of interest to the non-specialist on every aspect of the plays and their performance; those Japanese films released in the West have been exhaustively discussed in *Sight and Sound* and *Cahiers du Cinéma*.

Anderson, Joseph, and Richie, Donald, *The Japanese Film: Art and Industry* (Tokyo and Rutland, Vermont: Charles E. Tuttle Co., 1959).

Araki, J. T., *The Ballad-Drama of Medieval Japan* (Berkeley, California: University of California Press, 1964).

Arnold, Paul, *Le Théâtre japonais* (Paris: L'Arche, 1957).

Benazet, A., *Le Théâtre au Japon: Esquisse d'une histoire litteraire* (Paris, 1901).

Bohner, Hermann, *Nô: Die einzelnen Nô* (Tokyo: Deutsche Gesellschaft für Natur- und Völkerkunde Ostasiens, 1956).

Bowers, Faubion, *Japanese Theatre* (New York: Hermitage House, 1952).

—— *Theatre in the East* (New York: Nelson, 1956).

Ernst, Earle, *The Kabuki Theatre* (New York: Oxford University Press, 1956).

—— *Three Japanese Plays for the Traditional Theatre* (London: Oxford University Press, 1959).

Fenollosa, Ernest, and Pound, Ezra, *Noh, or Accomplishment* (London, 1917).

Haar, Francis, *Japanese Theatre in Highlight: a pictorial commentary* (Tokyo and Rutland, Vermont: Charles E. Tuttle Co., 1954).

Halford, Aubrey S., and Giovanna M., *The Kabuki Handbook* (Tokyo and Rutland, Vermont: Charles E. Tuttle Co., 1959).

Hamemura Yonezo and others, *Kabuki* (Tokyo: Kenkyusha Ltd, 1956).

Hironaga Shuzaburo, *Bunraku – Japan's Unique Puppet Theatre* (Tokyo: Tokyo News Service Inc., 1960).

Ishibashi Hiro, *Yeats and the Noh: Types of Japanese Beauty and their Reflection in Yeats's Plays* (Dublin: Dolmen Press, 1966).

Japanese National Commission for UNESCO, *Theatre in Japan* (Tokyo: Printing Bureau, Ministry of Finance, 1963).

Kawatake Shigetoshi, *Kabuki: Japanese Drama* (Tokyo: The Foreign Affairs Association of Japan, 1958).

Keene, Donald, *Bunraku: The Art of the Japanese Puppet Theatre* (Tokyo: Kodansha International Ltd, 1965).

—— *Nō: The Classical Theatre of Japan* (Tokyo and Palo Alto, California: Kodansha International Ltd, 1966).

Komiya Toyokata, Keene, Donald and Seidensticker, E. G., *Japanese Music and Drama in the Meiji Era* (Tokyo: Obunshi, 1956).

Kusano Eisaburo, *Stories Behind Noh and Kabuki Plays* (Tokyo: Tokyo News Service, 1962).

Nippon Gakujutsku Shinkokai, *Japanese Noh Drama*, 3 vols (Tokyo: 1955, 1959, 1960).

Nogami Toyoichiro (trans. Mutsumoto Ryozo), *Zeami and his Theories on Noh* (Tokyo: Tsunetaro Hinoki, 1955).

—— *The Noh and Greek Tragedy* (Tokyo: Sendai International Cultural Society, 1940).

O'Neill, P. G., *A Guide to Nō* (Tokyo: Hinshi Shoten, 1953).

—— *Early Nō Drama* (London: Lund Humphries, 1958).

Peri, Noel, *Le Nô* (Tokyo: Maison Franco-Japonaise, 1944).

Renondeau, Gaston, *Le Bouddhisme dans le Nô* (Tokyo: Maison Franco-Japonaise, 1950).

—— *Nô* (Tokyo: Maison Franco-Japonaise, 1953).

Richie, Donald, *The Films of Akira Kurosawa* (Berkeley: University of California Press; Cambridge: Cambridge University Press, 1965).

—— *The Japanese Movie: An Illustrated History* (Tokyo: Kodansha International Ltd, 1966).

—— and Watanake Miyoko, *Six Kabuki Plays* (Tokyo: Hokuseido Press, 1963).

Sadler, A. L., *A Short History of Japan* (Sydney: Angus and Robertson, 1963).

Sakanishi Shio, *Japanese Folk-Plays: The Ink-Smeared Lady and Other Kyogen* (Tokyo and Rutland, Vermont: Charles E. Tuttle Co., 1960).

Sansom, G. B., *Japan: a short cultural history* (New York: Appleton-Century-Crofts, 1962).

Scott, A. C., *Genyadana: A Japanese Kabuki* (Tokyo: Hokuseido Press, 1953).

—— *The Kabuki Theatre of Japan* (London: Allen and Unwin, 1955).

—— *The Classical Theatre of China* (New York: Macmillan, 1957).

Seiffert, Rene, *Zeami: La Tradition secrète du Nô* (Paris: Gallimard, 1960).

Shaver, Ruth M., *Kabuki Costume* (Tokyo and Rutland, Vermont: Charles E. Tuttle Co., 1967).

Shioya Sakae, *Chushingura: an exposition* (Tokyo: Hokuseido Press, 1956).

Stopes, Marie and Sakura, J., *Plays of Old Japan, the Nō, together with Translations of the Dramas* (London, 1913).

Suzuki, D. T., *Zen and Japanese Culture* (New York: Pantheon Books for the Bollingen Foundation, 1959).

Upton, Mr and Mrs Murakami, *A Spectator's Handbook of Nō* (Tokyo: Wanya Shoten, n.d.).

Waley, Arthur, *The Nō Plays of Japan* (New York: Grove Press, n.d.).

Wells, Henry W., *The Classical Drama of the Orient* (New York: Asia Publishing House, 1965).

Wilson, F. A. C., *W. B. Yeats and Tradition* (London: Victor Gollancz, 1961).

# Glossary

ARAGOTO — Flamboyant, bravura style characteristic of some aspects of *kabuki*.

BAKUFU — The 'tent government' established by the emergent Shogunate.

BENSHI — Narrators in the early Japanese cinema.

BIWA — The Japanese lute.

BUGAKU — Classical Japanese dance and music.

BUNRAKU — The classical Japanese puppet theatre.

CHAMBARA — Popular term for *samurai* films involving much sword play and violence.

DAIMYO — Provincial lords in the Japanese feudal system.

DENGAKU — 'Field' or 'rustic' music, springing from popular sources.

GAGAKU — 'Elegant and authorized music', particularly as cultivated by the Imperial Court.

GEISHA — Girls elaborately trained in the arts of entertaining, including the dance; also employed as dancers for certain religious purposes.

GENDAIMONO — Dramatic treatments of contemporary life.

GIDAYU — Chanted narrative of *kabuki* drama.

GIGAKU — 'Skill-music', imported from Korea and containing certain dramatic elements.

HANA — Literally 'flower'; in acting, the full bloom of an actor's performance.

| | |
|---|---|
| HANAMICHI | The long walkway running through the auditorium to stage right in the *kabuki* theatre. |
| HASHIGAKARI | The walkway connecting dressing-room and stage in the *noh* theatre. |
| JIDAIMONO | Dramatic treatments of historical subjects. |
| JORURI | Chanted narrative, existing first as a distinct art and later combined with the *bunraku and kabuki* performances. |
| KABUKI | The popular theatre, emerging in the sixteenth century as the favourite drama-form of the *bourgeoisie*. |
| KAGURA | The earliest form of Japanese sacred dance. |
| KANGEN | Classical Japanese music. |
| KANJIN performances | Performances given to raise money for some religious or civic cause. |
| KAWARA-MONO | 'Things of the river-bed', derogatory term applied to early *kabuki* actors. |
| KOJO ceremony | The formal taking by a *kabuki* actor of a new name within the company hierarchy. |
| KO-KATA | Child actors. |
| KORUMA NINGYO | A type of puppet play in which the operators work on wheeled stools. |
| KORUMBO | 'Black man', title given to stage assistant in *kabuki*. |
| KOTO | Japanese zither. |
| KOWAKA | Early type of choral recitation combined with dance. |
| KUSEMAI | Early ballad or dance. |
| KYOGEN | Explanatory interludes in *noh* play; comic playlets given between *noh* plays. |
| MANZAI | Brisk repartee; traditional form of entertainment in Osaka. |
| MIE | Contorted pose assumed by *kabuki* actor at moments of high dramatic intensity. |
| MIKO | Shrine maiden. |

| | |
|---|---|
| MOMEN SHIBAI | 'Cotton plays', descriptive of *kabuki* plays about peasant life. |
| MONOMANE | Imitation. |
| NINGYO SHIBAI | Puppet plays. |
| NINJA | Camouflaged commando warriors of feudal Japan. |
| NOH | The classical, Buddhist-inspired dance-drama of Japan. |
| OBEYA | 'Big room', the general dressing-room of the lower-grade actors in *kabuki*. |
| ONNA KABUKI | Early type of *kabuki* performed by all-female casts. |
| ONNAGATA | Female impersonators in *kabuki*. |
| OTAUE | Religious festivals connected with the transplanting of rice shoots and the fertility of the crops. |
| RAKUGO | Story-teller. |
| RONIN | Men without a lord or master. |
| SAMISEN | Japanese long-necked, three-stringed instrument, played with a plectrum. |
| SAMURAI | Warriors of the Japanese feudal system. |
| SANGAKU | Early type of popular music and dance. |
| SARUGAKU | 'Monkey music', possibly phonetic corruption of above. |
| SEWAMONO | Dramatic treatments of domestic subjects. |
| SHIMAI | Dance in *noh*. |
| SHIMPA | Modern dramatic treatments of traditional themes. |
| SHINGEKI | The 'new theatre'. |
| SHISHIMAI | Traditional lion dance. |
| SHO | Mouth-operated organ. |
| SH'TE | Principal actor-dancer in *noh* play. |
| SH'TE-TSURE | Assistants to the *sh'te*. |
| SUMO | Traditional form of Japanese wrestling in which opponents try to push each other out of the ring. |

| | |
|---|---|
| TATAMI | Straw mats covering the floor of a traditional Japanese house. |
| WAGOTO | Softer, more effeminate style of *kabuki* acting. |
| WAKASHU KABUKI | Early type of *kabuki* played by all-male casts. |
| WAKI | Supporting actor in *noh* play. |
| WAKI-TSURE | Assistants to the *waki*. |
| YARO KABUKI | Early type of *kabuki* played with casts of young men. |
| YUGEN | Indefinable quality of a *noh* actor's performance. |
| ZA | Guild; theatre. |

# Index

that is traditional in Irish poetry. For the soul bound by memories of past unhappiness to the terrestrial cycle, he substitutes the Christian concept of Purgatory, from which the forlorn spirit may be liberated by prayer or action, as the Old Man in *Purgatory* seeks to liberate his mother's ghost by sacrificing his own son and ending the doomed line that has cursed her memory. The present world is fleeting and illusory, and this is emphasized, as in *noh*, by the metamorphosis which his characters undergo. As in Zen Buddhism the timeless and ideal world, in which good and evil are as one, waits for all: his heroes, though they may be oblivious of divinity, carry within them an unconscious Platonic reminiscence of that world.

Yeats, like the *noh* writers, sees the arts as offering direct communion with the Absolute. In *The Player Queen* it is the drunken husband of the actress, the playwright, who perceives the symbolism of the Unicorn; it is the actress, mimicking royalty, who is a truer Queen than the legitimate incumbent. This confrontation by the Queen in life and the Queen in art is an interesting variation on the meeting of the Mountain Hag and the Dancer in *Yamamba*. In *A Full Moon in March* it is the singing swineherd alone who has the key to beauty. Although decapitated, his lips still sing, as the severed head of Orpheus went floating down to Lesbos. Writing on Blake, Yeats had said that 'After the flood, three methods of conversing with Paradise, the beautiful internal world, remain to men, poetry, painting and music.' Thus in his plays the strolling vagabond can touch eternity: for the austere discipline of the Japanese performing artist Yeats has substituted the romantic troubadour of Irish tradition – a dictum which might be applied equally well to Yeats *vis-à-vis* Zeami.

Yeats's dance-plays were designed for a limited audience, and it is this that they have received. The wider theatre-going public has taken little note of works which run so counter to the English dramatic tradition. Only *Purgatory*, perhaps, has continued to receive serious attention, and this more for its literary and sociological content than its dramatic effectiveness.

How successful were those adaptations? They were at their best when they drew from wellsprings of tradition and emotion

K 2